*The Best of Soccer Journal*
*An NSCAA Guide to Soccer Coaching Excellence*

D1316834

# The Best of Soccer Journal

## An NSCAA Guide to
## Soccer Coaching Excellence

Jay Martin (Ed.)

Meyer & Meyer Sport

British Library Cataloguing in Publication Data
A catalogue record for this book is available from the British Library

The Best of Soccer Journal
Maidenhead: Meyer & Meyer Sport (UK) Ltd., 2012
ISBN 978-1-84126-329-8

© 2012 by Meyer & Meyer Sport (UK) Ltd.
Auckland, Beirut, Budapest, Cairo, Cape Town, Dubai, Indianapolis,
Kindberg, Maidenhead, Sydney, Olten, Singapore, Tehran, Toronto
Member of the World
Sport Publishers' Association (WSPA)
www.w-s-p-a.org
Printed by: B.O.S.S Druck und Medien GmbH, Germany
ISBN 978-1-84126-329-8
E-Mail: info@m-m-sports.com
www.m-m-sports.com

# Table of Contents

## Chapter IV: Fitness and Nutrition ...................................... 169

## Chapter V: Coaching and Team Management........................... 213

© Craig Bohnert

# Chapter 1: Technique

# Principles of Teaching Techniques

**Manny Sanchez, TN Soccer Executive Director**
**USSF "A" License, NSCAA Premier Diploma, UEFA "A" Intermediate**

**Editor's Note:** *It is often good to get back to basics. Here is a quick refresher course for coaches to use to prepare their team technically.*

Players must have a solid foundation upon which to build before they can reach the next level of development. Teaching proper technique is a must for coaches working with young players. The coach can have the best intentions in the world, but re-enforcing bad technique or habits can be counterproductive in the development of our players. Bad habits, which are developed from repetition of bad technique, get harder to correct the more entrenched they become.

The old adage "practice makes perfect" is slightly off the mark when it comes to technique. In reality perfect practice makes perfect. The key is to repeat proper techniques. Proper fundamentals are necessary for developing good technique. If we get our players to repeat the techniques in a proper way over and over, they will start to form good habits that are fundamentally sound. This is definitely a key to creating good sound habits that will become second nature.

The purpose is to improve the player's technical ability and present them with activities, which will provide the repetition necessary to raise the level of individual proficiency and their comfort with the ball. Increased technical ability and better understanding of principles of play will help our players reach the next level in their development. But we must remember that this will not happen without a solid foundation. That is why it is so important that coaches know what to look for in teaching techniques.

Below you will find the principles of technique for heading, dribbling, passing, receiving and finishing/shooting. Utilizing these principles in conjunction with creating a perfect picture for them to see will help in getting the players on the road to creating good habits. I hope this will help the less experienced coach who might not have played the game in teaching proper techniques to younger players.

## Heading Principles:

- Eyes open
- Chin in, mouth closed, keep neck firm
- Attack the ball – don't let the ball hit you
- Contact the ball just above the eyebrows or forehead
- Arms help to propel the head forward as well as aid to balance
- Use legs and back for power - arch and uncoil
- Foot action – rocking motion, back foot to front foot
- Timing of jump is very important, make contact with ball at the highest possible point of the jump

## Finishing Principles:

- Accuracy is the key – finishing is merely passing the ball into the goal past the goalkeeper
- Power is determined by the speed of the foot at the point of contact and the technique used
- Body alignment – whenever possible, head and kicking knee over the ball and hips and shoulders square to target
- Firm ankle, toe down
- Non-kicking foot placed comfortably beside the ball – toe pointing to the target

- Eyes kept on the ball at the moment of contact, on approach to goal take a quick look up and pick out target – then focus on ball Many players try to look at the target while making contact with the ball
- Keep head still throughout the follow-through
- Follow through – ankle remains firm, toe down and follow through to the target
- Do not try to over hit the ball. Many players swing so hard at the ball that they usually swing around the ball and mis-hit it badly

## Passing Principles:

- Eyes on the ball at the moment of contact
- Non-kicking foot beside the ball: don't reach for ball
- Ankle locked on kicking foot
- Follow through ww target
- **Inside-of-the-foot pass:** Toe pulled up at a 90-degree angle; to keep the ball low, strike the ball at the midline or above
- **Outside-of-the-foot pass:** Toe pointed down; strike across the ball toward the target.
- **Instep drive:** For long passes in the air make sure that the player is making contact with the ball below the midline. When trying to drive the ball with less air under it, players should not follow through up into the air with their kicking foot.
- Practice passing with both feet at all times
- Emphasize the importance of pace and accuracy

## Receiving Principles:

- Go to the ball to be in a position to control early
- Prepare to receive the ball by opening up to the field
- Position the body directly in line with the flight of the ball and determine the surface to be used for controlling the ball
- At the moment of contact with the ball, the part of the body contacted is relaxed and gives slightly to kill the momentum of the ball

- Keep the ball close. Don't stop the ball completely. Guide the ball in the desired direction. The first touch must be constructive to prepare for next move (first time pass, dribble etc.) Use the various foot surfaces (inside/outside/sole) to redirect ball as it strikes foot. A bad first touch will result in losing possession
- Before the ball arrives, know the position of your opponents and teammates. The player should be thinking ahead: What will I do when I get the ball?

## Dribbling Principles:

- Lean forward and over the ball
- Knees bent, on the balls of feet
- Relax body
- Balance is a must
- Keep ball close
- Use inside/outside and instep of both feet
- Be creative, use imagination – develop own style
- Use body feints
- Change speed and direction: tight control v. open field
- Look up as much as possible
- Use body to shield/protect ball
- Don't be afraid to fail, take risks in offensive third of the field

# Dribbling: A Crucial Component

## Matt Robinson

**Dribbling:** *A vital technique for young players to develop, a crucial component of any team's attack, and a technique that is worthy of a specific training session. Most coaches would agree that that inclusive statement accurately describes the technique of dribbling. How to transfer technique into skill is the crucial coaching question.*

**W**ith an effective training session, a coach can make a difference with the individual players as well as the team. Through training, players can improve their individual skills and improve their tactical decision-making skills. As these physical and mental skills develop, the team will evolve into a more dangerous and intelligent attacking force.

This article will offer a logical progression of a training session devoted to dribbling. Ideas offered by members of the NSCAA National Coaching Staff are incorporated in the article, and the training session follows the progression that is emphasized in the NSCAA Coaching Academies. The training session focuses on the three types of dribbling – possession, speed and attacking – and will evolve from the warm-up to fundamental stage, then to the tactical stage, to match-related conditions and finally to match-condition stage.

## Warm-up

**Organization:** Designate an appropriate area on the field. The size of the space may range from the field's center circle to the penalty area to a half field. The size depends on the number of players and their skill level. The better the skill, the smaller the space (Diagram 1).

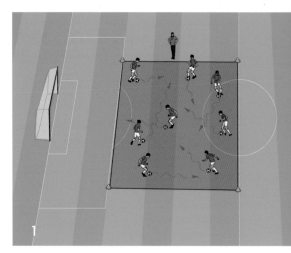

In executing the warm-up, the players dribble around the area following the commands of the coach. The commands may consist of dribbling with various surfaces of the feet, dribbling for tight control, to individual offensive moves, to changing direction with speed. If a coach or team is familiar with particular moves, (i.e. Coerver moves) they can be demonstrated and practiced during this time. It might be a good idea to have players individually demonstrate such maneuvers or individual moves you have noted they excel in. In this way you help in the development of their self-confidence and the honing of their leadership skills.

The intensity of the work should increase throughout the duration of the warm-up. Even though it is a warm-up, the coach should stress the importance of proper feinting and the explosion after the feint is executed. Also the players are working on their vision, as they must keep their heads up to avoid collisions with other players and to find open space.

This warm-up is economical in nature in that it is a mild cardiovascular workout while the player is becoming acclimated to the major emphasis of the training session.

## Fundamental/tactical training

The training session focuses on shielding, speed dribbling, and attacking with the dribble. With each type of dribbling, the coach can utilize a fundamental stage where there is no pressure and gradually introduce pressure to make the exercise more tactical in nature.

*Shielding: Protecting the ball from the opponent by putting your body between the ball and the defender.*

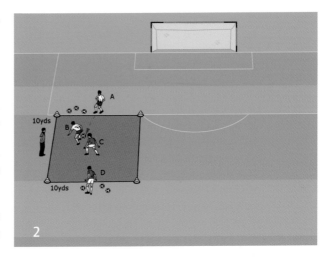

**Organization:** Make a 10x10-yard grid with four players to a grid (Diagram 2). To begin this part of the session, Player A plays the ball to Player B. B shields the ball (places his/her body between the ball and defender) from Player C for five seconds. C then receives a ball from Player D who will then shield it from Player B. The defensive pressure should intensify each time, but the defender should not steal the ball. This restriction is imposed in order to give players a chance to be successful in perfecting their shielding skill. The players in the middle will switch after five trials each.

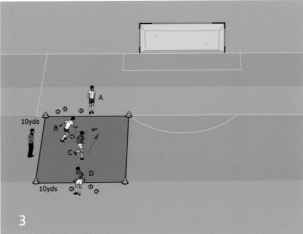

More pressure is added at the next stage (Diagram 3). Players should match up for a one-minute game of "keep away" in the grid. There are no goals, because the focus of the drill is possession by shielding. By rotating players through this several times, the coach can increase the intensity of the defender. At first the defender may be restricted from stealing the ball, but the intensity should be increased to the point it is an all-out game of "keep away." The players on the side have balls that can be put into play so that the players in the middle work the whole minute. When the minute is up, two players from the one side rotate with two players from the other side for their minute's practice. Perhaps of importance are the matchups in the grids. By carefully selecting which players are opposing each other, the coach can assure that equal 1 v. 1 competition is taking place in each work area.

The coach can use this part of the session to cover the major teaching points regarding shielding. These important fundamentals include keeping the body between the ball and the defender, playing the ball with the farthest foot from the defender, keeping the body at a right angle to the defender so that the attackers do not have their back completely to opportunities in front of them, legally using the arm to make space, and moving either laterally or away from the defender. The object is to keep possession as long as possible, and wait for the defender to make the mistake of overcommitting. If this occurs, the player can move to an open space and resume shielding.

Along with the technical training, players also will develop a tactical awareness of when to move to open space with the ball. All field players should participate in this training, for players in every position are placed in the situation of shielding. Finally, the one-minute grid work is very economical in that it is great fitness training for the players.

*Speed Dribbling: Dribbling the ball quickly without defensive pressure or defensive pressure from behind*

**Organization:** In a 45x90-yard area use two large goals (Diagram 4-5). The players are in lines at the end of the area as shown. Coaches may want to shorten the length of the field for younger players.

The players will speed dribble the length of the area. Emphasis should be placed on the player keeping the toe pointed down; using the instep, or laces, to strike the ball; playing the ball long on the first touch and increasing the number of touches on the ball and keeping the ball closer to the body as the player gets close to goal or to an opponent. The speed dribble then can be incorporated with shooting, executing a wall pass, and then a crossing the ball.

A defender then will be introduced. At first the defender will be passive. This will enable the attacking player to focus on keeping the ball closer to the body and increasing the number of touches as the defender and attacker are about to meet. It is effective to have the defender move towards the attacker to make the situation more game-like. Rarely in a game does an attacking player dribble toward a stationary defender.

After a few repetitions, the restrictions are taken off the defender and the attacker must attack with the speed dribble and work to get past the defender. The coach should encourage the player to look for the opportunity to play the ball behind the defender and explode past the defender to get the ball first in the open space. Once in that space, the attacker should cut off any opportunity for a recovery run by the defender by cutting in front of the defender. If the defender wins the ball, they attack to the opposite end line (Diagram 6).

This is excellent functional training for outside backs and midfielders who must attack the flanks

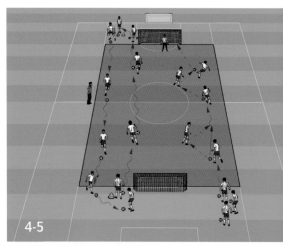

4-5

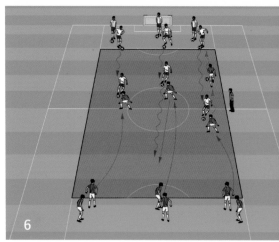

6

regularly, and an excellent conditioner for all field players as they work on this segment of dribbling.

*Attacking with the Ball: Dribbling to beat an opponent*

**Organization:** Set up a 20x30-yard grid with four players to a grid.

Attacking with the ball is the opportunity for players to utilize offensive moves they have developed. In this exercise, the attacking player will receive the ball from the defender at the other end of the grid and look to attack over the end line. After each exchange, the roles of the players in the grid are reversed (Diagram 7).

Again, the intensity of the defense will move from passive to full as more repetitions are completed.

The two players outside the grid can receive balls and will be rotated in by the coach. After rotating players, the exercise progresses to the dribbler attacking towards a small goal and if the defender wins the ball, he/she attacks the end line (Diagram 8).

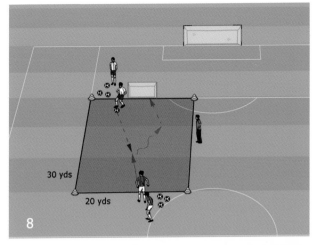

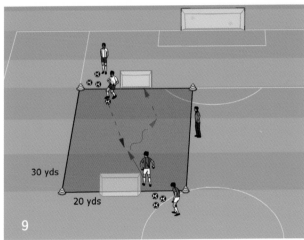

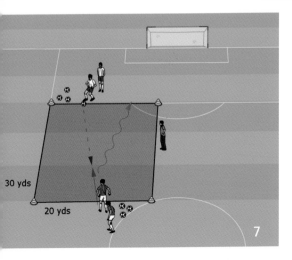

Finally two goals are set up and both players will attack the small goals. Again two players with balls can ensure that the drill continues for the duration of time selected by the coach.

Coaches need to remember that dribbling is largely an anaerobic exercise to ensure quality the right dosage of time-needs to be determined (i.e., a minute for high school player, more for mature players, less for youth players). This will assure that quality effort is given each time (Diagram 9).

The drill also can incorporate the shielding aspect of dribbling by having an outside player playing the ball to the attacker, and the attacker shielding until the opportunity presents itself to turn and attack the goal (Diagram 10).

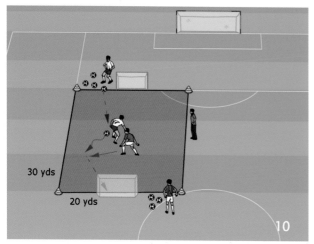

30 yds

20 yds

10

This exercise offers opportunity for a coach to emphasize the technical skills of attacking with the ball. The player should be encouraged to attack the front foot of the defender, for it is with the back foot a defender will tackle. Again the player should be encouraged to look for the opportunity to play the ball behind the defender; explode past the defender into the open space, and cut off any opportunity for a recovery run by the defender by cutting in front of the defender. It also should be emphasized that a change of speed and direction is vital in a successful attack with the ball.

## Game-Related

**Organization:** The field is 44x90 with clear markings of the thirds of the field. Twelve field players, two goalkeepers and two servers next to each goal are on the main field. One player from each team is in a channel on each side of the field as shown in Diagram 11.

Balls are played from the servers at the end of the field and also by the coach at midfield.

The player is presented the opportunity to utilize the three techniques of dribbling in a tactical situation. In this exercise, the concept of dribbling in different parts of the field is emphasized. In the back third, a player should dribble sparingly and play the ball simply. A dribbling mistake in the back third may prove costly in the form of an uncontested counterattack goal. In the middle third, the player may need to buy time by possessing and shielding the ball before playing it forward into the front third with the dribble. In the front third, the player should be encouraged to attack the defender with the dribble and to take chances. A coach may insert a rule that states the front player, once receiving the ball, must attack the defender with the dribble.

In short, the tactical decisions being made by the back players are much different than those being made by the front players. The back players must be cautious if they must dribble, while the front players should be encouraged to be daring and creative in order to enhance the number of opportunities to score. The progression of the exercise entails the players at first being restricted to their respective thirds by a pass. The

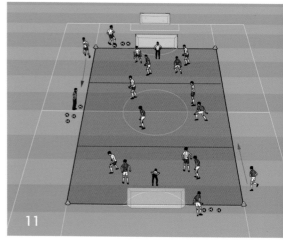

11

coach then lifts the restriction and players are permitted to move into other thirds to support, or they may make penetrating attacks with the ball into other thirds.

## Game Condition

**Organization:** The same field size as game-related stage, but eliminate the thirds of the field markings.

In the game condition stage, the coach lifts the restrictions from the game-related stage. The servers from the end become sweepers. Even though the markers of the thirds are gone, players must realize which third they are in and make the proper tactical decision.

## Conclusion

Dribbling, without question, is one of the vital skills of the game. Coaches should devote time to the skill so the players are proficient technically and tactical in the same skill. As stated earlier, dribbling itself is worthy of a specific training session, and a coach may even feel compelled to focus specifically on one aspect of dribbling if needed. This decision should, as always, be based upon the needs of a particular team.

© Craig Bohnert

# Fast Footwork

## Frans Van Balkom

### Introduction

In today's game it is important that players are comfortable on the ball. Fast footwork skills and drills are designed to develop confidence with the ball in tight spaces. The objectives of a fast footwork practice are:

* Coordination of feet
* A "feel" for the ball
* Flexibility and agility
* Speed and quick movements
* Creativity and confidence
* Conditioning

### How it Works

There are a number of skills taught when working with fast footwork sessions. Players begin slowly and increase speed until they can execute the skill at a fast pace. After executing a skill the ball is played rapidly back and forth between the insides of the left and right foot for a combined total of six or eight touches. The skill is then repeated or another skill is performed. Many of the skills can be used in game situations.

### Fast Footwork – Individual Basic Moves

The basic move: With the weight forward on the balls of the feet, the ball is tapped (passed) repeatedly from the inside of one foot to the other, touching the ball once with each foot. The player is relaxed and the knees are bent for good balance. Start slowly and then increase the speed.

The basic move plus the push: Start with the basic move with 5 or 6 touches. Without stopping, push the ball softly forward with the inside of the right foot. Immediately plant the right foot; reach out for the ball with the sole of the left foot and pull the ball back between the feet. Repeat the basic move. Without stopping repeat the move using the left foot to push the ball forward and the right foot to pull it back. Always perform the basic move between skills.

The basic move plus the diagonal push: Start with the basic move. On the last touch with the inside of the left foot, play the ball diagonally across so the ball is in front of the right foot. Reach out with the sole of the right foot and pull the ball back to the inside of the left foot. Repeat the basic move and repeat the skill starting with the right foot. Continue the skill alternating feet.

Basic move plus outside of the foot: Start with the basic move. Push the ball softly in front. Immediately pull the ball back using the sole of the right foot on the top of the ball. Quickly move the foot off the top of the ball and using the outside of the right foot push the ball slightly to the right. Quickly move the right foot to the outside of the ball and using the inside of the right foot pull the ball back to the left foot. Pull the ball back with the left sole and repeat the skill.

Play the ball forward softly with the right foot: Step over the ball with the left foot and using the outside of the left foot pull the ball back. As you do this pivot to the left on the right foot. With the left foot now planted pull the ball back across your body with the outside of the right foot. Add in the basic move and repeat.

Using the sole of the right foot: on top of the ball, pull the ball back towards you. As the ball is about to pass the standing leg (left), move the right leg away from the body and using the inside of the right foot pass the ball behind the

## Drills

1. Have the players work in a confined area. This will help the players learn to keep their heads up while performing the moves. Perform a series of skills in sequence always using the basic move as the start point.

2. In a confined area divide the players into two groups. Each player in one group has a ball. This drill simulates a 1 v. 1 situation. Ask the players with the ball to perform a series of fast footwork drills against a passive opponent. The player on the ball performs fast footwork skills and practices shielding the ball from the defender. The players without the ball move around the area and approach any players with the ball.

3. 3 v. 1 in a confined area of 12 yards x 12 yards. In order to get the players accustomed to pressure and at the same time, force them to use various fast footwork skills, which include shielding, feinting and dribbling moves, we put a condition on this drill. Each time a player receives the ball they must touch it five times before they can pass it. If the defender wins the ball they change places with the player who lost the ball.

left foot. Immediately plant the right foot and pivot to the left. Raise the left foot and bring it over the ball. Using the sole of the left foot bring the ball in and start the basic move. Repeat in the opposite direction.

Begin with the basic move: Using the inside of the left foot, softly push the ball forward. Follow the ball by reaching out with the sole of the right foot and stop the ball with a light touch. Immediately after stopping the ball the right foot continues forward and is planted on the ground beyond the ball. Transfer the weight to the right foot and pivot 180 degrees so you are facing the ball. Pull the ball back with the left sole between your feet and begin the basic move again. Repeat the above skill starting with the right foot.

Begin with the basic move: Stop the ball with the sole of the right foot. The first contact is high on the ball. Roll the ball to the right with the sole of the foot. Let the right foot move over the ball and using the inside of the right foot pull the ball back to the middle of your feet and begin the basic move. Repeat using the left foot.

## Teaching Method for Fast Footwork Skills

1. Start with the basic move with each skill

2. Introduce a new skill in practice. Don't move to the next skill until the players have mastered the new skill

3. Combine the basic move with every skill

4. Introduce a new skill

5. Using the basic skill before starting each skill-combine the two skills learned

6. Introduce a new skill

7. Using the basic move before each skill, combine skills one, two and three

8. Continue in this manner until all skills are learned

It is recommended that fast footwork skills be practiced 15 minutes each day.

# Shielding

## Frans Van Balkom

## Definitions

Shielding: A skill that allows players to possess the ball by placing their body between the defender and the ball.

Playing the ball free requires a number of specifically developed skills, including shielding and feinting, which allows a player in possession to create space to play/pass the ball or to move away from an opponent. In tight situations playing the ball free presents a lower risk factor than when trying to dribble past opponents.

## Fundamentals

The fundamentals necessary to help a player successfully receive the ball under pressure and to create more time in preparation for shielding or playing the ball free include:

- Good basic ball control skills
- Moving into free space before receiving the ball
- Proper timing of when to come off the marking defender before receiving the ball
- Good understanding between the player passing the ball and the player receiving the ball
- Pace and accuracy of the pass
- Observation of the surrounding field of play before receiving the ball
- If possible, the pass should be made to the unmarked side of the receiver
- Feinting before receiving the pass

## When and How to Practice Shielding

Once young players are fairly well coordinated and have a good basic skill level, specific practice for shielding and playing the ball free should start. Important points to remember when practicing shielding practice are:

- Sufficient space to work – 10 players in the 18 yard box (18 yards x 44 yards) as a guide
- Each move should be explained and demonstrated by the coach
- Each player works in their own space at their own pace
- Up to six moves can be introduced and practiced in this fashion
- Practice the moves in pairs. The player on the ball is put under light pressure by their teammate. Alternate ball possession
- All players, each with a ball, practice shielding in a 20 x 20 yard grid. The players move around at random and use each other to shield the ball. The coach could indicate which move to use
- Players can use their imagination to use cones, teammates, or lines as opponents to practice shielding

## Drills

- Each player has a ball and they work in pairs. The pairs are spaced about 6-7 yards apart as shown in Diagram 1. The drill begins with the last pair who dribble forward with the ball on the outside of the line. Each time they reach another pair, they execute a shielding move and then take a standing position 6-7 yards past the last pair. Then the next pair repeats the drill. The line moves the length of the field and back. The same principle can be used in a single line zig-zag formation as shown in Diagram 2.

- Each player has a ball in a 20 x 20 yard grid. The players try to kick the ball of their teammates out of the grid while protecting their ball. The last two in the grid win

• Same as a above but with additional pressure. All but three have a ball. The three free players have one minute to kick as many balls out of the grid as possible

• Three players are in a 10 yard x 10 yard grid with each standing in a corner. A tries to dribble to the open corner. C runs over to prevent A from getting there. If A can't get into the open corner they dribble back to the original corner and B tries to get to the open corner. C tries to prevent B from doing so. Change C up often. It is tiring

• Four players are in a 10 x 10 yard grid with two playing 1 v. 1 in the grid. The other two are stationed on the line outside the grid on opposite sides. The object for the player with the ball is to keep it. The player in possession can use the outside "walls" to support them. The player with the ball can change places with the player on the side at any time

• 4 v. 3 in a 30 yard x 30 yard grid. The four players have the ball and work to keep it from the defending three. Set a time for each bout of work

• 3 v. 4 in a 30 yard x 30 yard grid. The three in possession try to keep the ball under tough defending situations with four defenders. The players in possession must use all ball shielding skills to be successful

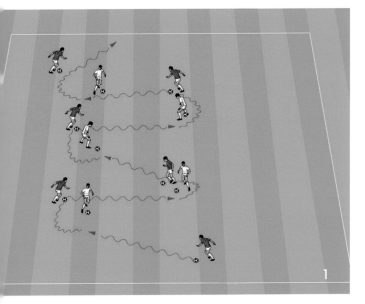

## Shielding and Playing the Ball Free Moves

Outside of the foot shield: Dribble the ball with the outside of the right foot. Make sure you touch the ball every

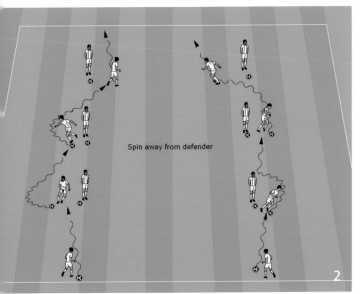

Spin away from defender

time the right foot comes forward. To change the dribbling foot, step to the right with the right foot. The ball is now in position to be played by the outside of the left foot. Important points:

- Keep the ball close to your feet
- Don't look at the ball ONLY. Look around the field and see what problems may arise
- Start at a slow pace and increase speed as you get comfortable
- Add pressure by dribbling with teammates in a confined area or adding a defender

**The V Move:** Use the instep of the left foot; dribble the ball forward at a slight angle toward the right foot. Keep the toes of the dribbling foot pointing down. Pull the ball back with the sole of the left foot, pivot to the left on the right foot and push the ball forward with the inside of the left foot. The ball forms a "V" shape. Repeat the move every five yards and alternate feet. Important points:

- The V move works well under pressure to play the ball free
- After the completion of the V move, the player changes pace for three or four yards

**The Roll Back Turn:** Dribble the ball forward on the right foot. Reach out and pull the ball back with the sole of the right foot. Pivot turn on the left foot. Plant the right foot and play the ball forward in the opposite direction with the instep of the left foot. Important points:

- When you pull the ball back, let it roll, don't stop it
- Turn quickly, plant the right foot and go
- This can be used for shielding OR playing the ball free

**The Pull the Ball Behind the Standing Foot Move:** Dribble with the instep of right foot. Use the sole of the right foot to pull the ball back. Don't plant the right foot. As the ball rolls past the standing left foot use the inside of the right foot and then play the ball left with the outside of the left foot. Important points:

- Reach out to the ball with the right sole to start the move
- Practice the move and alternate sides
- Once the move is mastered insist that it be performed at high speed and have the player accelerate with the move

**The Step over the Ball Move:** Dribble the ball with the right foot and envision a defender coming at you from the left. Step sideways – right to left – over the ball. Plant and pivot on the right foot and play the ball away with the left inside of the foot. Important points:

- When the challenge comes from the left side, step over the ball with the right foot across the top of the ball. It should be a long step toward the opponent. That will shield the ball from the opponent
- If the challenge is from behind, step straight over the ball on the right side, pivot and go in the opposite direction.

**The Tap Outside Foot Move:** Dribble forward with the right foot. From well behind the ball, take a long step over the ball. As you step, turn the right foot so you can play the ball with the outside of the right foot. Chop the ball back in the opposite direction and let your left foot make the next touch. Important points:

- Stretch out the right leg from well behind the ball
- Bring the leg straight over the ball
- As the right leg is passing over the ball, rotate the right leg to the right
- Chop the ball by the foot actually touching the ball before the ground
- When learning this move use slowly rolling balls

**The Inside Turn:** Dribble forward at a slight angle with the right foot touching the ball each time the foot comes forward. Roll the ball back towards the body with the sole (toes) of the right foot. Pivot and touch the ball with the inside of the left foot. Dribble five yards and do it again. Important points:

- Practice the pivot and turn without the ball
- Reach out with the sole (toe) of the right foot pull it back quickly and shield the ball
- Once the move is mastered, increase the speed
- Practice with both feet

The Pull Across the Body and Step over Move: Dribble with the instep of the right foot. Reach out with the sole of the foot and drag the ball across the body to the left side. The right foot then steps forward, providing a shield against an opponent, and the ball is pushed left with the inside of the left foot. Important points:

- Practice at first with a ball that is not moving
- Practice the drag and step by itself first
- Practice the complete move with a ball that is not rolling
- Later roll the ball slowly
- As always start slowly and increase speed

Shielding moves should be learned by age 14. These can be practiced every day. Using some of these activities in a warm-up will help the players become comfortable with shielding the ball.

# Tackling
## It takes both: Proper technical skills and good tactical decisions

### Jeff Tipping

When defense is discussed it is often in the context of the team. Yes, the defensive system employed by a coach, whether a man-to-man or zone, is important, but what is as important and often overlooked is the individual technical and tactical defensive abilities of the individual players.

All coaches want players who are aggressive on defense, but if this aggressiveness is not tempered with sound technical skills and tactical decisions, the aggressiveness can lead to breakdowns in the team defense. Common individual mistakes include a player overrunning an attacker rather than closing down and containing, players not tackling at the proper moment, or a player reverting to slide tackling in the open field as a first resort rather than a last resort.

The following is a practical session that addresses the individual skills of tackling, closing down, and containing from the front and back as well as exercises that incorporate these skills into a team's defense.

## Warm-up Exercise

**Organization:** Two players to a ball on either the end line or sideline.

The warm-up will serve two purposes: preparing the player both mentally and physically for the session. The players will be introduced to tackling, closing down, containing while also getting their bodies acclimated to the physical demands of the session.

To begin the warm-up, Player A1 passes to Player B1 and closes down on Player B1. Player B1

dribbles at A1 who backpedals, keeping the ball and Player B1 in front until they get back to the line. The players then switch roles. Several pairs of players may be executing the same exercise at the same time (Diagram 1).

Player B1 should not be concerned in beating player A1 with a penetrating dribble at this point. The attacker is helping with the defensive warm-up.

Although it is still the warm-up, the coach should stress to the defender the importance of moving quickly after playing the ball, but slowing down as they get closer to Player B. Young players especially have the tendency to overrun the attacking player.

In the second stage of the warm-up, Player A plays the ball between Player B's legs. As Player B chases the ball down, Player A closes down and prevents Player B from turning (Diagram 2).

Again, even though a warm-up, the coach should stress the importance to Player A of keeping

the approach as they near the attacker. The defender should begin with long strides to cover long distance, but as they near the opponent, small steps should be employed to slow down and to be ready to defend. The defender wants to transform the attacker into a ball watcher. When an attacker's head is looking down at the ball, they cannot see teammates who may be open or who have potentially better scoring opportunities.

When slowed and in a position to pressure the attacker, the defender should adopt a sideways stance. This is done for several reasons.

about an arm's length distance between themselves and Player B.

In the final stage of the warm-up the two players will work on block and poke tackling. Each player will stand about a foot from the ball. On the coach's command, both players will plant their left foot and follow through with their right foot to execute a block tackle. A second exercise is to reverse the roles of the feet.

Next, the players will be on angle to the ball. On command they will use the toe of the front foot to knock the ball past the other player.

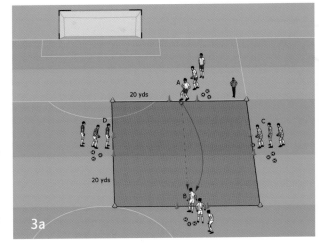

## Fundamental Stage

**Organization:** Four cone goals are set up on each side of a 20 x 20 grid. Four lines of players are positioned as shown in Diagram 3A. In stage one of the fundamental stage, Player A1 passes to B1 and closes down from the front. B1 now attempts to beat A1 with the dribble and go to goal. When either a tackle is executed or a goal is scored, Player C1 plays to D1. At the conclusion of the drill players A and B switch, as do players in lines C and D.

A key coaching point should be the importance of the defender closing down quickly but slowing

First, for proper block tackling one foot must be planted for the follow-through foot to make contact on the middle of the ball. With one foot in front of the other, the plant foot is set. The motion needed includes starting with a low center of gravity and following through with the other foot. If the feet were set side by side, it would take two motions, first planting the foot and following through, to execute the block tackle.

Second, the player is in proper position to execute a poke tackle. The defender can use the toe of the front foot to knock the ball from the attacker.

If the defender attempts the poke, they must be able to recover if the poke is unsuccessful.

Third, if the defender is beaten, they need only to turn 90 degrees rather than 180 degrees to make a recovery run.

Finally, the defender can channel the attacker to a second defender or toward the sidelines, which in essence is a defender itself. This makes the attacker predictable in regard to the direction they are moving.

The main object is delaying. In a game situation, if the defender on the ball is able to delay the attack, it allows teammates to apply pressure to the attacker from the rear and also allows teammates to organize a collective defensive effort behind the defender on the ball.

Another important coaching point at this stage is the decision when to tackle. The player should be within one step of reaching the ball, and should tackle the instant the attacker last touches the ball. Even with good tackling technique, a poor decision on when to tackle can lead to a team breakdown.

The second stage involves A1 playing the ball to B1. B2 follows B1 and must prevent B1 from turning and scoring (Diagram 3B). After play is finished with either a goal by B1 or a tackle by B2, A1 moves to the B line, B1 moves to the A line and B2 becomes B1 and will play the ball to A2, who will come to meet the ball and be challenged by A3. The C and D lines follow the same progression.

An important coaching point here is the necessity of the defender keeping the attacker's back to the goal and their head looking down at the ball. When an attacker's back is to the goal, their view and options are limited to the back view. When their head is down, they cannot utilize other forward, more penetrating and dangerous options.

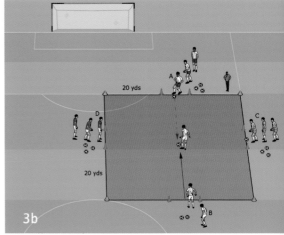

3b

A defender should prevent the attacker from turning and wait for the attacker to make a mistake. The defender should keep an arm's length so if the attacker turns, the defender is in a position to block tackle. By being too close, the defender runs the risk of fouling or over-committing and allowing the attacker to move into open space with the dribble or to flick the ball behind to pentetrate.

Stage three calls for a 1 on 2 situation. The tactics of individual defending now are combined with the concept of cover and balance. A1 passes the ball to B1 and A1 and A2 go to defend (Diagram 3C). A1 is the first defender, but A2 should be in a support position with proper angle and distance. The angle should be 45 degrees on the side A1 to which is channeling the attacker. This position is taken so A2 can be in position to tackle or close down if A1 is beaten. By being too close, A2 could be beaten at the same time as A1. If too far, A2 might not be able to make up the ground necessary to tackle or close down the dribbler.

The fourth and final stage calls for a 2 v. 2 situation. Again, balance and cover are emphasized. In this case, A2 is still in a support position, but also must be concerned with a second attacker, B2. If B1 does play the ball to B2, A2 must close down to become first defender, while A1 adjusts and

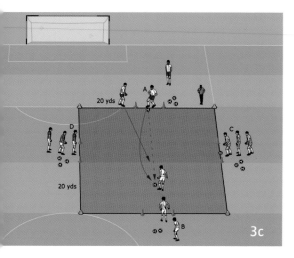

3c

should still be conscious of their player and goal, but also of assisting in providing cover.

An easy way to emphasize the concept is to refer to it as "squeezing centrally behind the ball." An attacker who is beaten should always have a backup, a covering player in position to step up. If the ball is on the opposite side of the field, a defender can afford to move centrally behind their teammates. If the ball is played long across, the defender has time to adjust and step up to apply pressure on the ball while teammates make the adjustments to squeeze centrally behind them.

gets into a support position with proper angle and distance while still focusing on B1, who is now without ball.

After the A-B teams conclude their exercise, the C-D groups play. This gives each group a chance to reorganize and creates a good playing rhythm.

In Diagram 4 we see how, when play begins with Player A, these types of collective defending strategies are invoked.

## Focus Stage

**Organization:** Split the full field into two halves. Put four sets of five-yard goals (here use the flat, platter-like cones) on each half of the field. There are eight players in each half of the field, each with one ball as shown in Diagram 4.

In this functional training game each player has the primary responsibility of defending their own goal and player, but should also be concerned with providing cover for teammates.

Important coaching points in this stage again include the necessity of applying pressure on the ball and the importance of being in a position both in angle and in distance to assist a fellow defender if is beaten by the attacker. The defender on the ball should apply pressure so that the attacker becomes a ball watcher, and the other defenders

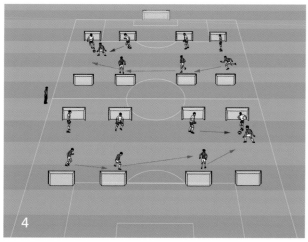

4

## Technical/Tactical Training Session

**Organization:** Move goals to penalty spot to have field 96 x 60. Eight field players to a side in a 3-3-2 alignment plus a goalkeeper, as shown in Diagram 5.

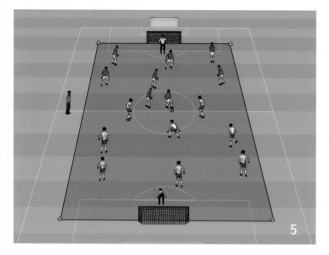

5

The technical and tactical skills presented in the earlier stages of the workout are now incorporated into match-like conditions.

The object of the game is for a team to chip a ball to the opposing goalkeeper. A point is awarded if this is executed. The defensive team must apply pressure on the ball at all times to prevent an attacker from having the time to lift the ball towards goal or change field. All principles of tackling, closing down and cover and balance are incorporated in the exercise.

This stage offers an opportunity for a coach to address players' tendencies to slide tackle. A slide tackle should be a last resort. With a slide tackle, the player is committing their whole body. A slide tackle should only be used if the defender knows they have support or the play is near a sideline or end line. If neither is the case and the attacker beats the tackle, they can attack without pressure. A slide tackle, although effective, should not be used in every tackling situation. It must be used with discretion.

## Match Conditions

Goals are moved back to the end line and a full scrimmage is played with no restrictions. Defensive principles are still emphasized in the scrimmage. Play should be stopped if a teachable moment occurs. Since the theme of the session is defense, if an individual defense lapse occurs the coach should address it and not write it off as a good play on the part of the attacker.

## Conclusion

Individuals make up a collective defensive effort. An individual breakdown can and in most cases will lead to a collective team breakdown. Some coaches may have the tendency to focus on offensive concepts and neglect the defense. This will catch up with the team in the long run.

Ample practice time should be spent on proper technical skills and tactical decisions as regards tackling. Good, hard and clean block tackles are key to strong collective defending. Proper technique, along with good judgment in regard to when to tackle, will make a team a strong defensive unit. The time spent on tackling will be worthwhile, for in the end it will be the team that benefits.

# Receiving

## The first touch is the most important

### Ron McEachen, Tim Schum and Jeff Vennell

In arranging practices that focus on receiving the ball, coaches should generally divide the first part of the session into two parts: The first will focus on receiving balls on the ground; the second will concentrate on receiving balls in the air.

The coaching points covered in each of the sessions will build on each other but the major emphasis will be on "preparing the ball" so that it is as close as necessary depending on the situation (degree of pressure the receivers find themselves under). Another definition might indicate that the technical receptions of the ball need to be as efficient and quick as possible in order that continued possession can be tactically maintained by one's team. In discussing the reception of balls from the air, particular emphasis should be placed on players' choices in terms of which body surface is used to receive the ball.

The progression of this technical session will proceed from a fundamental to a match-related to match-condition phases.

In the case of the fundamental exercises, they have been labeled B for beginning level players, I for intermediate players and A for advanced players. In some cases they are applicable to more than one group of players. Obviously, by using restrictions, coaches can gear exercises to reach any level of players (i.e., more space for an exercise allows more time for players to react to a situation).

## Fundamental Phase: Ground Passes

1. 5s in 20 x 20 yard grid, one ball (use cones) (B level)

A. Pass right to start exercise and follow the pass. Review fundamentals of reception, including:

- Receive ball across body with farthest foot (right foot in case of the first phase of this exercise)

- Look at the next target before the ball gets to you so that you already know how to position body or where **you** are going to pass the ball – take a mental picture of the situation

- Receive the ball with the toe pointed upward and the ankle locked to increase the surface area hitting ball

- Do not stop the ball, keep it within close range to draw the defender, then move it away from them toward the next target

- Under pressure, look to play the ball away from the pressure with a long first touch; use feints or false cues as appropriate in this situation

- Make eye contact with the next receiver so that they know when to begin the run and then strike the ball so that the receiver can receive it in stride

- Keep hips open to target for efficiency of passing movement and to allow maximum passing options

B. Pass to left as second phase of activity

**C.** Can conduct drill with more players (up to 12) and race against the clock, with drill concluded when the first passer returns to the starting point. If two groups, have a competition.

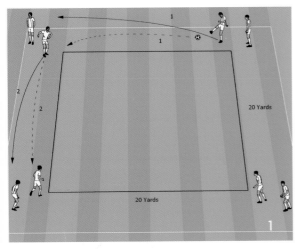

**2.** 5-6 in 20 x 20 yard grid, two balls (B Level)

**A.** Two balls with outside players, with central player to control and prepare the ball so it can be played onto one of the players without a ball on the perimeter of the grid. Review fundamentals, including:

- All of points covered in 1
- Eye contact by receiver with pass as checks to receive the ball
- Practice turning quickly with the ball
- Emphasize timing of run to ball (eye contact with passer)

**B.** Change on one-minute intervals

**C.** Add defender (using either frontal pressure or pressure from behind) and do the following:

- Prepare ball away from defender
- Use reception to beat defender
- Use outside and top of foot for deception

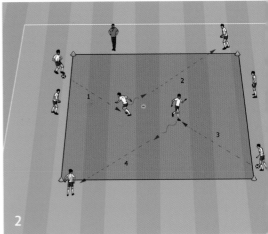

**3.** Three teams of two players each (six total) in 30 x 40 yard grid (I level)

**A.** Working in pairs (three teams of two players, As, Bs, Cs), dribbler controls the ball and waits for the receiver to run to farthest line in grid, then checks to receive the ball with the front foot, two-touch for control, play back to dribbler and repeat the process. After one minute, change roles. Review fundamentals, including:

- All points covered in 2
- Find place in crowded grid to receive the ball
- Checking run to ball must be at match speed

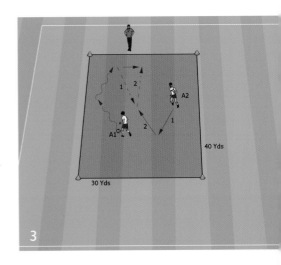

B. Instead of playing the ball back, the receiver accepts the ball with the foot open to the same side as that which the ball arrives and turns in that direction (i.e., ball played to the left side of the body, turn to the left) and sprint dribbles to farthest line in the grid and plays it to a checking receiver, who waits until dribbler has turned and faces them before the checking run is made (a reversal of roles from A.); one minute. Review fundamentals, including:

- All points covered in 3
- Observe ability of receiver to coordinate with dribbler

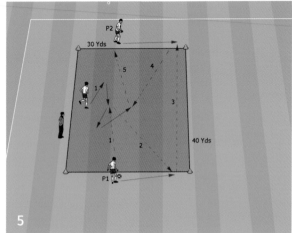

5. 16 players in a 40 x 30 yard grid (I-A levels)

A. X1 is linked with O1, X2 with O2, etc., each player outside grid with a ball. Play is continuous between each pair of players, with O1 checking away and working on timing as checks back to receive ball. Exchange roles

B. Xs pass to any Os, who checks for the ball; reverse roles

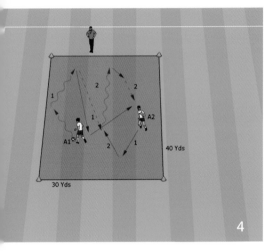

4. Three players in 20 x 30 yard grid (I level)

A. The receiver initiates pass with run to ball, controls ball, returns it at angle to passer, moves away as ball is played to opposite corner. Upon control by third player, receiver checks the ball and repeats control and angled pass back; one minute, change roles.

B. All return passes two-touches by receiver

C. Various surfaces of foot used on first touch

D. One touch receptions

E Add defender

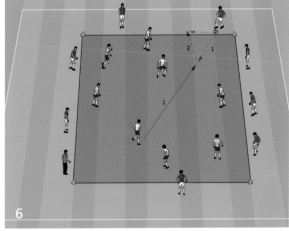

6. 12 players, four groups of three players (A level)

   A. Player in grid receives ball, takes a mental picture and identifies the position of the third member of the group, then moves body so they are in a good position to pass the ball to the third member

   B. Add two to four defenders. If defenders win ball, replace player who gave up the ball. One minute maximum for defenders

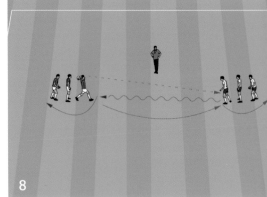

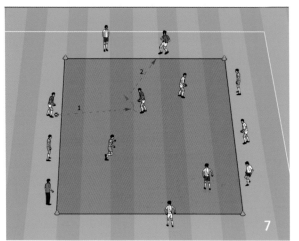

## Fundamental Stage: Air Balls

7. Warm-up, two groups of three players (B level)

   A. Passer using throw-in technique throws ball to a receiver, who controls and dribbles past the tossing player, who rushes forward to apply pressure. Both players continue to the end of the line they are moving toward, with dribbler leaving ball for the next tosser

8. Dutch warm-up, team exercise (B-I-A levels)

   A. Half the group with the balls, half without. The players with the ball are on the outside of a circle. Player with ball tosses to another player for designated receptions (i.e., chest

reception). Receive five tosses from different players around the circle

   B. Add to A by having the first player to receive five balls from four different players declared the winner

   C. Add to A by having receivers control balls from as many different players as possible in 90 seconds. Players rotate from being passers to receivers.

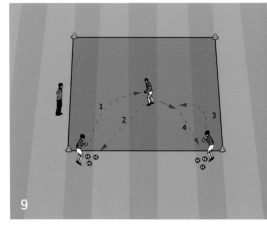

9. Three in grids, several balls with each server

   A. Two players serve balls (from hands, from village kick, from surface [advanced players] to checking player.) Services below knees, above knees, to chest areas. Server plays to receiver,

receiver prepares return ball to passer, faces second server and repeats. One minute and rotate roles. Review fundamentals, including

- Get in line of flight with ball
- Judge flight of ball to decide which body part to use for control
- Present body part to the ball
- Relax body part at impact if ball is to be collected
- Move ball from the landing area
- Win the ball early, don't wait for it

B. Control and play ball out of air to self and then to third player

C. Sprint to far line of grid and check back to ball at speed and prepare return

D. Add services from various angles, left and right, use two servers

E. Add a defender

reception and preparation by P3 checks to him/her and the whole process repeats itself. Review fundamentals

- All covered but with emphasis on receptions/ support of longer passes, timing of checking runs

B. Add defender to checking player

C. Add fourth player, P4 behind P3. Once pass is made, player follows pass each time. P1 receives, lays ball to P2, takes P2's place; P2 plays long ball to P3 who supports at angle, runs to middle and receives pass from P3; lays ball off to P3, who plays long pass to P1 and runs to support, etc

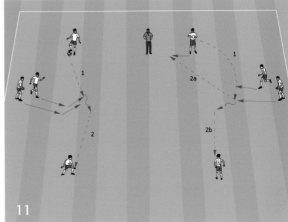

11. Four players, defensive pressure

A. P1 plays ground pass to checking receiver O and under the pressure of defender X, the receiver turns ball and plays to P2. X now becomes the receiver, etc.

B. P1 plays air ball over top of O to X, who depending on degree of control can play either to P1 or P2, then O receives the next air ball

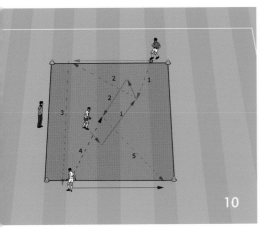

10. Three-four in open field, one ball

A. Receiver checks (P1) to ball, plays back at angle to initial passer (P2). P2 now plays a long (30- to 40-yard) air ball to P3. While ball is in flight, P1 checks away and upon

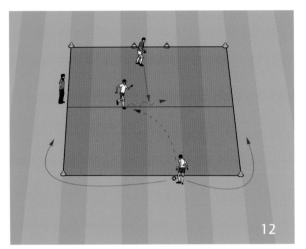

12

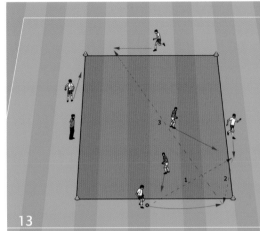

13

12. Three in grids, server plays ball in air to receiver who turns and takes on defender to goal. Use cones for goals

**A** Defender moves initially on the first touch by the receiver. Play 1 v. 1 and upon completion of play, repeat. One minute and rotate roles. Review fundamentals:

- All covered in 6 and 7
- Ability to control ball out of air with change of direction
- Prepare the ball away from the defender (spin turn technique can be used here)

**B.** Defender moves on flight of ball.

## Match-related

13. 4 v. 2 in 20 x 30 grid

Review fundamentals including:
- Watch support movement to ball such that body position is open to all support players;
- Emphasis on good reception and positioning relative to being open to pass to any of the three supporting players
- Four play for possession with two-touch restriction. Emphasis on splitting two defenders with a through ball

- All points covered in other exercises
- Use of first touch in preparing the ball for next pass
- Use of feints, ball runs to deceive defenders, buying time for easy possession

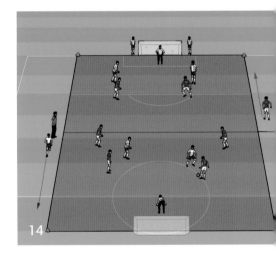

14

14. 6 v. 6 to two goals

**A** Unlimited touches. Play 4 v. 2 in each half, including goalkeepers defending each full goal. Field is 60 x 40 yards with no one allowed over the halfway line. Four attackers v. two defenders in each half. Defending team marks 2 v. 2 in other half with two others retreating into goal until possession is regained, at which time it can play 4 v. 2 until ball is played to its strikers in other half (2 v. 2 again!). Use restrictions in match (touches, etc., if objectives are not being achieved). Review fundamentals:

- When in possession, be composed
- Use first touch to
    1. relieve pressure, angle of touch, distance of touch (i.e., can beat defender with a good first touch)
    2. attack non-pressurizing defender
    3. set up a pass or shot- distance of touch
    4. keep possession-distance of touch
- Control made easier by good body position for reception

## Match Condition

The session should end with a 6 v. 6 match from 18-yard line to 18-yard line with a 44-yard wide field. While there has been some designation as to the level of expertise demanded by the fundamental exercises discussed in this practice session, the match-related exercises and the concluding match can be conditioned in various ways by the coach in order to achieve certain objectives, dependent upon the ability level of the players being instructed.

Conditions that can be imposed include:

- Number of touches (two or three touches generally; one touch for expert players)
- Long, narrow field for more vertical passing
- Wider field encourages wing play
- Channels on the touch lines of the field encourage crossing/heading play
- Four goals encourage mobility of play by the participants

© Mflippo/Dreamstime.com

# Learning to Make Quick Decisions

## Ed Trimble

Development of proper technique is the No. 1 requirement for coaches when training youth players. Our young players must develop a high comfort level with the ball, even when faced with pressure. Activities should be organized to allow for the maximum number of touches on the ball for each player. Emphasis should be placed on economical activities that allow for quality repetitions during the session. During the activities the coach can sprinkle small amounts of tactical decision-making related to the use of the technique (skill) the players are performing. The following session will emphasize the following tactical decisions:

- Move immediately after your pass
- Make a quick decision whether to dribble or to pass
- Read cues from receiver
- Read cues from sender
- What to do and where to move in small game situations

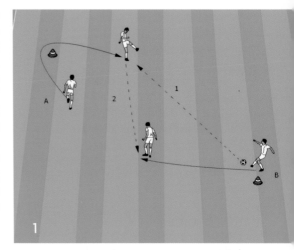

## Exercise 1

Organize players in pairs, each pair with a ball. Player A (without the ball) runs away from the ball, then back to it with a checking run. When Player A turns (checks) back to the ball, Player B plays the ball back to A's feet. Player A uses one-touch to return the ball and Player B immediately runs to collect the ball. Repeat the sequence several times and then switch the roles (Diagram 1).

### Coaching points:
- Quality inside of the foot passes with pace, play to feet
- Player A moves away from the direction of the pass, then explodes back

- Play A relaxes and returns the ball with different surfaces (instep, outside of foot, alternate feet)
- Player B moves to the ball immediately after the pass – a quick decision is made

## Exercise 2

Player A performs a checking run as in the earlier exercise. Player B passes ball to Player A, who then must read the run of Player B and react in one of two ways:

### Option 1:
If Player B follows the pass and runs toward Player A, Player A's response is to two-touch the ball and play it back to Player B. Player B collects the ball and repeats the exercise (Diagram 2, option 1).

### Option 2:
If Player B runs away from the direction of pass, Player A collects the ball and dribbles while Player B moves away. Player B then checks back to Player A and the roles will be switched (Diagram 2, option 2).

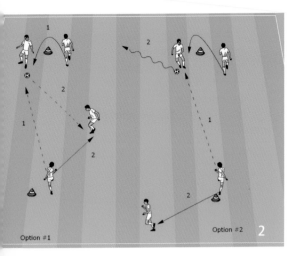

Option #1

Option #2

The attacking players must now read each other's actions. If a player cannot turn, the second player must make a quick run to support the ball and the ball must be played to that support. The original receiver must now seek to buy space (check away) so that after a few touches the two again can attempt to combine to beat the single defender (Diagram 3).

### Option 4: 2 v. 2 Game
Here the forward player can turn, and the supporting player makes a quick run to get in advance of the ball for a pass (Diagram 4).

### Coaching Points:
- If the player cannot turn, support for the ball must take place at the correct angle and distance
- If the player can turn and go to goal there is no immediate need to support the play from behind, so the support player should make a quick, attacking run in advance of the ball
- Allow the forward players to vary what they do so the support players must read the situation each time and make the correct decision on where and how to move

### Coaching Points:
- Both players must execute a quality pass and reception of ball
- Player A must read the run of Player B and perform the correct technical skill
- Player B must make a quick decision to follow pass or move away

### Option 3: 2 v. 2 Game
The players are now placed in a two-goal 2 v. 2 game. When a team has the ball, one of the other team's members must retreat to goal, creating a 2 v. 1 situation for the attacking team.

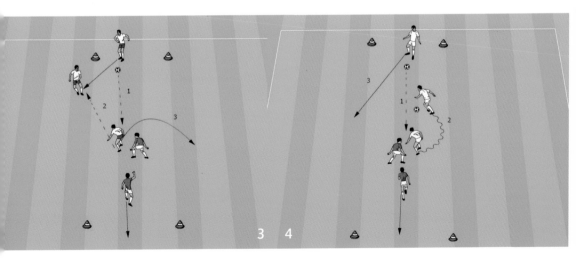

## Exercise 3

*2 v. 2 v. 2: Option 1.*

Organize the group into three teams of two playing to three goals. Make sure there is a good supply of balls behind each goal in order to keep the game moving. The aim is to try to protect your goal while on defense. When on offense try to dribble over either of the other two goal lines for a point. After a score the team who is scored against attacks (Diagram 4).

### Coaching Points:

- Organize young players to take chances and dribbling for points
- Players in possession of the ball must read the actions of the teammate. If they follow the pass, then play it back. If they move away, then dribble yourself
- Quick decisions must be made, either pass or dribble
- If the dribbling option is taken, the player must dribble at speed for goal

*2 v. 2 v. 2: Option 2.*

Same organization as Option 1. This time one point is given for a pass through the other two goals and two points for a dribble through.

### Coaching Points:

- Encourage players to take chances to score and go forward to goal
- During the game encourage players to look for cues from earlier exercises, encouraging quick decisions
- Players must read each other

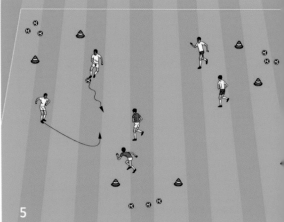

# First Touch – Fine Tuning Technique

## Dr. Tom Fleck

Arguably the single most important touch for a soccer player is the first one. This touch can be with any part of the body as a means of receiving or redirecting the ball. The word 'arguably' was purposely used to counter those who may suggest that the last touch that results in a goal is the most important touch.

For as many years as memory serves me the expression 'trap it' was directly associated with the first touch. Players were told to trap the ball with the chest, the thigh, various parts of the foot and in some instances, for the more advanced or risk taking, the head. The instructional point of the exercise was always the same: stop the ball. Semantics not withstanding, the idea in today's modern, more dynamic game is not to stop the ball, but rather to receive it and maintain control while keeping it in motion. Stopping the ball means the player must start it again, all of which takes time. This time spent stopping and starting, though inconsequential on the clock, is most inefficient on the part of the individual receiving the ball. Further, the timing of the teammate runs and/or defender movements is directly related to the technical speed of the player receiving the ball.

In some instances this simple technical action can mean the difference between finding a penetrating channel or being forced to play back or square and reload the attack. Generally penetrating spaces open briefly and must be exploited with technical efficiency, hence the need for a clean, productive first touch – not stop and go.

Following are exercises to train the first touch:

In Diagram 1, A dribbles forward and B runs off A to receive a pass. B must one-touch a pass through the cones to a space in front of C, who is timing a run for a shot on goal. Repeat this exercise by changing player positions.

A proper first touch into space can also be used by players to get out of tight or bad spaces on the field. A well timed, paced, and directed first touch can spring an alert player between or around defenders and free them to receive a return pass on the way out of the back.

In addition to the receiving first touch being used as a control technique, it can also be used as the touch that prepares the ball for the following pass or dribble. Receiving a ground ball by playing it first touch in a 45-degree angle gives the player the opportunity to play the next touch immediately without further preparation. If there is need for a ground pass, then the receiving touch should be short and kept close to the body for a quick release.

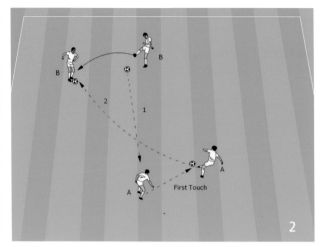

2

an air ball can be served to C. The distance of the ball from the body allows for the leverage needed for the airborne serve.

A throws air ball to B, who must redirect the serves with one touch of the head, thigh, chest, foot to C who is moving back and forth behind A. This requires B to play with the head so the direction that C is moving can be seen. This activity can be done with all three players moving (i.e. A and B forward and back with C continuing to change direction behind the server).

In Diagram 2, A passes a ground ball to B. B plays the ball on a 45-degree angle with the first touch and then plays the ball back with the second touch. Play is continual.

When the player wishes to send a long or lofted ball, the receiving touch must be played away from the body (still at 45-degrees) so that the entire leg can be used for both power and leverage when striking the ball.

A plays a ground ball to B. C makes a run off A to the flank. B's first touch upon receiving the ball must be far enough away from the body

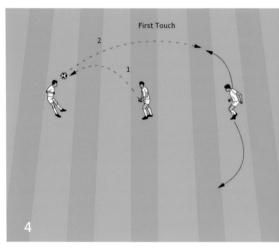

4

Once players have achieved relative success at the fundamental level, then appropriate pressures of time, space, and opponents must be applied to move the training to game situations. After all, that is why we train, isn't it?

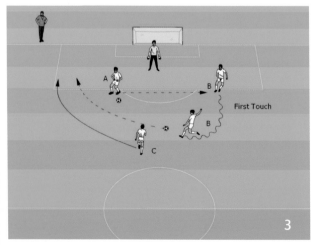

3

# Heading

## Dr. Tom Fleck

Heading or using the head to direct the ball, is unique to soccer. It is an essential technique to learn, but it can be difficult to teach young players. Many young players become fearful headers, developing habits such as blinking and ducking as the ball approaches. Through proper teaching methods and activities, these habits can be corrected.

As the ball approaches players must keep their eyes open and trained on the ball. The back should be arched, knees bent and heels raised from the ground as contact is made in the desired direction.

Heading should be taught with activities and not drills. Standing in line and heading is boring and does not allow for any creativity. Players need to be given a problem and the opportunity to solve the problem through activities. If the activity is challenging, keeps players moving and is game related, essential techniques will develop.

The follow are some activities that you can use to teach heading:

## Warm-up Exercises

Start with some confidence-building activities.
- Walk in any direction, throw the ball in the air, head into the air and catch
- Jog in any direction, throw the ball into the air, head into the air and catch
- Head the ball twice consecutively; after the second head, touch the ground with your hands before the ball touches the ground and catch it
- Walk in any direction bent over with the ball resting on the bridge of the neck
- Repeat above; go down on all fours without losing the ball

- Head ball three times consecutively and then settle the ball on the ground with your foot
- Head the ball twice and turn without letting the ball touch the ground then head the ball twice in the other direction

## Partner Warm-up Exercises

Players want to have fun and fun is touching the ball.
- In a seated position: A performs sit-ups while B serves ball to head
- Standing position: A and B hand ball to each other over a cone or ball placed between them on the ground
- A and B take turns throwing the ball to each other in the air to be returned with the head
- A and B head the ball back and forth consecutively. Count the number of touches before the ball lands on the ground

## Competitive Activities

If the players are not being successful, stop the activity and coach/help. Always start the ball with hands.
- In groups of four, head the ball back and forth consecutively and count the number of touches
- Players head the ball back and forth and move across the field from one sideline to the other (Diagram 1). Here you can see how 5, 4 or 3 players would perform this task
- In groups of three players, volley the ball with the head short/short/long. Count the number of touches and compete against the team (Diagram 2)

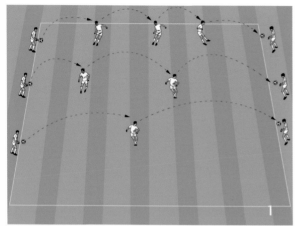

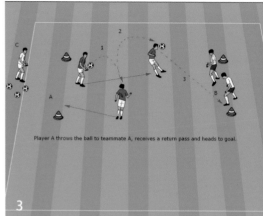

Player A throws the ball to teammate A, receives a return pass and heads to goal.

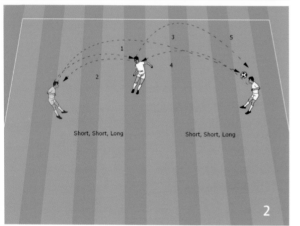

Short, Short, Long          Short, Short, Long

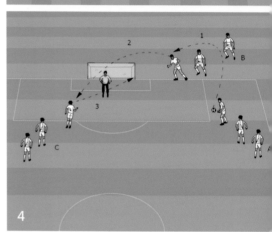

## Power Heading Activities

Never serve the ball to the head, but to space in front of the teammate, which allows the player to whip the head into the ball.

- Player A heads the ball toward the goal. A goal must be scored below the waist of Player B, who is in the goal trying to block the ball. After the shot Player A sprints back to protect their goal. Player C backs up the goal and chases the ball to keep the drill moving (Diagram 3)

- Team Handball: Team A starts with the ball in the hands. They throw and catch with each other down the field trying to attack a goal. A goal is scored only with the head. To get the ball Team B can intercept the ball or tag a Team A player who still has the ball in the hands. Each player is allowed only four steps

- **Variation:** Two players must head to goal (i.e. one heads to a teammate for the final shot)

## Closing Activities

Always finish with successful activities around the goal

- A serves the ball underhand to B, who heads to C for shot on goal

- **Variation:** Add a defender to create vision problems

- **Variation:** Add a defender to "bump" C on the shot

- **Variation:** Add goalkeeper – ball must be scored below the keeper's knees (Diagram 4)

# Elevating Passing Skill

## Coaches learn techniques at all levels in Academy course

### Ron Ost, Karen Stanley, Tim Schum, and Jeff Vennell

As with all techniques that are taught at the NSCAA Academy level, a session on passing will begin at the fundamental level, proceed to the game-related stage and finish with a match (5 v. 5 with keepers).

Passing ability must be developed in every practice session to some degree. The coach must recognize that the two main considerations in achieving a high level of passing skill are the direction (accuracy) and speed (sometimes referred to as the "weight") of the pass. Also important is good communication between the passer and the receiver.

Coaching passing is somewhat laborious. It demands repetition and coaches can seek to bring diversity to their practices by using different methodologies to achieve passing skill in the team. Numerous exercises can be applied in the team setting to upgrade the team's passing ability including possession games, conditioned games (limited touches), grid work, small-sided games and shadow play.

It might be noted that passing practices are really receiving practices with the opposite emphasis.

## Warm-ups

1. In twos, checking and passing with the emphasis on the receiver checking to the ball at an angle. Player X2 dribbles the ball, X2

observes X1 and when X2 looks up to play the ball, X1 checks back at an angle.

- X2 plays ball to close foot (foot closest to passer) and X1, upon reception, plays the ball back to X2
- X2 plays ball to farther foot (foot farthest from passer) and X1, upon reception, controls ball and turns with it

The coaching emphases in this exercise include:

- Weight and accuracy of the pass
- Checking run made when passer's head is up
- Checking run made at an angle

2. In threes, while X1 and X2 inter-pass, X3 looks up and then checks back at an angle to receive the ball, then plays it back to the person not playing them the pass.

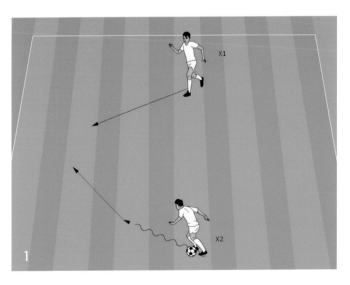

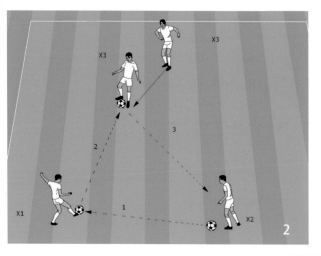

- Angled checking runs
- Getting ready in terms of selection of pass by looking at the next player before the ball gets to you

4. In fives, passing against the clock in a 20 x 30 grid. Clocked time each passing sequence. Player passes across corner to next player and follows pass. Continue sequence until everyone resumes their starting position. Total elapsed time is goal for each group. The coaching emphases should include:

Repeat the drill, adding which foot you want ball played to, etc.

3. In an open area, in threes and fours, each player with a number. Pass to each other in sequential order, No. 1 to No. 2, etc. Each time the player receiving ball must control, dribble and look up to find the next receiver, who must check at angle, etc. The coaching emphases should include:

- Angled passes (if runs are angled, passes are angled)

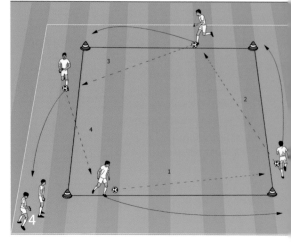

- Pass to teammate's front foot (play to space)
- Receive ball across body
- Use one-touch restriction if possible
- Check position of receiver as ball is getting to you

5. In fives, pass and follow pass. Open ended in terms of space. The coaching emphases should include:
- Pass at angle
- Receive ball across body
- Pass to the front foot (play to space)

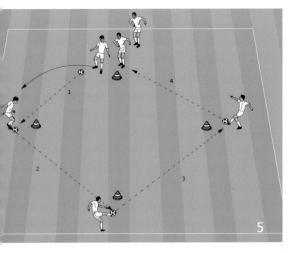

5

## Match-related

7. Same game as No. 6 above but teams go to goal by carrying ball over halfway line or passing over it and going to goal. Always have 2 v. 1 advantage. Play restricted passing (two-touch, etc.).

7A. 2 v. 2 in 20 x 40 grid. Attempt to pass to a target player who can move along end line. Team that "scores" maintains possession and goes the other direction. Can add a support player on each sideline to make exercise easier.

- Move from two-touch to one-touch restriction
- Look at the next target before ball arrives

6. Possession game to teach third man passing. 40 x 20 grid divided into two halves. 2 v. 1 in one half and 1 v. 1 in the other. The two in 2 v. 1 must keep possession while using their teammate in 1 v. 1 for third-man combination.

   If opponents get ball, they become 3 v. 2 by activating the idle player and the other team drops off a man.

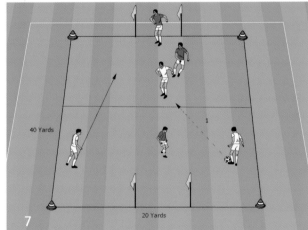

7

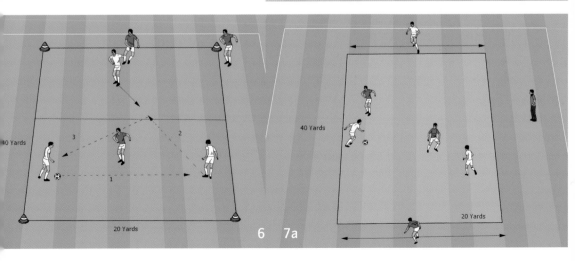

6   7a

## Teaching angled passing

8. Field 60 x 45 yards (three 15-yard wide zones). Goals at the end of each zone. Play 2 v. 2 in each zone (6 v. 6 in total). Players must stay in zones; ball cannot be passed into player in same zone
9. Same as No. 8, but players can go into other zones, but ball cannot be passed to a player in the same zone
10. Same as No. 8 and No. 9, but remove zones, leaving only two goals on end lines of field

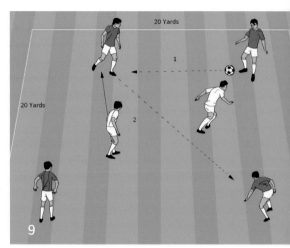

and letting it run to opposite foot, etc.) prior to passing the ball

12. 2 v. 2 in 30 x 20 rectangle. The emphasis is on playing the ball forward immediately.
- The players can only score by first playing the ball to one of two targets at the side of their goal
- They can receive a vertical 1-2 off the target or the target can play to a third man for a shot on goal
- Targets are limited to one-touch passing

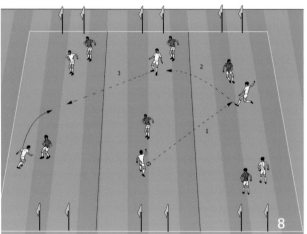

## Teaching penetrating passes

Remembering the soccer motto "The best pass you can make is the longest pass you can make and still keep possession", the following exercises are designed to emphasize the penetrating pass.

11. 4 v. 2 in a 20 x 20 area. Keep possession until you can split the two defenders with a through ball. Emphasis on one-touch and two-touch passing to create the through ball. Also work on various forms of deception (i.e., faking to receive ball

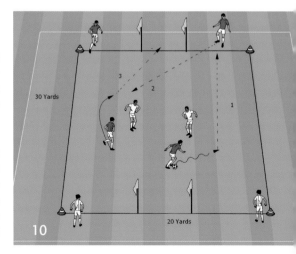

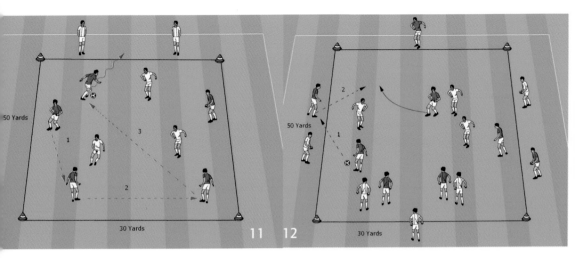

13. 5 v. 3 to line. Ten players in 50 x 30 grid. Five attackers attempt to maintain possession v. three defenders and try to play through ball for a teammate to control and dribble under control over the goal line
   - Teams exchange roles following a goal, with two spare players joining the exercise and two players going off
   - Play ball sideways if no forward pass is available

## Match-condition

14. 5 v. 5 to two end line goals in 50 x 30 area. Both teams have both end line (one for each team) and sideline players (one for each sideline) to use for additional support
   - Players score with combination play off end targets and must dribble over line for score
   - Players can relieve pressure by using a sideline support pass
   - Emphasis on making a penetrating pass and the role of the third player in support of pass

15. 5 v. 5 with keepers would conclude the activity with no restrictions

# Finishing: Technique and Repetition

## Sigi Schmid

The beauty of the game and its most difficult task are embodied in finishing. The ability to score goals can make a player a hero overnight. But as coaches can we create a goal-scorer through training? A true goal scorer has great instinct. The "nose for the goal" is inbred and cannot be taught, but coaches can work on goal-scoring technique. This can improve a player's chances to score when the situation arises. But remember, we cannot make a diamond from a rock. These exercises can only help polish the diamond!

## Consistent striking of the ball

Warm-up 1: (Note: All warm-up exercises are done without the goalkeeper)

Players work in pairs, with one partner serving the ball with the hands to the other. After 10 to 15 strikes, the partners change roles. The types of returns:
- Instep volley
- Side volley
- Thigh trap and volley – receive the ball on one thigh and volley with the opposite foot
- Chest trap to volley
- Heading

### Coaching points:
- Strike the ball cleanly
- There should be forward rotation on the ball
- Power is generated with the "snap" of the knee

Warm-up 2:

In Diagram 1 you see that the coach stands on the end line and serves diagonally across the 18 yard box to shooters. After the shot the player returns to the back of the line. Use both feet

and attack from both sides. The progression would be:
- Jog to the ball and shoot with the inside of the foot
- Jog to the ball and volley the ball
- Jog to the ball and half volley into goal

### Coaching points:
- Strike the ball cleanly
- Hit the lower third of the net
- Count clean hits from 10 serves

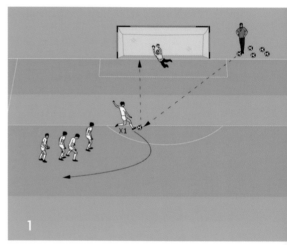

1

Warm-up 3:

In Diagram 2 the coach serves the ball to players on the top of the 18 yard box. The players face the goal. The coach varies serves (i.e. on the ground, bouncing ball, in the air etc.).

### Coaching points:
- React to the ball quickly
- Shoot first time
- Strike the ball cleanly
- Hit the lower third of the net

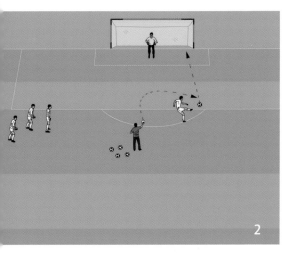

2

shooting line. After taking 10 to 15 shots, the shooters go to the other side of the box. A good variation will have the players beating the cone to the inside (Diagram 3).

**Coaching points:**
- The players must TAKE A LOOK at the goal
- When the player beats the cone they must look at the near post. If the near post is open, shoot there. If the near post is covered, shoot to the far post – it is open!

The square shot:
The coach sets up a square with cones in the 18 yard box. The size of the square and

## Repetition training

Remember, training the finishers on the team is a practice for forwards, NOT goalkeepers. These exercises are set up to maximize the effectiveness for forwards.

Dribble and shoot:
Use two goalkeepers and three to six shooters. The keepers switch every few shots. Set up cones 16 yards from the goal one yard inside both posts. The shooters will dribble at the cone, perform a feint, beat the cone to the outside and shoot on goal. The shooter retrieves the ball and goes to the end of the

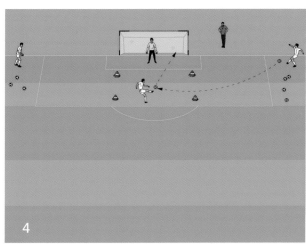

4

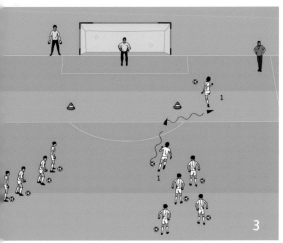

3

the placement in the 18 yard box are at the discretion of the coach. Two teammates serve the ball, alternating from each side. The shooter has a maximum of two touches to finish. The shooter should take ONE LOOK at the near post (from where the serve came). If the post is open, shoot it there; if not, automatically shoot to far post (Diagram 4).

Three quick ones
As seen in Diagram 5, the coach serves a ball to the shooter who has checked to the coach from the penalty spot. The shooter turns and shoots.

The coach immediately serves another ball for the shooter, who plays it first time or turns and shoots. A third ball follows. After three shots another shooter goes into the box. The resting players collect the balls. The coach varies the serves (i.e. bouncing ball, on the ground and in the air).

**Coaching points:**
- Watch how often players are shooting from positions practiced earlier
- Clean strikes on the ball
- ONE LOOK only
- React quickly to the ball

## Conclusion

The above exercises try to improve the player's confidence in and ability to strike the ball cleanly, at first with no pressure and later with self imposed pressure and then game pressure.

Simplify the forward's task. Take ONE LOOK, preferably to the near post. There is no need for a second look. Get the shot off. The shot is best placed to the right or left of the keeper. A shot at the post usually misses.

## 5 v. 3 game

Using one third or one half of the field play five attackers against three defenders. The coach serves the ball. The serves are varied (i.e. to the forward, to the wide player, to the back player etc.). After two or three minutes the players change roles.

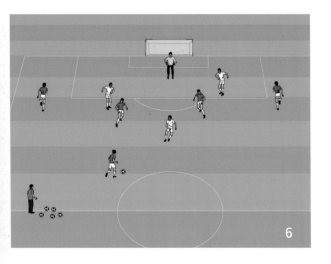

Goalkeeper Training...The DiCicco Method

# Training the Basics for Handling – Part 1

## Tony DiCicco

Goalkeepers at all levels are required not only to handle the ball but to handle all routine shots and crosses successfully. Yet, in every game, we see, regardless of the level, mishandled shots or crosses.

At the *NSCAA Goalkeeping Academy,* we train coaches to train goalkeepers to minimize mishandled shots through the following sequence:

1. Identify or name the handling techniques. There are only 4 ways in which a keeper has to handle any shot. Also identify the associated handling positions and there are only 3 of these.
   **By simplifying the position, you allow the keeper to make easier technical decisions and also allow them the appropriate reference points so that they can coach themselves.**

2. Train each handling technique separately to make sure the key aspects are understood and repeated and then train them collectively so

that the keeper has to adjust from one handling position to another based on the shot, location and pace. Remember when training techniques, make sure there are many, many repetitions.

However, before we even begin to identify and train handling, we must first perfect the goalkeeper stance and ready position. The stance is consistent with any athletic starting position. The knees are slightly bent and the feet are about shoulder width apart, the weight is forward onto the "ball of the feet" and the feet are only slightly toed out. A key aspect of the proper stance is that the elbows are also flexed at about 90 degrees with the hands forward, relaxed and with the palms facing down (Picture 1). A flat piece of cardboard should slide up along the body with the elbows slight in front. The head is still and slightly forward and also relaxed. The important aspect of the stance is that the overall position is relaxed, not tense and that it facilitates movement.

Movement is created by a "transfer of momentum" initiating from the hands and arms (the smaller

The four handling positions are *(Pictures on p. 53)*:
1. **Basket Catch** – balls played along the ground or up to mid-trunk that allow the keeper to get behind the ball (Picture 2).
2. **Contour Catch** – balls played at mid-trunk or higher that allow the keeper to get square behind the ball. The question always arises, when do I go from a basket catch to a contour catch? The answer is when the ball is to be first touched by the forearms then use the basket catch. When the ball is going to hit your body first, then use the contour catch (Picture 3).
3. **High-Contour Catch** – balls such as crosses that can be caught above the challenge use the same technique as the contour catch but with extended or nearly extended arms so to catch above any field player's challenge (Picture 4).
4. **Side-Contour Catch** – balls that are slightly to the side, not allowing the keeper to be square behind the shot, require a side-contour catch. This catch is again the same as the contour catch but just turned on its side. The head, hands and ball come together to secure the catch (Picture 5).

levers of the body) and then transferring to the legs and back (the larger levers of the body). Common mistakes with the stance are:

1. Rigid, tense muscular positions,
2. Palms facing out (either above the waist or from below the waist),
3. Arms allowed to hang down too low,
4. Feet staggered and not balanced or square
5. Poor head position.

## Training Methods:

### Warm-up (Diagram 1)

GK-2 begins between back 2 cones, spaced shoulders' width apart, on command from GK-1, GK-2 steps forward and sets in front of top 2 cones – 2 yards apart and handles ball delivered by GK-1. Continue. Train each technique in 2-3 minute intervals.

**Use hand distribution to maximize repetitions to train the basic techniques to handling:**

1. Basket Catch (baseball throw a skipped ball)
2. Contour Catch (sling throw the ball towards the chest/head)
3. Side-Contour (toss the ball just outside the frame of the body)
4. High-Contour (toss the ball into the air in front of GK)

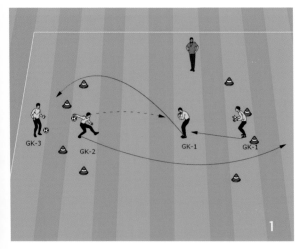

**Variations:**
- Foot distribution: off the ground, half-volley, and volley should be used for intermediate to high level goalkeepers
- Coach serves the goalkeepers; goalkeepers rotate through the exercise

### Phase 1 (Diagram 2)

**Set up:**
Utilizing the goal. Cones are placed 3 yards off the goal line representing the middle third of the goal. 3 goalkeepers train. GK1 in goal, between the cones. GK2 and GK3 outside the goal on each post. Coach (C) serves from 14 – 16 yards.

**Note:**
Emphasizing the middle third of the goal enforces the goalkeepers to use proper footwork, which should eliminate diving and reaffirm utilization of basic techniques. The coach should stipulate no diving and encourage good footwork.

**Sequence:**
- GK1 starts between the cones with a ball. GK1 bowls ball to coach. Prior to first time redirection from coach, GK1 should pre-stretch and set. GK1 reacts to shot using proper handling technique. After making the save, GK1 exits the goal towards GK2. GK2 enters the exercise and continues the sequence
- GK1 starts between the cones facing the goal. Coach has the soccer balls. On command, GK1 will turn to handle a shot from coach
- GK1 starts outside the cones. On command, GK1 will shuffle and set in between the cones to handle a shot from the coach

**Variations:**
- Coach serves volleys and drop-kicks
- Incorporate agility: start goalkeepers on their stomach or sides
- Have goalkeepers face the flank outside the cones. This will force the goalkeepers to use a drop-step and/or cross-over step
- Have goalkeepers shuffle and touch the cone or footwork around the cones

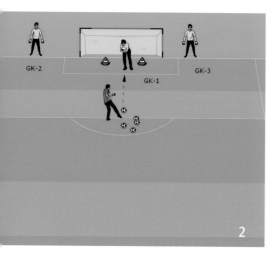

2

## Coaching Points:

- Focus on setting feet and using proper ready position to handle shots
- Utilize proper techniques to catch the ball.
- Emphasize footwork and getting the body behind the ball
- Maximize the number of repetitions to train technique

## Phase 2 (Diagram 3)

### Set up:

Utilizing the goal, GK1 will stand in the center of the goal. GK2 and GK3 will be positioned outside the corners of the 6 yard box with 2 medicine balls each. Coach is 16 yards away with soccer balls.

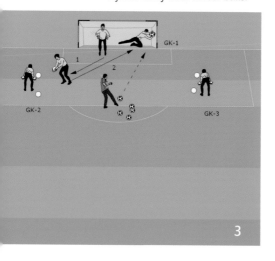

3

## Note:

Kwik Goal medicine balls are useful tools to assist goalkeepers with using proper technique and increasing strength.

## Sequence:

- GK1 will footwork to GK2 and handle a bowled ball using a front-smother save. GK1 will then recover back to the center of the goal, set to handle a shot to a pre-determined side to train the collapse dive. Repeat sequence to the other. After completing the sequence, GK2 replaces GK1 in goal; GK1 becomes a server
- GK1 will footwork to GK2, set to handle a bowled ball to the right side using a collapse dive. GK1 will then recover back to the center of the goal. The coach will then play a ball in front of GK1 for them to make a breakaway save. Repeat the sequence to the other side. The only change is having GK1 make a collapse dive to their left
- GK1 will footwork to GK2, set to handle a ball played to either the sides or at GK1 to make a collapse dive or front smother save. GK1 will then recover to the center of the goal, set, then handle either a shot or respond to a loose ball for a breakaway save

## Variations:

- Replace medicine balls with regular soccer balls
- Incorporate a live breakaway from the top of the penalty area
- Provide foot service from the angle positions
- Increase the intensity level; each segment of the training exercise should be continuous

## Coaching Points:

- Stress the importance of the technical set position
- Goalkeepers need to bring in the forearms when making a front-smother save
- Encourage saving through the ball when making the breakaway save

- When making a collapse dive save, the goalkeeper's body momentum should come forward towards the ball

## Phase 3 (Diagram 4)

### Set up:
- Mark out a field: 25 x 44
- Divide 18 players into 4 groups, each with a different color. Arrange four teams of 4 and 2 goalkeepers
- The game is 2 v 2 + 2 neutral players
- Utilize resting team players as neutral players.
- 2-3 minute games

### Note:
Goalkeeper coach should be behind the goal evaluating the goalkeeper's performance. Feedback should be provided after the 2-3 minute intervals.

### Sequence:
- Teams play 2 v 2 + 2
- The objective is to create as many shots as possible on goal
- After 2-3 minutes, alternate the 2 resting players from each team, as well as the neutral players and play another game. Winning team will remain on the field

### Variations:
- Add two neutral players to the flanks. This will add the dimension of dealing with crosses (high-contour)
- Eliminate directional play; allow the teams to attack either goal

### Coaching Points:
- Emphasize positional play; ball-line and angle arch
- Use proper distribution
- Tactical decision making

## The associated handling positions are as follows:

1. **Front-smother** – this is an extension of the basket catch, used to control hard low shots (Picture 6).

2. **Break-away technique** – this is an extension of the side-contour catch. The Break-away save, technique and tactics will be discussed in a later article but as you can see, the technique requires the side-contour catch position as the keeper sprawls to win a through ball or an open ball in their penalty area (Picture 7).

3. **Collapse Dive** – this techniques is again an extension of the side-contour handling position requiring a diving save. The collapse dive is when

the keeper catches the ball before the save but their momentum requires a controlled collapse with the ball (Pictures 8 and 9).

Remember, when training techniques the key component is repetition. You should coach to build self-confidence in your keeper. Don't overanalyze...sometimes you do everything right as a keeper and get scored on, and other times you make a number of mistakes but the ball stays out of the net so be selective with your coaching.

Briana Scurry, probably the best woman keeper to ever play was not a great technical goalkeeper. Some of her catching or handling was not perfect

BUT, she made the save so I didn't over-coach her. That is what I mean by being selective. It's more important to have a self-confident keeper than a keeper suffering from paralysis by analysis!

Good luck and enjoy working with your keeper...the time spent will make a difference for your team.

*Tony DiCicco, in addition to winning an Olympic Gold Medal and World Cup Championship as Head Coach of the USA Women's National Soccer Team, has recently been appointed as the Director of the NSCAA Goalkeeping Academy. For information on the NSCAA Goalkeeping Academy please go to www.nscaa.com.*

# Advanced Catching and Diving
# Goalkeeper Training Part 2

### Tony DiCicco and George Kostelis

*This is the second of a two part series from Director of the NSCAA Goalkeeper Institute Tony DiCicco.*

During a season, there will be moments within a match when the goalkeeper will be called upon to make the special save. The save will be recorded on the score sheet like any other shot attempt. But to the seasoned professionals, the importance of this save could be the difference between winning and losing, as well as promotion and relegation. The spectacular save not only changes the complexity of the match, but it re-energizes a team and awakens their fighting spirit. Spectators may view this save as "unexpected," but to the goalkeeper who puts countless hours of training into every week this save is the result of hard work and commitment to their craft.

Through numerous years of training goalkeepers, we have come to believe that a goalkeeper's ability to dive is truly special. Every aspiring goalkeeper who trains conscientiously has the intention of making that extraordinary diving save, but not every goalkeeper has the athletic ability to fully propel themselves through the air and catch the ball (Picture 1).

In addressing this topic of "Advanced Catching and Diving," the following three saves will be covered: 1. Extension Diving, 2. Parrying, and 3. Tipping Back to the Bar. Furthermore, the article will identify the physical, technical, tactical and psychological implications needed to make these types of saves.

## The Diving Saves

**Extension Diving:** There are two types of diving saves. The more elementary version is called the Collapse Dive. A collapse dive is when the keeper catches the ball before *diving*. The other type of dive and the type we are identifying and training is Extension *Diving* or diving first and catching while flying towards the ball.

This is an explosive save used to cope with shots struck initially outside the reach of the goalkeeper. Using quick footwork, the goalkeeper transfers momentum by forcibly flexing the knee and driving the arms. This propels the body through the air allowing the goalkeeper to catch the ball in mid-flight. Unlike the collapse dive, the feet are airborne.

**Parrying:** Deriving from the extension dive; the goalkeeper utilizes one or two hands to redirect the flight of the ball outside the goal. Balls that cannot be caught can be redirected using the fingertips for softer shots or the heel-of-the-hand for hard driven balls (Picture 2).

**Tipping Back to the Bar:** While using proper footwork to get back to the goal line and having precise timing, the goalkeeper extends up into the air to redirect the ball over the top of the crossbar (Picture 3).

## The Four Pillars

Like other players, to examine the goalkeeper's capabilities to make the dynamic diving save, we will use the "Four Pillars", which are commonly known as the physical, technical, tactical, and psychological components of the game. Assessment and evaluation of the goalkeeper using the four pillars allows coaches to pinpoint areas of concern, as well as track the amount of progress made in their development. Obviously, higher level goalkeepers possess extraordinary abilities in reference to the four components. In preparation to making these types of saves, goalkeepers must consider the following implications:

**Physical**
- Height – will determine starting position. Smaller goalkeepers may stand closer to the goal line; taller may stand further off the goal line
- Power (explosiveness) – 1) main attribute used to dive for balls struck outside the comfort zone, 2) vertical jump
- Strength – assists with propelling body off the ground, as well as absorbing contact with ground
- Agility – the goalkeeper's ability to change direction (up/down, side to side, forward/backward)
- Foot Speed – main ingredient used to make these saves; sprint, shuffle, cross-over step, and drop-step
- Reaction Speed – quick reflexes
- Flexibility – being limber

**Technical**
- Extension Dive – take forward step with the foot closest to the ball. Place weight on that leg as you bend. Using your arms and opposite leg, transfer momentum and drive your body towards the ball. Upon catching the ball, continue to drive through the ball while descending towards the ground. The ball should be the first thing to hit the ground, being used to absorb impact while also using the ground to help secure the catch
- Parrying – progression is the same as the extension dive. Being fully extended in the air, the goalkeeper can use two different surfaces of hand to redirect uncatchable shots. 1) Fingertip: used for shots hit soft enough to be redirected around or over the goal. 2) Heel-of-the Hand: used for shots hit too hard to be caught or redirected with the fingers. The heel is the part of the hand at the bottom of the palm, just above the wrist. Use of the heel of the hand will allow the goalkeeper to deflect hard shots with force far away from danger. Avoid trying to slap or stop the ball; make the decision to catch or parry

2

- Tipping (Back to the Bar) – goalkeeper starts in a sprinter stance. They immediately drop-step and move into a cross-over step after reading the flight of the ball towards the goal. At the last moment, they leap off the back foot and drive the closest hand up to the ball. Contact with the ball is made with strong fingertips, using a subtle jab through the center of the ball

## Tactical

- Assess the distance and position of the ball to determine vertical and lateral positioning
- Assess whether there is pressure on the ball and which foot the ball is being struck with on goal
- Recognize that if the ball is bouncing, the goalkeeper's position should be closer to the goal line
- Recognize the approach of the shooter. Usually, a strong/faster approach towards the ball

indicates a shot with power; if the shooter slows down, it represents a possible chip
- Weather Conditions – should influence the goalkeeper's decision to catch, box or parry.
- Anticipation – the goalkeeper who reads the game well and anticipates the next touch (pass, dribble or shot) generally arrives in the proper position to make the play sooner

## Psychological

- Confidence – goalkeepers must believe that they can make the spectacular save
- Concentration – maintaining focus throughout the match; including stoppage time/overtime. Knowing that at any given moment, they may be called upon to make the special save
- Composure – be relaxed under pressure; embrace the moment
- Courage – this is the biggest hurdle for youth goalkeepers. When learning and training these types of saves, most fear hurting themselves. Also, many youth goalkeepers favor diving to one particular side; they need to address these "mental blocks"
- Training Ethics/Motivation – success is equated with preparation. To achieve and maintain a high level of goalkeeping, you commit yourself to training. Incredible saves should only surprise those who are unprepared to make them

Without question, saves of this magnitude reverberate for years. To this day, people refer to Gordon Banks' save on Pele' during the 1970 World Cup as the greatest save ever made. In the women's game, the diving save by Brianna Scurry on a penalty kick during the 1999 World Cup Finals set the stage for Brandi Chastain's winning goal. On the biggest stages, such as the World Cup and Olympic Games, world class goalkeepers will emerge with world class saves. It is this intangible quality that separates them from other players.

# Extending the Keeper's Range

## In practice session, players learn to go for and hold more shots

### Chris Ducar, UNC Women

Of all the games that goalkeepers play at camp, "keeper wars" is by far the most popular. It has everything we want: competition, kicking, diving, throwing, positional play, psychology, and last, but not least, fun. As a player, I have to admit, this game was one I always looked forward to playing.

I have created an environment with this one simple game that is both fun and competitive for the keepers. Out of these sessions, not only do I get a better understanding of where each keeper is technically, but I also get a view of the players' competitive fire.

### Set Up:

- Two full-size goals facing each other 18-22 yards apart (the distance depends on ability of keepers)
- A bunch of balls placed outside the posts of each goal
- Outside boundary: the edge of the six-yard box

### Rules:

- A keeper with a ball starts on his or her goal line
- He or she has two steps to either kick or throw the ball into the other keeper's goal

© Perry McIntyre

- If a goal is scored, the scoring keeper regains possession and repeats
- If the defensive keeper makes the save, he or she can throw or kick from where the save was made
- If a save is made but the ball is dropped, the keeper must start on the goal line
- If the throw or kick goes high or wide, the goalkeeper on defense gets possession
- Rebounds (off the post, crossbar or keeper) must be shot first-time if the ball remains in bounds
- The game is played to three (although scoring is up to you). Always compete for a winner

In the game I describe above, there are no restrictions on how the attacker/keeper can score. So if you have a keeper who can hit a laser of a drop kick, then that player will likely dominate that particular game.

Restrictions can be placed on both the attacker (keeper with the ball) and the defensive keeper. All keepers have their own strength when it comes to the distribution side of the game. While it is good that they are proficient in a particular area, a coach must demand that they bring up the level in their weaker areas. At the higher levels of play, it is inevitable that weaknesses will be cruelly exposed. In these training environments, don't let your players hide their weaknesses.

## Restrictions

- In a game to three, players cannot score the same way all three times. The good drop kicker would have to score another way (i.e., a throw) in order to win the game
- Players must score with a kick or throw from their "weak" side

### Consequences for inaccurate shooting or throwing:

- Each miss is a strike
- Three strikes equals a goal against the attacke.

In the basic game there was no real consequence for dropped or parried balls other than the fact that they must return to the line to start. I want my keepers to hold everything they can and not give rebounds or corner kicks. The reward for holding the shot on the first try is that they can play it from where they caught it. If they used any angle play at all, the distance to the other goal has decreased and they have an excellent chance to score. The consequence for tipping the ball over or punching it is a "corner kick" given to the other team. What that really means is that the other keeper gets another crack at scoring.

One of the main reasons I put this restriction on is because keepers, as a whole, are pretty smart. They figure that the key to the game is to get possession. Without the corner kick rule, any save the least bit uncomfortable will be tipped over or touched wide knowing they get the ball back. I want the keepers going for, and holding, the uncomfortable save. Of course there are those shots that merit a tip or a deflection. But with the corner kick rule, you can be sure the keeper used that type of save only as a last resort.

I have seen a significant improvement in the UNC keepers to go for and hold shots that they had traditionally thought out of their range. They are no longer willing to concede corner kicks so freely.

With more than two keepers at a training session, play so that the winner stays on. Or hold a team competition.

In the end these types of environments benefit everyone. The keepers get high repetitions of the different types of distribution and shot handling and the coach will be able to evaluate what technical aspects need more focus in future sessions.

# Training to Save the Breakaway

## Amy Allmann

### Stage One - Warm-up:

With the keeper in a large goal, the coach lines up with soccer balls 35 yards out. The coach serves balls to the goalie such that the ball is slowing down 12-15 yards away from the keeper. The coach serves the balls at different angles so the goalie can make decisions as to which balls are within their range and which are not (Diagram 1).

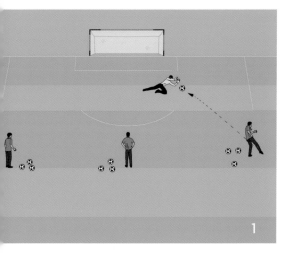

### Stage Two - Game-Related Saves:

Here there are two or three players serving as attacking players. In the beginning stage, the coach plays serves that are 60/40 in favor of the keeper, then serves 50-50 balls and finally serves that are 40-60 balls with the attackers in control (Diagram 2).

#### Organization:
- Players have no more than two touches to get the shot off
- A chasing/recovering defender can be added to create a more realistic "game pace." Emphasize the same technical coaching points as in Stage I

#### Coaching Points:
- The goalkeeper must possess a "next touch is mine" mentality
- Goalkeepers must commit themselves to save the breakaway when it is a 50-50 ball or better in their favor
- This decision should be made as soon as the player touches the ball

### Coaching Points:
- Drive the hands to the ball; make a barrier along the ground for as long as possible You are late if you are not horizontal when the shot is taken
- Spread the body to cover as much area as possible, with legs and arms slightly bent to protect the body
- Time the run to the ball so that momentum is still strong when the keeper meets the ball in order to go "through the save, not just make the save"
- Keep head/face behind the "window" that the forearms create
- Keep the body between the ball and the goal. Do not loop the run

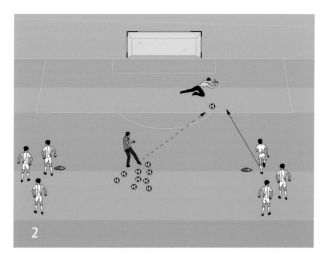

- If the ball is more in the attacker's favor, or when they have control, the keeper should simply close down the angle and be set for a shot or be ready for the next touch
- When you commit, call "KEEPER!"
- The biggest problems for goalkeepers are: lack of patience, committing to balls they cannot get and charging out to make a breakaway save when the attacker clearly is in control of the ball
- If goalkeepers are patient and wait for the touch that they can pounce on, it will slow play down and give teammates time to recover. An impatient keeper will speed play up and rarely result in defenders being able to recover to help

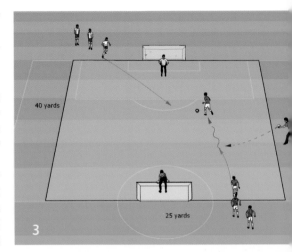

## Small-sided Games for Breakaways: "Flying Changes"

### Organization:

- Two equal teams
- Two goalkeepers in regulation goals
- 40 yards x 25 yards playing area
- Ample supply of balls
- This game can be played from 1 v. 1 to 4 v. 4

Coach starts play with a ball to one team. Both teams then try to win the ball and shoot on goal. If there is a score or the ball goes over the end line, the attacker stays to defend and a new opposing attacker comes on with the ball. There should be plenty of breakaway situations presented in this game (Diagram 3).

### Coaching Points:

- Same as in Stages I and II, both technically and tactically
- Watch for early decision-making and patience.
- Watch for approach angle to the ball and using the body as a barrier for as long as possible behind the ball

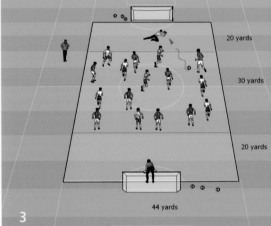

## Final Game: 8 v. 8 (with Goalkeepers) to Large Goals

The field is divided into three zones. In a restricted game, the objective for the teams is to dribble into their attacking zone. Once that happens no defender can follow. This creates obvious breakaway opportunities.

The training session finishes off with unrestricted action, with the coach watching for breakaway opportunities and how they are handled by the goalkeepers (Diagram 4).

# Dealing with Crosses

## Goalkeepers must make quick decisions in controlling their area

### Bob Barry

Goalkeepers are often judged on their ability to control the goal area and how they deal with crosses. Many factors have to be taken into consideration before a keeper can effectively deal with this type of service. Where do you position yourself in the goal? When do you come out? What if there are players blocking the path to the ball? Should you always try to catch the ball? If not, should you box or deflect? What type of communication is needed with your teammates?

Let's analyze each of the following areas: position, communication, catch or box, and technique.

## Position

Flank players who are moving toward the goal line will find themselves in one of three positions. Diagram 1 shows the flank player in three different areas outside of the box.

In the first position he can strike directly on goal, therefore he is still the primary danger. The keeper must protect the near post while also anticipating a crossed ball (secondary danger). In second position, the flank player has moved to the goal line and no longer has a good shooting angle. The area in front of the goal becomes the primary danger. At this point, the GK moves back toward the middle of the goal, where he can anticipate a crossed ball. In position No. 3, the player with the ball is now moving to the goal, where a ball can be served on the ground or in the air. The GK must now position himself to (1) cut out the cross and (2) not allow the ball to pass between him and the post. A goalkeeper must always determine the primary and secondary dangers on the field.

## Communication

Goalkeepers will have to communicate with their teammates who are marking opponents or space in front of the goal. Keepers need only to use two verbal commands: "keeper" or "away." Each is clear and with practice it can be made clear how the keeper has decided to deal with the ball. It should be clear that support is needed in the goal whenever the GK yells "keeper" and comes off his line to deal with the cross. When the communication is "away," the keeper has instructed his teammates to clear the ball to safety.

## Catch or Box

There are several reasons why a keeper might box instead of catching the ball. Box the ball if (1) there is too much traffic (too many players) in the box to catch the ball safely; (2) the weather has made the ball slippery and difficult to catch; or (3) the GK has an injury which prevents safely catching the ball. Whichever technique you decide to use, remember to box forward if you are moving forward and box backward (over the crossbar) if you are moving backward. If you are close to the goal, deflect the ball over the crossbar with an open hand.

## Technique

The keeper must work on the technique of catching air balls, the technique of boxing with two hands (to change direction), and with one hand (to continue the flight of the ball in the same direction). In addition to catching and boxing, the keeper must improve the technique of deflecting the ball with an open hand.

## Practice Drills

1. Having an understanding of the position in goal, serve balls to flank players who move down the wing and cross balls into the box. The flank players should vary the services — early balls from the edge of the box and others served on or near the goal line (Diagram 2). The keeper now has the opportunity to work on his timing and technique in dealing with the crossed ball.

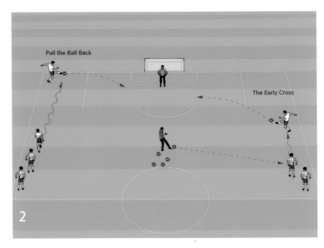

2. Add a back defender and repeat the same drill (Diagram 3). The keeper must now give instructions to his teammates. Remember that the defender must give the keeper support if he leaves his box to deal with the cross.

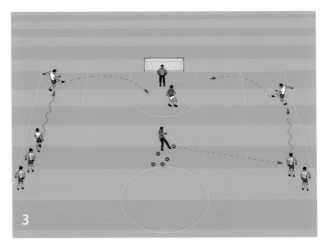

3. The drill now progresses towards a game-related situation. Add an opponent to strike on goal. The decision to catch or box will become apparent as the keeper now must deal with a striker in the box (Diagram 4).

4. Add a second striker to create a 2 v.1 situation in the goal mouth.

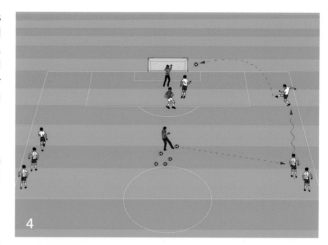

5. Place two goals 40 x 44 (approximately two penalty boxes apart). Flank players will attack both goals that each will have three attackers and two defenders in each half of the field (Diagram 5). Play begins when the keeper distributes the ball to a flank player who dribbles into the other half and crosses the ball. All players must stay in their respective halves of the field but attackers may position themselves to strike poorly cleared balls back on goal.

## Conclusion

Several years ago I attended an English FA International Coaching Course, where the acronym WADA was used when dealing with crossed balls. "W" means wait for the crossed ball to come and don't leave too early. "A" means analyze the cross to determine whether it is going to the near or far post. "D" means decide if you are going to catch or box and finally "A" means to act. Come late and hard to catch or clear the ball out of the area. This is excellent advice to all keepers when dealing with crosses.

# Integrating The Goalkeeper in a Team Training Session

## Giovanni Pacini, NSCAA National Goalkeeper Academy Staff

Not every team is blessed with a goalkeeper coach; that person educated and experienced in the training and development of goalkeepers. I always use the phrase "training and development" as virtually anyone can "train" a 'keeper. But if that person does not have the capability to indentify the areas where improvements must be made; then the training session is nothing more than a series of exercises, which may only perpetuate bad habits. It is the responsibility of every soccer coach to become formally educated in the training and development of goalkeepers. Armed with that knowledge, not only can the coach work with the goalkeeper on a one on one basis, but in the realm of integrating others. Specifically, modern goalkeeper training and development breaks down into three training realms:

Goalkeeper Coach – Goalkeeper

Goalkeeper Coach – Goalkeeper – Group of players

Coach – Team - Goalkeeper

Goalkeeper Coach – Goalkeeper is simply one on one time between the coach and goalkeeper. The second option involves groups of players, who will assist the coach in creating game like dynamics that serve the goalkeeper in a training environment. The last area involves the entire team and how the goalkeeper fits into the grand scheme of both attack and in defense.

Let's go back to the beginning; you don't have a goalkeeper coach. Maybe you're a high school or club coach in a situation where your time is limited relative to training the team. How can you integrate the 'keeper in a session that not only addresses a topic for the field players, but allows for the goalkeeper to get an effective training experience as well? I have outlined one session

that is designed to focus on passing and receiving, but shows how the goalkeeper can be effectively involved. Involved without compromising the integrity of the session as a whole.

### Warm-Up

Given that the topic for this session is actually "passing and receiving of the soccer ball"; we can see how this lends itself to integrating the goalkeeper. Here, the players move around within a grid passing the ball. The goalkeepers are allowed to either use their feet or make an appropriate save depending how the ball is played to them. Periodically, the coach will instruct the players to perform various types of passes as well as those receiving to handle the ball in a particular way (Diagram 1).

In Diagram 2, one group of players dribbles in the grid looking to pass (accurately) to those situated between the cones which are 2 yards wide (wider with younger players). Upon receiving the pass, the players between the cones one-touch the ball

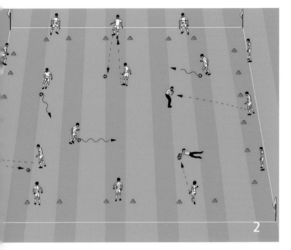

2

to pass the ball back and forth. The receiving player makes a short run away from the passer. Upon checking back to the passer, the pass is made. The coach instructs the receiving player about the various methods by which the ball is to be played (first touch) and straight versus angled checking (Diagram 3).

Each group has a number; once that number is called by the goalkeeper, the receiving player takes a touch and shoots on the goalkeeper. The 'keeper then distributes to the other player. Players are asked to take specific types of shots as directed by the coach.

back. When the goal-keeper passes, a shot is taken by the player between the cones. Next, players switch positions; i.e. when the ball is passed between the cones, the receiving player now enters the grid to dribble and the passing player takes the spot between the cones.

When a dribbling player goes to a goalkeeper between the cones, the "pass" is now made either inside or outside the cones, forcing the 'keeper to now execute the appropriate save.

Players are now paired off forming a circle around the the goalkeepers. Players are asked

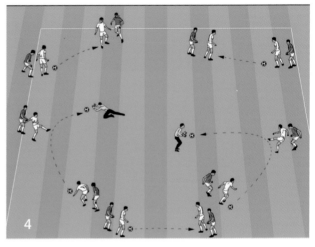

4

In Diagram 4, players are grouped into four. The phase is the same as that noted in Diagram 3, but now with pressure. The passing player must now read the defending player's pressure and then make the appropriate pass. The coach must insure that both straight and angled checks take place. As was the case in Diagram 3, the groups are given a number.

When a group's number is called, the player receiving the ball now dribbles in on the goalkeeper simulating a breakaway situation. Over the course of several repetitions, attacking players may either shoot or dribble in.

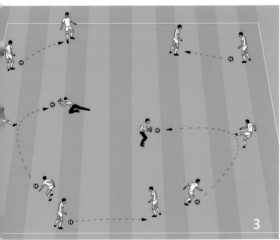

3

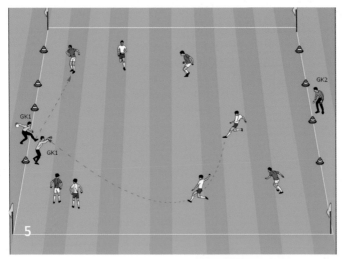

In this 4 v 4 game, players are directed to recognize appropriate attacking shape (diamond) and to understand the importance of fluid movement in support of the ball. The objective of the game is to find the goalkeeper. The 'keeper plays the ball with either their feet or hands depending upon the ball played. In Diagram 5, the goalkeeper saves the ball and releases to the red team.

The session concludes in a 6 v 6 game using full goals. At the coach's discretion, restrictions can be made on the players (2-touch, 5 passes before shooting...), so as to heighten the pressure of executing quality passes and necessity of being able to receive the ball so as to set up the subsequent pass. The goalkeeper is allowed to play freely, however a training flag is placed 1-2 feet beyond the posts. The 'keeper is expected to defend "flag to flag", as this will assist in enhancing the goalkeeper's range (Diagram 6).

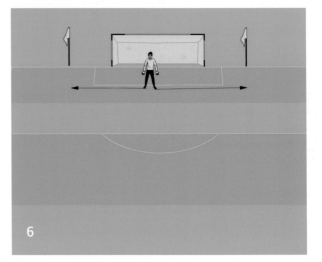

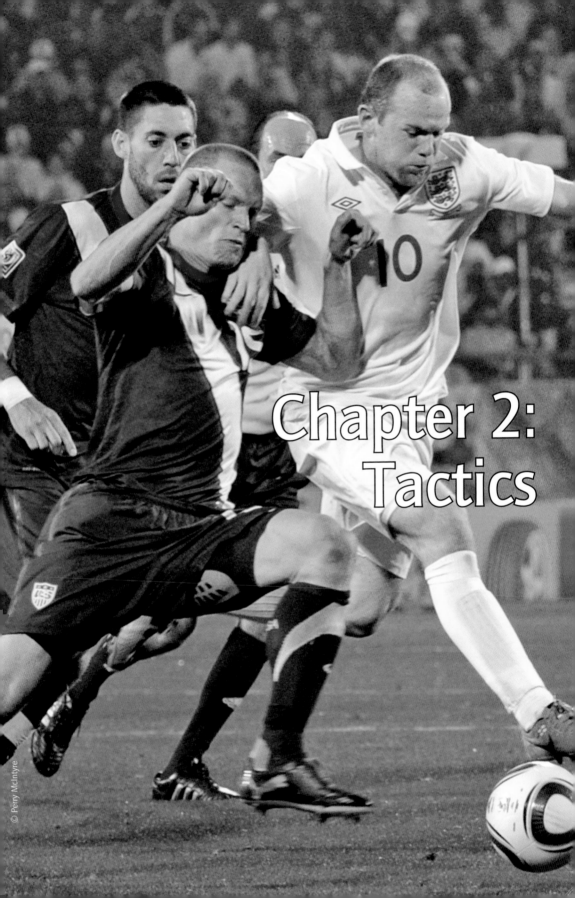

Chapter 2:
Tactics

# The Evolution of Systems

## John Bluem

In this article, we will trace the development and evolution of the game of soccer through the growth of systems of play. Today's modern game clearly can be traced back to the late 1800s.

## The Dribbling Game

On Oct. 26, 1863, representatives from a group of clubs met at the Freemason's Tavern in England to draw up the first official rules. The rules were accepted on December 18, 1863.

Rule 6 stated "when a player has kicked the ball, any one of the same side who is nearer to the opponent's goal line is out of play" (offside!). The lifeblood of the early games was the skill of dribbling. The forward pass was banned. Rule 6 was changed in 1866 to permit advanced players to receive a pass, providing there were at least three opponents between themselves and the goal line.

There still was little difference in the way the game was played. In the 1870s, soccer pundit C.W. Alcock wrote about "the grand and essential principle of backing up." This first recognized principle of play was understood to mean the following closely of a fellow player in case possession was lost. There was no mention of passing.

The first international match saw Scotland play England in Glasgow, where the English played a 1-2-7 and the Scots a 2-2-6. It was the Scots who realized the potential of the 1866 rule change and began to employ the short pass. Despite the large number of forwards in the game, the result was a 0-0 tie.

Players now had to think about their positional play due to the new weapon, the pass. By the

1883 Football Association Cup final, the English had developed the long passing game. Blackburn won the finale easily, using the long pass to change the point of attack from wing to wing.

By this time, new skills had been introduced to the game − the ability to hit a long ball and the skills necessary to receive, intercept or clear long passes. Heading, chest trapping, receiving on the run and volleying were skills now emphasized.

## The Pyramid System

By 1890 the favored system of play in England had evolved to the 2-3-5 formation. A pyramid shape was described, as one would draw lines from the two wings on either side of the field back to the goalkeeper. The key player was the center halfback, who was supposed to come forward on attack and also serve to organize the five-person defense (versus the five attackers of the opponents). Note that the system utilized only two defending backs (Diagram 1).

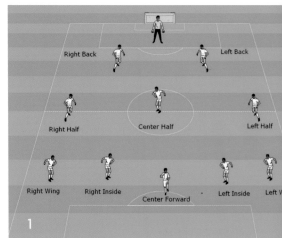

## The W-M Formation

The offside law was amended in 1925. From then on, attackers needed only two opponents between themselves and the goal line at the moment the ball was played. If justification for the rule change was needed, it emerged from the matches themselves. The number of goals in the English First Division shot up 40 percent, from 1,192 in 1925 to 1,703 in 1926.

Defenses had to be strengthened, and Arsenal coach Herbert Chapman, who had taken over the London club in 1925, drew up a new tactical plan.

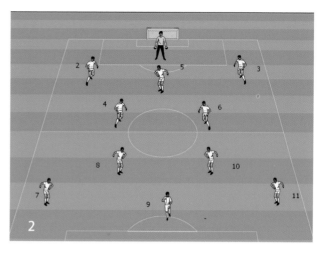

The center forward was doing the most attacking damage in the game, so Chapman dropped the center half to the position of fullback to mark him. This position became known as the "stopper" and represented the birth of the modern man-to-man marker style. Defensive responsibilities were now reassigned, with the original fullbacks moving wide to mark the wingers and the wing halves assigned to look after the inside forwards.

For the next 25 years, the new center back or "stopper" and the pivot of the other backs to provide cover and balance dominated the game. Basically, if the ball was with a winger, the outside back marked that player; the center back provided cover and the weak side back was concerned with balancing things.

Any system of play stands or falls with the men who put it into practice. Arsenal's W-M prevailed because of the genius of Chapman in finding the right players to fill the roles he had established. The key to the attacking success of Arsenal was in the playmaking abilities of one of the withdrawn inside forwards, Scotsman Alex James.

Chapman died in 1934, but between 1927 and 1938 the team that he built won the league championship five times and the FA Cup twice. By the late 1930's the W-M was the standard formation of every English club (Diagram 2).

Outside of the English game, the attacking center half continued to flourish, particularly in Hungary, Austria and South America. In the first World Cup in 1930, both finalists, Argentina and Uruguay, utilized the 2-3-5 pyramid formation.

Artistry was the essence of the South American game, which often emphasized individual talent to decide games while collective tactics were minimized. Asked about the role of coaching in those days, Uruguayan left back Ernesto Mascheroni replied, "What are the coaches for? Only the player can solve the problems on the field. What does a player do when he meets another who makes a fool of him? Ask the coach?"

The Uruguayans won the first Cup by the score of 4-2, and opinions were expressed that they were a better-organized team. With the score 3-2 and with Argentina doing all the attacking, Uruguay laid back and then used a quick counter to score on a breakaway. This type of play now would become a tactic for some teams.

## The Italian *"Metodo"*

In Italy, Vittorio Pozzo, an undistinguished player who, as a coach, had a great interest in tactics, coached the national team. For the 1934 Italian World Cup team, he devised a scheme based on the classic 2-3-5 as played by the Austrians,

Czechs and Hungarians, the so-called Danubian School of soccer.

The Danubian School had emerged from the Scottish short-passing game brought to central Europe by a remarkable Englishman named Jimmy Hogan. His philosophy was that soccer was a game in which the ball belonged on the ground, and he used the phrase "keep it on the carpet" to describe how he wanted the ball to be passed.

The Danubian style, based on the 2-3-5, was faithful to Hogan's artistic approach to the game. By 1934, the Austrians had raised the style to its pinnacle under national coach Hugo Meisl. The Austrian "wunderteam" was considered the strongest in continental Europe.

Pozzo could not simply copy the Danubian model because he lacked the player to fill the vital playmaking center half role. This role was taken over by two players, the inside forwards, who were withdrawn into midfield. Thus Pozzo's metodo, as it was called, retained elements of the 2-3-5 (particularly the marking assignments under which the fullbacks guarded the penalty area and the wing halves marked the opposing wingers), but used the M formation for the forward line (Diagram 3).

The *metodo* proved ideally suited to the Italian player. It stressed methodical defense and gave birth to the lightning counterattack, which was to be the basis of the Italian game for a long time. As one journalist put it, "The other team does all the attacking, but Italy wins the game."

In the 1934 World Cup final, the *metodo* triumphed over the Danubian 2-3-5 of the Czechs. However the general feeling was that it was Italian strength, stamina and ruthlessness that actually determined the 2-1 outcome.

The 1938 final resulted in a similar match-up, the Italian *metodo* against the Hungarian 2-3-5. It was an easy 4-2 win by the Italians, whose system proved capable of accommodating a new, faster, more athletic type of game.

The 2-3-5 was stagnating and the tactics of its defensive system were about to be exposed. As the world prepared for war, there were three systems of play throughout the world: The W-M, the standard formation in England; the Italian *metodo*, part W-M, part 2-3-5; and the 2-3-5, the Pyramid, still favored in South America, Czechoslovakia, Hungary and Austria.

## The "Swissbolt"

Within the various systems, soccer had become a game for specialist players, each with certain rather limited functions (i.e., wingers). There was one system that went against this trend, a system that at the time didn't receive the study it deserved. In part this was because it was developed in Switzerland, which was not considered a bastion of soccer thought, and in part because it was a difficult theory to put into practice.

Karl Rappan, a former Austrian international who from 1931 on coached club soccer in Switzerland, concocted the system. The aim of the "bolt" system was to create a team that

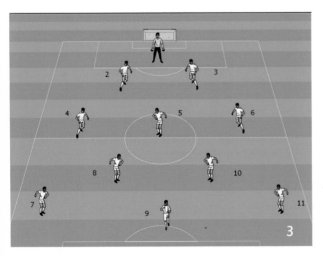

would outnumber opponents in both attack and defense. On attack, the bolt had a 3-3-4 shape complete with an attacking center half, with all the players, including the three-man fullback line, moving well upfield (Diagram 4).

When ball possession was lost, all 10 players retreated. The function of the four forwards was to harass the opponents and slow down the attack. The other six players raced deep into their own defensive half of the field. The attacking center half now became the center back, while the former center back retreated to an ultra-deep position behind every one else. From this deep position that player could move laterally across the field, covering the other three backs and functioning as the sliding "bolt" to lock out opposing forwards.

The bolt system required great fitness from its players. They had to be capable of high-speed running and have the ability to function both as attackers and defenders.

The system was not widely utilized, but it did introduce the two ideas: a retreating defense and the lone fullback playing deep. Its attacking and defending shapes are shown in Diagrams 4 and 5.

Uruguay's 2-1 victory over Brazil in the 1950 World Cup final remains the most astonishing upset in World Cup history. The Brazilians produced an attack-oriented version of the W-M that they called the diagonal system to start the tournament and dismissed Mexico, 4-0. They then were held to a 2-2 tie by Switzerland, which frustrated them with their bolt system. Changing to a more traditional W-M, the Brazilians regrouped and defeated Yugoslavia, 2-0, Sweden, 7-1, and Spain, 6-1.

Meanwhile, the Uruguayans were plodding along with their version of the metodo. In the final the Uruguayans utilized a deep-lying fullback and tight man marking everywhere on the field. In reality, the team looked more like the 4-3-3 of the future than the metodo. Although the Uruguayans trailed 1-0 at halftime, their counterattacks exposed the fragility of the Brazilian defense to capture the Cup. The Uruguayans, an Italian journalist commented, had become the world champions of marking (Diagram 5).

## The Hungarian Team, 1953

By the 1954 World Cup, the attacking center half was on his last legs and the attention now switched to the center forward, in particular the so-called withdrawn center forward utilized by the Hungarians.

Chapman's invention of the third back killed off the attacking center half and also changed

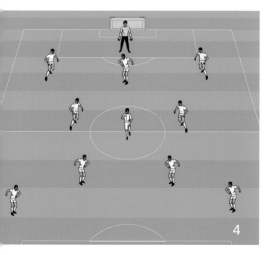

4

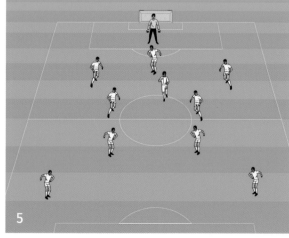

5

the role of the center forward, from the talented all-rounder to the strong, powerful battering ram who battled the stopper (Diagram 6).

Brawny center forwards were not available in Hungary. Marton Bukovi, coach of a top club in Budapest, Voros Loboga, got around the problem by bringing the center forward back to play in midfield. The role of the center forward was assumed by the two insides. The M had been turned upside down. These changes were the basis for the great Hungarian national team formed in the 1950's by Gustav Sebes.

The weakness of the three-back game was exposed when coaches began to think about attacking space. By withdrawing the center forward, the center back had to make a choice – follow his man and expose the central attacking space, or leave his man free to protect the central space. The fullbacks, when confronted or not confronted by the withdrawing wingers, were faced with the same problem. Defenders always have had two responsibilities, to mark and to cover.

In 1953 Hungary crushed England, 6-3, at Wembley. The following year, to prove it was no fluke, Hungary defeated England, 7-1, in Budapest.

Through a series of training drills known as three-man combinations, the Hungarian players Puskas, Kocsis, Bozsik and Hidegkuti built up a great understanding. First developed around 1951, the combinations largely were based on positional switching allied to the wall pass. Later, between 1954 and 1956, these combinations were further developed to involve not two players, as in a wall pass, but three (Diagram 7).

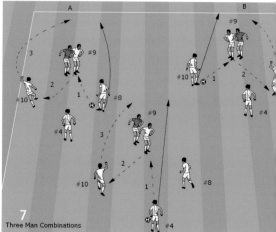

**7**
Three Man Combinations

The great Hungarian team of 1953-54 had one player who was generally considered to be inferior to his colleagues. At the time no one could understand how left half Joseph Zakarias managed to keep his place in the team. It is now clear that Zakarias was not a left half at all but a left-center back.

Way back in the 1860s, the English had started playing soccer with one fullback; in 1872 the Scots had made it two; in 1925 Arsenal had introduced the third back, and now here were the Hungarians with approximately three-and-a-half fullbacks.

## The 4-2-4 Formation

The essential features of the 4-2-4 system introduced by the attack-minded Brazilians in 1958, two center forwards and two center halves, already had been seen in the Hungarian game.

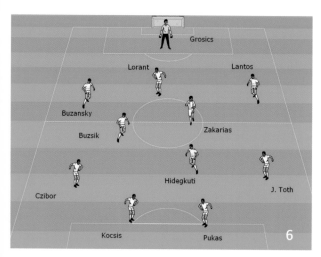

Grosics
Lorant
Lantos
Buzansky
Buzsik
Zakarias
Czibor
Hidegkuti
J. Toth
Kocsis
Pukas

6

While the Hungarians concealed their system through place-changing, the Brazilians' rigid formation had Vava and Pelé clearly operating as twin center forwards. It was no longer possible for any opponent to play with one center back. Within 12 months of Brazil's World Cup success, almost the entire world had switched to the 4-2-4 (Diagram 8).

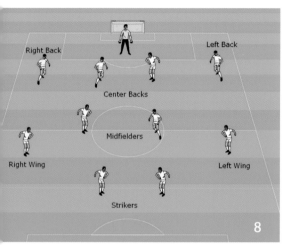

8

The 2-3-5 and 3-4-3 formations that have been discussed were not referenced in a numerical way at the time. They were simply the Pyramid and the W-M. Following 1958, all the talk was about the 4-2-4. Methodical coaching was on the rise, and identifying formations with numbers gave them a more modern scientific sound.

Despite the four fullbacks, the 4-2-4 as played by the 1958 Brazilians was far from a defensive scheme. An exhilarating feature was the attacking role of the two outside fullbacks. On attack, the formation became 2-4-4, enabling Brazil to commit as many as eight players to the offense.

The new role demanded fullbacks who were quick-moving, with a fair share of the forward's talents, the ability to exchange short passes, and, once in attack, to shoot accurately.

Quite a change from the W-M days when a fullback's main functions were to stay deep, win the ball through hard tackling and deliver long downfield passes. As Brazil spent most of its time on the attack, little attention was paid to its defensive adjustment. When its opponents had the ball, Brazil's left winger, Mario Zagallo, quickly withdrew into midfield, changing the alignment to 4-3-3.

The 4-2-4 succeeded in 1958 because the Brazilians' extravagant attacking talents allowed them to maintain relentless pressure on their opponents. But it contained a serious weakness. When forced into a defensive mode, the 4-2-4 was dangerously "under populated" in midfield.

## The 4-3-3 Formation

The 1962 World Cup featured a 4-3-3 system of play employed by the Brazilians as the altitude of the Chilean site demanded a bit more defensive posture by the participating teams. The use of three midfielders gave greater strength to the midfield and their more central alignment still allowed for attacking runs by the outside backs. The midfielders themselves could be staggered in a number of ways (one up, two back; two up, one back, etc.) (Diagram 9).

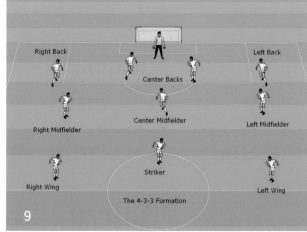

The 4-3-3 Formation

9

Of interest was the fact that the average number of goals scored in World Cup matches during the period of 1954-1962 decreased from 5.38 per game to 2.78 per game. Clearly the emphasis of coaches was more on the defensive side of the game than on the attack.

*Catenaccio*

The Italians continued the trend toward defensive soccer during the 1960s. They had perfected a system that used the deep-lying fullback seen in Switzerland's 1950 Verrou formation. *Catenaccio* ("large chain") was the name the Italians gave their system (Diagram 10).

Three of the fullbacks were given strict man-to-man marking duties. The "*libero*," or "free man" because he had no specific opponent to mark, played deep behind the markers. His job was to patrol the entire center of the defense and to quickly close any gaps that might be opened by other defenders' errors.

The history of *catenaccio* tells much about the development of soccer tactics. There was absolutely nothing positive about its origin. It was designed not to win games, but rather to avoid losing them.

The Italian Serie A (First Division) had long been an unbalanced league, with a few rich clubs regularly carrying off all the honors. In 1947, Nereo Rocco took over at Triestina, a small club that was barely surviving. It was Rocco who loosed *catenaccio* on the soccer world. He had immediate and dramatic success. In 1948 Triestina climbed to second place in the league. Noting the team's success, other Italian clubs began to utiltize the *catenaccio* system of play.

Herrera perfected the system with Inter Milan, which won the European Cup twice using its own brand of *catenaccio*. So even the wealthier, more powerful Italian clubs adopted *catenaccio*. It would become more than a style of play; it became a mentality that dragged Italian soccer down to a style of game that emphasized negativity at the expense of creativity.

*Catenaccio* had a special appeal for the Italians because it relied so heavily on the sudden counterattack to score goals. The quick breakaway, the rapid switch from defense to attack, had long been a feature of the Italian game. Now it had been given an almost scientific basis.

## 4-4-2 System of England

The English acknowledged the coming of the *libero*, but coined their own term for the position. They called the player the sweeper, the man who moved about at the back of the defense, cleaning up the errors of his teammates.

Wingers were an endangered species and what looked like their burial took place in 1966 when England won the World Cup using a formation that included no wingers at all. It was dubbed the "penguin" formation. Wingless! Sir Alf Ramsay, England manager, was said he had experimented with wingers, but found none to his liking (Diagram 11).

An increasing emphasis on not conceding goals led to the packing of numbers in midfield. Just as the 4-2-4 formation had lost a forward

Right Back
Libero - Sweeper
Left Back
Center Back
Right Midfielder
Center Midfielder
Left Midfielder
Right Wing
Striker
Left Wing

The Italian Catenaccio

10

to midfield and became the 4-3-3, the process continued and the 4-3-3 became the 4-4-2.

England's World Cup-winning side included a novelty in midfield – the evolution of the screen man. Nobby Stiles fulfilled this function as a defensively oriented player detailed to mark or act as a sweeper between the back four and midfield.

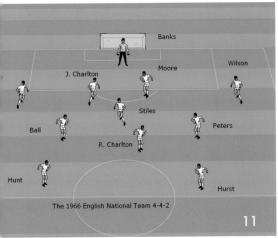

The 1966 English National Team 4-4-2

11

## Tactical Trends, 1970-1998

Brazil won the 1970 World Cup due to the brilliance of Pelé and the goal scoring of Jairzinho, who scored in every game. The Italians' deep sweeper and counterattacks were not enough to win, but they would be heard from again.

"Total soccer" burst on the scene in the '70s, with the emphasis on players fit enough and skilled enough to play any position on the field and intelligent enough to know exactly when to switch roles. The style reached its zenith with the Dutch National Team of 1974, which featured the brilliant play of Johan Cruyff under the direction of Rinus Michels.

The Germans won the World Cup that year, however, led by the equally brilliant Franz Beckenbauer, who had revolutionized the role of *libero* in soccer by reshaping the position so he could utilize his immense attacking talents.

By 1978 total soccer had begun to dissipate, primarily because its two most inspirational players, Cruyff and Beckenbauer, had retired from international soccer. The Cup-winning side from Argentina had reverted to a traditional 4-3-3 and reintroduced the long-forgotten wingers to defeat the Dutch in the Buenos Aires final.

In 1982 the Italians used Paolo Rossi to effectuate their counter-attacking game as they overcame a solid but somewhat unimaginative German team in the World Cup final in Madrid. By 1986 Maradona was playing as a midfield schemer behind the double forwards. His skill at both freeing others and scoring goals himself led the Argentines to the title in Mexico. Maradona was covered by what had now become known as a defensive midfielder. That player's job (not unlike Stiles in 1966) was to break up play and play balls forward.

By 1990 and 1994, World Cups were becoming marked by strong defensive play, with no goals scored from free play in either final match. Germany won on a penalty kick in 1990 over Argentina in the Italian staging of the event, while Brazil prevailed in a penalty kick shootout over Italy in Los Angeles in 1994.

## Selecting a System

Your choice of a system can be based on the following factors:

- Technical ability of the players on the team
- An understanding by the players of their roles in the game
- The level of fitness necessary to play a system
- The system the other team is using

The principles of the game must be the foundation upon which systems of play and tactical considerations are developed. Instruction in the basic principles will result in a greater

## The 4-4-2

**Strengths:**
- Team consists of two equally balanced vertical halves of the field
- Four midfield players receive the ball facing forward
- Allows two players in each central channel
- More space for the two strikers
- Easy to change the point of attack
- Eight defenders behind the ball
- Difficult to unbalance
- A good high pressing system

**Weaknesses:**
- Numbers down in midfield against a 3-5-2
- How do you match up against two forwards?
- Susceptible to the counter attack if midfield balance is lost
- Forwards can get isolated

## The 3-5-2

**Strengths:**
- Creates the ability to balance in central midfield
- Numerical advantage in midfield
- Immediate support for the strikers
- Easier to spring flank midfield players
- Effective against teams that play an indirect style
- Allows assignments for man-to-man coverage
- The holding midfielder prevents the counterattack

**Weaknesses:**
- Concedes space on the wings
- Difficult formation for high pressure
- Difficult to prevent opponents from building out of the back
- Fewer numbers in the back leads to cover and balance problems

## The 4-3-3 / 3-4-3

**Strengths:**
- Front line is ready to attack when the ball is won
- Three targets rather than two
- Easier to attack critical space
- Width in attack is assured
- Allows for pressure closer to the opponent's goal
- Puts tremendous pressure on weak opponents
- Forces your opponent to adjust

**Weaknesses:**
- Three front players can be played out of the game immediately
- Three players with their back to goal
- Can be out numbered in the midfield
- Defends with only seven players

understanding of the game by the players and give the coach an opportunity to assess the ability of the players in a variety of situations. Through this evaluation, the coach may evolve a style of play that allows the players to perform to the best of their ability.

The development of a system of play is the recognition of where space is on the field. Through the specific arrangement of players on the field, the coach tries to close dangerous spaces while defending and find open spaces while attacking.

A system must fit the abilities and playing characteristics of the team members. If the players cannot perform in the chosen system, it doesn't fit the team.

Too often a system is seen as the solution to all coaching problems. Just because the system is popular does not mean it is right for the team.

The system must be elastic to enable different players to use their strengths and to allow quick changes when necessitated by the opponents.

## Principles of Defense

**Delay** means that you force the attacking team to take time in organizing its attack so defenders have time to build a collective defending action between the ball and the goal. The first defender should work on the concept of delay.

**Depth** means the organization of the players behind the first defender to provide cover. This is specifically the work of the second defender.

**Balance** means positioning of the defenders relative to the possibilities of penetration by attackers away from the ball. This is specifically the work of the third defender.

**Concentration** means that players limit space and time by "squeezing" centrally behind the ball. This will prevent balls from being played over the top or through the defense.

## Principles of Attack

**Penetration** is getting the ball behind the defenders by shooting, dribbling or passing. The first attacker makes this decision.

**Depth** is the organization of players behind and in front of the first attacker. The players in these positions are the second attackers and they help the first attacker with penetration by combination play and possession.

**Mobility** is the attempt by the attacking players to penetrate and unbalance the collective defending action. The third attackers do this work.

**Width** is the disposition of attackers across the field to pull apart the collective defense.

# 4-4-2 – A Balanced Attack

## Schellas Hyndman
## Coach: FC Dallas: MLS

The 1982 World Cup in Spain gave birth to the 4-4-2 systems which was introduced by the Germans. It was developed because the attackers realized that the defenders were too strong. Thus, one attacker retreated to reinforce the midfield. The strikers get help from the midfield players when their team is in possession of the ball.

The 4-4-2 system has four defenders and four midfielders who are capable of covering the width of the field in both attacking and defending play, while the two strikers have space to play in the attack. This system offers a balanced attack, with a mirror image from left to right side of the field.

The 4-4-2 system can be played in many different ways – this is only one way. Up top, play is with two in the attack (Nos. 9 and 10). A diamond shape is shown by the four midfielders, with No. 8 as attacking midfielder and No. 6 as defending midfielder. Nos. 7 and 11 are wide midfielders. The wide defenders are Nos. 2 and 3, while No.

4 is the center back and No. 5 plays deep as the sweeper (Diagram 1).

## Attack

The forwards are Nos. 9 and 10. The two forwards always create opportunities for each other by interplay or by opening space for each other. Checking back to the ball on angles is very important to the forwards. They also make diagonal runs to the flanks to receive the ball on the move from the back. They will go wide to create a 2 v. 1 situation with the wing midfielders on the flanks. The timing of runs to the near and far posts is extremely important. The forwards need to complement each other in terms of playing characteristics – No. 9 might play higher and be the target player, while No. 10 might be better at showing back to collect balls from the midfield and defense.

The attacking midfielder (No. 8) is very important in this system. This player must possess excellent penetrating ability with the dribble, as well as very good passing technique to penetrate the opponent's defense with well-timed, accurate balls. This player can unbalance the defense with his creativity and has the ability to combine with the forwards. Usually playing in the center of the field, the attacking midfielder should possess a powerful shot. This player also can be classified as a withdrawn forward.

The defending midfielder (No. 6) is a pivotal player in this system. This player gets the majority of balls from the defense. His primary role is to move the ball from one flank to the other as quickly as possible. He should always make himself available for touches. The defending midfielder usually will stay in the

1

center of the field while checking back on angles and maintaining good body position to switch the ball to the opposite flank. The defending center midfielder must be tactically sound to make good decisions, such as whether to play the ball wide or to start the counterattack in a more central fashion.

The two central midfielders must understand the functions of the positions. No. 8 has to view his position as 70 percent attacking versus 30 percent defensive responsibilities. Meanwhile, No. 6 has the opposite percentages of responsibility. They must understand each other's role and offer balance in the midfield – both cannot attack at the same time. They must work to give support to strikers and one (hopefully No. 8) must support them if at all possible.

The wing midfielders, Nos. 7 and 11, play wide on the field. They must have good speed and constantly make runs behind the defense. The wing midfielders should have good dribbling ability and good tactical sense, such as knowing when to take an opponent on, either individually or combining with a teammate. This player must be able to cross a quality ball while under pressure.

The job of the wing midfielders is to get behind the defenders, either by individual penetration or by playing balls into the valuable space behind the defense. They look to create a 2 v. 1 situation on the outside of the field. Defensively they must be able to pressure the ball.

The wing fullbacks (Nos. 2 and 3) attack from the back. Both should possess pure speed and good passing ability on both short and long passes. They should have good tactical sense in terms of supporting the ball, as well as knowing when to go forward on overlapping runs.

The wing fullbacks must have a high work rate since they have to be able to move up and down the perimeter of the field. They must

possess good 1 v. 1 defending skills. Technically they must be able to deliver good crossing balls as well as bend balls to players. A player such as Maldini has the ability to play a long diagonal ball and penalize a team if it doesn't have depth in its defense. Such a player also can help a team penetrate centrally by playing a ball to a striker's diagonal run behind a drawn-up defense.

The center back must be able to defend 1 v. 1 and be a good header of the ball. The ability to play with both feet also is a plus for this player. The center back (No. 4) usually is a supporting player who plays simply and primarily stays in the middle of the field.

The sweeper (No. 5) is very important in this system. This player must have good soccer sense; he is the playmaker with the wing fullbacks and can switch the ball from one flank to the other. The sweeper should have very good passing skills, including the ability to hit 40-yard passes behind the defense. The sweeper also can carry the ball from the defending third into the middle third.

Examples of changing the point of attack through the midfield (Diagram 2) and developing attacking play out of the back (Diagram 3) in the 4-4-2 are illustrated.

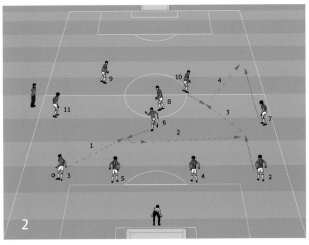

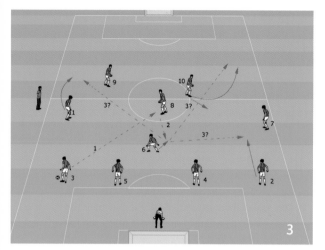

## Defense

Defenders wear Nos. 2, 3, 4 and 5. Nos. 2 and 3 are fullbacks, No. 4 is the center back and No. 5 is the sweeper.

The first priority of the fullbacks (Nos. 2 and 3) is to play in a disciplined manner. They must have good speed to mark players. The fullbacks must have good tactical awareness to know when and where to give coverage, usually with the third defender giving balance to the defense.

The center back (No. 4) has the special responsibility to be the man-marker (he marks the opponent's best attacker out of the game). This player must possess good athletic ability, speed, quickness, jumping ability for heading and the determination to win every 50/50 ball. The center back is the physical strength of the defense.

The sweeper (No. 5) is the defensive leader. He must be sound tactically in order to make good decisions on the field. The ability to communicate and give directions to the other players is extremely important. The sweeper must have the speed to give immediate coverage to teammates as well as to cover runners coming through with or without the ball. The sweeper must be a sure tackler, since the position generally is the last line of defense before the goalkeeper.

The defensive strength in a 4-4-2 system is in the midfield. The two wing midfielders (Nos. 7 and 11) have a great responsibility of channeling opponents into more pressurized situations. The wing midfielders work extremely hard throughout the game. Both players must be tactically sound and disciplined and play within the team's structure. The ball side midfielder can put immediate pressure on the fullback or mark the opponent's wing midfielder. The weak side midfielder will come into the center to condense the opponent's space, but still must be aware of the long diagonal ball by opponents as they attempt to switch the point of attack.

The defending midfielder (No. 6) must mark man-to-man any opponent who attacks through the center of the midfield. This player must be tactically sound, knowing when to go with runners and when to give coverage. It is helpful if No. 6 has the ability to win air balls from goal kicks or goalkeeper punts.

The attacking midfielder (No. 8) must be able to give direction to the two strikers in addition to being positioned well in the passing lanes. No. 8's defensive role is to prevent the opponents from penetrating the center of the field or switching the ball to the opposite flank.

The two forwards (Nos. 9 and 10) must work together to force opponents to the flanks. The forwards' role is not to win the ball on tackles, but to make play predictable and force opponents to play into pressure. They should not let opponents play back to switch the ball from one flank to the other.

The 4-4-2 allows for high pressure defending. If opponents are playing the ball successfully down the flank, the 4-4-2 can be adjusted with the outside midfielder pushing up and combining with the striker to double-team the player of the penetrating ball. The players closest to the ball on that side of the field tighten up on potential receivers while the balancing players provide

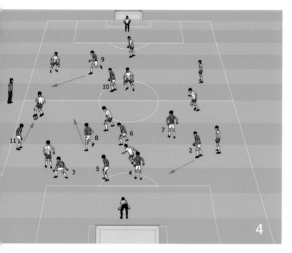

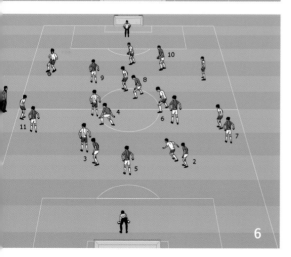

zonal coverage away from ball. It also can be structured to allow for low pressure defending (Diagrams 4 and 5).

Playing a 4-4-2 against a 3-5-2 would have an outside back push up, while the third central midfielder would play the fifth opposition midfielder or zone in back or forward of the midfield line (Diagram 6).

The defense can push together with all four no more than 40 yards across the field. This allows for pressure on the ball in the final third, with the balancing defender offering wide space that should be able to be covered.

Defensively, the team shape should emphasize compactness, with the ideal being about 12 to 15 yards of distance between the three lines. In this way, the group should be able to surround the ball. Such compactness also favors the use of the offside trap as a means of squeezing a team's space. A central back can dictate this if there is pressure on the ball and the line is held.

In terms of combating the offside trap, an exchange of position between a central midfielder and striker with service from an unpressured wing midfielder is the ideal manner of beating the offside trap.

# 4-4-2 – The Defensive Strategy

## Mike Noonan
## Clemson University

While there is no formal warm-up, coaches may want to organize players into 4 v. 2 or other possession games with the focus on the work of the two defenders. Here pressure on the ball, angle and speed of approach might be the points of emphasis. Have everyone work as defenders, with stretching to be interspersed between each bout of the exercise.

## 6 v. 7 – Beginning the Practice

Two sets of training vests should be on hand and the balls placed in the goal. Field size should be 75 x 80 yards. One regular goal is placed on one end line and two target goals established at either side of the 80-yard line.

Six attacking players work against seven players plus a keeper coming out of the back. Play starts with one of the attacking players taking a shot on goal. The keeper collects it or a ball from the goal and distributes to a wide back. As soon as this occurs, all six defenders get behind the ball.

As the ball is on the way from the keeper, the outside midfielder (No. 11) on that side of the field moves forward to defend. If the attacker is not clean in controlling the ball or looks to play the ball back to his support, then the nearest striker (No. 9) looks to double-team or press. If the player in possession cannot be highly pressured, the striker will take a position to cut out the back pass (Diagram I).

If high pressure is "on," the second striker (No. 10) cuts out the possibility of a pass to the keeper or, if not, moves more centrally to zone the opponent's central midfielder.

The No. 6 player will push up if pressure is on or drop back to mark space otherwise. Likewise, No. 8 pushes up to compress play on the weak side while No. 7 looks to take a position that allows interception of a long diagonal pass. The possibilities are shown in Diagram 1.

## 6 v. 7 – Strikers Defend Outside Backs

The defenders' objective is to defend the attacking outside backs and invite play to be made with either of the opponent's central backs by spreading the two strikers (Nos. 9 and 10) into wider initial positions.

This invites the keeper to play the ball short to the center back and the striker (No. 9) on the outside of the field tries to channel play to the central part of the field. No. 10 keeps play in front while eliminating the pass to the other outside back. No. 11 looks for passes to the right midfielder. Nos. 6 and 8 would shift to cover the midfield spaces (if No. 11 must defend), while No. 7 looks to intercept any long diagonal ball to the attacking team's opposite side midfielder (Diagram 2).

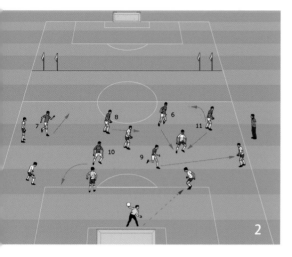

midfielders shift toward the ball in a zonal fashion with No. 7 again looking to cut out a long diagonal or lateral pass from the player with the ball (Diagram 3).

One advantage of this system is that the two strikers are in good forward positions to be played to for a quick counterattack. I let play take place with an emphasis on commitment to defense by the defending team with particular emphasis on team compactness in the midfield, so as the ball moved into the mid-third of the field it could be pressured and the players farthest from the ball could seek to balance the field.

It is important that the coach sets the line of confrontation (in relation to the penalty area) and who will apply the pressure (either No. 9 or 10, depending on which side of the field is being attacked).

## 6 v. 7 – Strikers defend central backs

The third option for the defensive team is to have the two strikers mark up or defend the center backs when the ball is distributed to the outside back. This forces No. 11 to step up to defend the outside back – channeling play into the interior of the field – while the other defending

## 7 v. 9 – Playing Off the Strikers

Here a central striker and a fourth midfielder are added to the attacking team and a central defender is added to the defending team. The forwards were free (depending on communication to play any of the three options introduced earlier in the practice (drop centrally, play wide or play the opposing cornerbacks)).

I emphasized that the defenders' midfield should "play off" how the strikers channel play (centrally or wide) through the positioning they are able to take relative to the ball. I also wanted the players to put an aggressive mentality to work in the practice while marking on the goal side of the ball at all times. If the ball were to be played back or square by the opponents, the defending team should use that as a cue to impart high-pressure tactics (Diagram 4).

The defensive emphasis is for the defending team to be able to adapt high or low pressure tactics and counterattack or possession tactics once the ball is won. By focusing on the ability of the central strikers to read the game, the defending unit can react in the correct fashion.

I emphasized that the ability to scout a team and determine its capabilities in the back

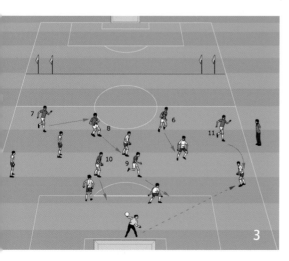

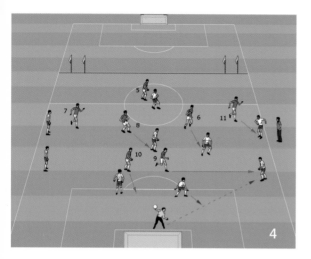

usually dictates before the game which way the strikers will play and thus how the midfield and backs will defend collectively.

## Shape of Defenders — 5 v. 6

As for how the back four in a 4-4-2 should be aligned, I stress compactness, no more than 60 yards wide and about 15 yards between each defender. They want to hold the line at a reasonable distance behind a midfield line so as not to get beaten vertically or diagonally by pace. This varies from team to team and opponent to opponent. The outside back furthest from the ball should be ahead of the other backs. This helps in playing teams offside as vertical and diagonal running takes place, as few players have to step forward for the tactic to be employed.

In order to ensure that the shape of the back four is right, the ball is moved from side to side by the attacking team, and as it moves the backs react accordingly.

Meanwhile the single defensive midfielder seeks to use positioning to put enough pressure on the midfielders to force play into one side of the field, making matters more predictable for the four backs. An emphasis here was for the defenders

to get goal side of the ball and realize that they need to see both attackers and the ball. The deeper the ball goes, the more difficult it is not to "ball-watch" (Diagram 5).

## 8 v. 8 with Counterattack

In this segment of the practice, the attacking team starts in the midfield and tries to penetrate. It must complete five passes before it can shoot on goal. The attacking team has five midfielders and two strikers, while the four backs and four midfielders are in place for the defending team, which tries to counterattack to the two goals situated on the perimeter of the expanded (80 x 75 yard) field.

The defensive emphasis in the game is for the back four and the midfield four to remain compact, to pressure the ball. Let them go around you, but not through you.

If there is pressure on the ball and the back four are compact, they can push up prior to the ball being played and draw the attacking team offside. If there is not pressure on the ball, the unit must retreat as a unit and try to cut out the ball over the top (Diagram 6).

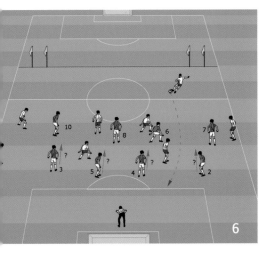

The collective objective of defending in the 4-4-2 is to make the opposition play negatively, and if penetration occurs, that it happens on the flanks, but in front of your defensive block.

Finally the defensive principles must be at work at all times, namely pressure (on the ball), ball winning (1 v. 1), compactness and denial of penetration (cover).

## 11 v. 11 - Full-Sided Play

In the concluding full-sided match, one team is instructed to play high pressure with the emphasis on quick counterattacks. If the pressure breaks down, the whole team must try to get behind the ball, with the back four conceding space to prevent a through ball. The second group plays low pressure and tries to possess the ball and penetrate collectively for strikes on goal.

## Reminders

Each of the segments of the coaching session might occupy one pre-season practice for a team. Repetition and collective talk as well as corrective coaching will help the team's building blocks achieve the needed coordination.

The coach needs to "build pairs" within the 4-4-2 with coordinated play between the outside backs and midfielders, the two strikers, the two central midfielders and the two center backs as part of the team selection process. The playing characteristics and chemistry of the "twos" are concerns as the team is finalized. The "twos" also are built into playing triangles and how these are constructed is of additional concern.

# 4-4-2 – The Attacking Strategy

## Schellas Hyndman
## FC Dallas

This article is based on a training session conducted by Schellas Hyndman at the NSCAA Premier Course.

## 5 v. 2 (4 + GK v. 2 Strikers)

One of the two strikers starts play with long shot on goal, which the keeper will field, and play to one of the outside backs. The closest central back offers support for the ball as the outside back dribbles forward and tries to get to the middle third. If closed by one of the two defenders, the player plays the ball to his closest supporting defender who tries to prepare the ball and send to the opposite outside back. The key here is the technical ability to deliver a long diagonal ball to the opposite outside back moving forward (Diagram 1).

## 7 v. 3 (6 + GK v. 2 Strikers and a Central Midfielder)

Two goals were established for the defensive team to score on at midfield. Add two central midfield

target players (No. 6 and No. 8) for the defensive team to play to at midfield (Diagram 2).

Have ball played to central back, who dribbles forward and creates 2 v. 1 with team's outside back. In turn seek to play the ball forward to one of the central midfielders who lays the ball off for the score.

2

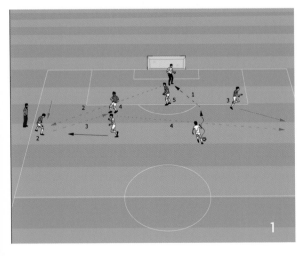

1

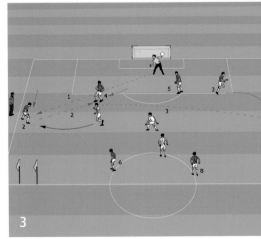

3

If the outside back gets shut down, play the ball back to supporting central back who tries to play long diagonal ball over the top to his opposite outside back (Diagram 3).

## 8 v. 3 (7 + GK v. 2 Strikers and 1 Central Midfielder)

A new central defensive midfielder (No. 6) joins with four backs and two midfielders as the team seeks to work the ball to play to the central midfielder in midfield area. No. 6 can run wide to receive ball from outside back or receive a ball from a central back and play to an attacking outside back (Diagram 4).

## 11 v. 6 (2 Strikers and 4 Midfielders)

Now add outside midfielders to each team and a second central midfielder to the defending team with the objective of the attacking team to move the ball to the attacking third of the field.

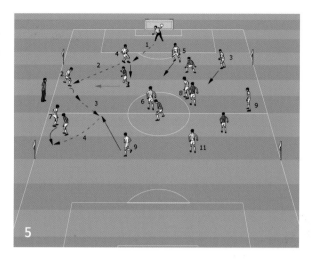

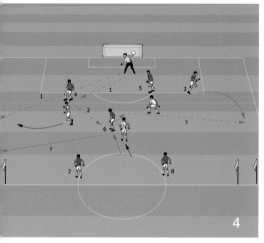

If there is no pressure on the outside back following distribution from the keeper, then the supporting midfielder (No. 7) takes his defender away and the outside back attacks with the dribble and can play to checking the central striker who turns or walls ball off to attacking outside midfielder (Diagram 5).

## 11 v. 8 – Play from the Midfield to the Attacking Third of the Field.

Add two central marking backs to the defending team. Emphasis on combining play with the tightly marked No. 6 in midfield and having that player turn the ball and switch play either to his opposite midfielder or opposite outside back. The ball side midfielder clears space by taking his marker away. Keep compactness between lines at all times. Also, once the ball enters the central midfield area, the attacking team must remain composed, slow play down, make simple passes and not give the ball away.

Hyndman noted that it is vital to build 2 v. 1 combination play between the attacking team's outside back and outside midfielder. If the midfielder is tightly marked, play the ball back and run to space behind the defender (Diagram 6).

If tightly marked, the outside midfielder can take the defender inside and open the space for outside back to run into and play a 1-2 with that player (Diagram 7).

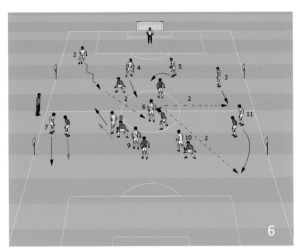

6

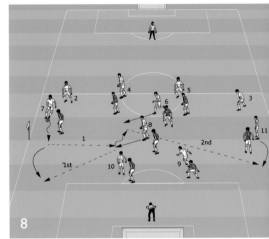

8

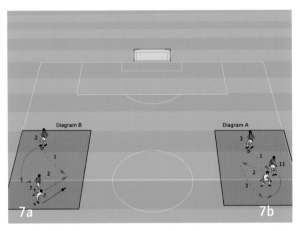

7a 7b

### 11 v. 9 – Moving from the Mid-Third to the Final Third

A goalkeeper is added to the defending team. The emphasis should be on playing balls to a midfielder (No. 8) so that individual can: 1) play square or through balls to the outside midfielder closest to the ball, or 2) support the ball and switch play behind the defense to the opposite outside midfielder. Watch for extra touches and play the ball simply (play the way you are facing) (Diagram 8).

### 11 v. 9 – Play from Midfield to Attacking Third of Field

Two central defenders are added to the defending team. Keeping the ball side midfielder wide, outside back plays ball to central striker and while ball is on the way, but before the ball reaches the striker's feet, the outside midfielder runs to space to be played to (action - reaction) (Diagram 9).

A coordinated checking to the ball by the outside midfielder and the attacking midfielder as well as lateral runs by the two strikers can open up the long diagonal ball to opposite outside midfielder (Diagram 10).

9

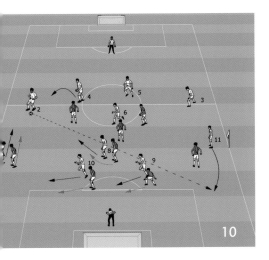

## 11 v. 11

Both teams play 4-4-2 with the triangles playing a direct style of play and while the attacking team plays an indirect style (looking for 2 v.1s);

Any time ball is played past the attacking central midfielder (No. 6), that player must seek to run to support the central strikers.

Restrict both teams to five passes before they can shoot on goal.

## 11 v. 11

Add two outside backs to the defending team. When attacking the outside midfielder (No. 11) needs to attack with two strikers when ball is played wide. Generally player (No. 6) offers a target for pullbacks on the cross and also looks for knockdowns in box for scoring opportunities. The central supporting striker (No. 9) does not want to take his defender into the space of the outside midfielder. Open it up, if anything (illustration in Diagram 11).

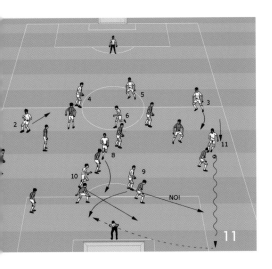

# 4-3-3 – A System that Works

## Jerry Smith

The 4-3-3 system is easy for players to understand and has been used with the U.S. National Girls U-19 Team. The players come together and have to learn a tactical plan quickly. The 4-3-3 system works well in that situation.

In terms of systems of play, we are talking team tactics. This is the least important of the four components of coaching. Technique, fitness and the psychological dimension come before tactics, but tactics cannot be dismissed.

## Why Play the 4-3-3 System?

Players' strengths can be accentuated and weaknesses hidden in a 4-3-3 system. Players have tendencies and must be organized tactically so that collectively they reach their potential as a team. The 4-3-3 begins at kickoff, but once the ball is in play it is the principles of play that will dictate how players react. Pressure, cover, balance and depth must be understood defensively. Penetration, depth, width and mobility must dominate the thinking while on attack. The team should play from the 4-3-3.

We started playing with the 4-3-3 at Santa Clara following a 1997 road game at Washington where the team had won to improve its record to 3-0. It was a good team that won in spite of not playing well. Among other things FIFA's goalkeeper rule had come to college soccer. Santa Clara liked to use three forwards but the old rule allowed defenders, when under pressure by the forwards, to use keeper to thwart that pressure. So something had to change. We changed from a 4-4-2 to a 4-3-3.

## How to Play at the Back?

Brazil's Carlos Alberto Parriera, says that the best defense is when a team possesses the ball. So to a degree, defense starts with the idea that, if you have the ball the majority of time you will have a good chance to win the game.

It is hard to defend with all the senseless running at back if playing a man-to-man marking system. So the team plays a zonal system. The flat back four offers simple concepts while having the advantage of keeping the team in its best attacking shape. It is not necessary to adjust if there are four backs at onset. If the other team plays two, three or four forwards, Santa Clara still plays four at the back.

## The Organization of the Midfield

Look at your personnel before you decide how to play in the midfield. It is important that you have the players to play this system. The team was playing 4-4-2 prior to the switch to 4-3-3. Wing midfielders had to work hard in the 4-4-2.

In 1997 while preparing Santa Clara for a match at Washington State following the aforementioned Washington win, I used a napkin to align the team to play in a 4-3-3. The feeling was with the team playing badly and still unbeaten, they couldn't play any worse! The grand experiment turned out great!! The team played great! The team played with three midfielders who were pulled in tight in the middle (Diagram 1). That left the outside backs responsible for the flank attack.

## Coaching Points

After the back line and midfield were set, it was time to look at the forwards. After games the coaches evaluated shots and action in box. I don't worry too much about the number of shots. Take some time to view old Ajax tapes and watch how those teams used extra passes to penetrate defenses. Santa Clara emphasizes the number of quality chances created and the percentage of shots made. Along with quality shots, all dangerous opportunities are charted.

In the years playing 4-3-3, Santa Clara has outshot every opponent. In 1999 the team scored 99 goals and allowed only five. During that time in games against major collegiate women powers, Santa Clara outshot every team. In the 1997 season, the team lost to North Carolina on two free-kick goals while outshooting the Tarheels 14-13. In 1998 Santa Clara lost to Florida 1-0 while on top 13-11 in terms of shots. Losses to Notre Dame during the four-year period saw Santa Clara on top in shots by a combined 34-7!

Coaches need to be objective and recognize that other factors impact a result. A hot goalkeeper, lapses on free kicks, injuries, etc., all affect the result. The selection of a system of play has nothing to do with results but has everything to do with your personnel.

## Positional Playing Characteristics

I believe the goalkeeper must possess a sweeper mentality. She must be mobile, quick to the ball, have good range and skills with both feet, as she needs to cover ground in a forward and

lateral fashion. In addition her ball receiving skills must be good.

There are two different types of backs, the wide backs and the central backs. The central backs need to be able to play both the stopper and sweeper roles interchangeably. The wide backs are seen as the playmakers. Good soccer players are needed in these positions. Often the wide backs are left undefended and so are presented with real opportunities to go forward and attack. I prefer a left-footed player on the left side. In either case, such individuals must be able to penetrate on the dribble and serve the cross both early as well as in the box. The outside backs will have a lot of time with ball and so have to be good passers. They also will get exposed 1 v. 1, so they also need to be good individual defenders.

In the midfield the deep midfield player is very important. She must be the team's most complete player. She must be a good defender and playmaker. For the most part this individual doesn't get defended a lot. Usually the opposing player nearest this player is the other team's playmaker, so if teams do defend against the deep midfielder they usually are taking their best attacker out of the game.

In terms of forwards, the coach needs to be flexible. The alignment depends on your players' strengths. If the players are genuine strikers, they like to play central and have a scoring mentality. So if there are three strikers, they would play central. If the strikers are more wing types (dribblers, passers, crossers of the ball, playmaking types) then they would allow a wider alignment with a central striker in the middle. Most scorers like to be in front of goal.

What does the 4-3-3 formation concede? I don't believe we have ever lost a game if possession is lost and we are in the formation's vulnerable area, the flank areas in the midfield. In terms of defending the flank area (Diagram 1), don't allow players to make

too many decisions. Don't shift too many players to defend the area. The rule is that usually in the defensive third the person most responsible is the outside striker. In the middle third it is one of the two inside midfielders who moves out, while in the back third the outside back defends wide.

Generally I like to have players working in twos or even threes, as combinations are the ultimate way to win ball back in the outside areas. So the playing characteristics of the outside three players and their coordination by the coach are a must for successful defending in the "weak zone" of the 4-3-3.

When does the outside back step up? Players have to know principles of play to make intelligent decisions regarding stepping up. Defending is best begun with a sprint to the ball when it is on its way to the receiver. If a defender can't get to the opposing player, she stays and defends the space. Play for the interception, to delay, to let player come and tackle the ball or finally, to take a defensive position to make play predictable (channeling).

The nearest forward must work back to get the ball. What looks like weakness can become a strength. Three players must work together. The outside midfielder must slide and put pressure on the ball. If play is on the touchline and that midfielder doesn't challenge. The team has to regroup when the ball gets into the vulnerable space.

When there is minimal pressure in the outside midfield area, the central backs must read the game and drop back. Here they must have good technique in terms of heading and dealing with balls out of the area. If pressure can be placed on the ball, the central backs and the outside back on the ball side step up and compress the attacking space. All of this must be in coordination with the goalkeeper.

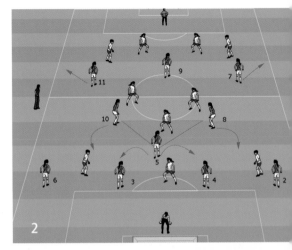

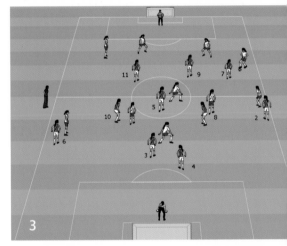

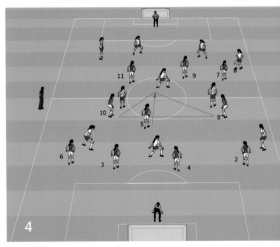

## Adjusting with the 4-3-3

How do you play another team that utilizes a 4-3-3? Presented with this problem today, Smith noted that Santa Clara would have played its own forwards wide so they could have been made available (Diagram 2). Also the team would have taken its outside backs wide and let the central backs play-make out of the center who, along with the deep-lying central midfielder, would have created a 3 v. 1 or possibly a 3 v. 2 situation in the middle of the field.

What if teams "pack it in" using a 4-5-1 or similar strategy? Here the adjustment would be to move the outside backs higher, playing them in the zones occupied by the opponents' outside midfielders. Very little adjustment is needed when playing 4-3-3 against various other alignments (Diagram 3).

In terms of defending against a formidable, deep-lying central midfielder, simply reverse the central triangle with the more forward midfielder marking the playmaker (Diagram 4).

© Bernd Mai

# Examining the 3-5-2 System

## Chris Petrucelli

## Part 1:

### Structure and Shape

- Re-enforcement of numbers in the midfield
- Only one player on each flank
- Three defenders in back

Note the re-enforcement of numbers in the central corridor and concomitant open space on flanks and in the back. Tactical flexibility is necessary to supply numbers in these open areas in attack and defense (Diagram 1).

### Tactical Arrangements and Player Functions

A. Defending Block
1. Can utilize man-to-man markers and sweeper playing behind markers.

- Markers must be athletic. Speed and anaerobic capacity are critical in order to track opposing forwards

- Markers must be aggressive, yet under control in 1 v. 1 duel as attackers have a lot of space to play in

- Markers usually paired vs. attackers (i.e., a fast marker vs. a fast forward, or a disciplined tactical marker vs. a very technical forward or a good header vs. a tall forward)

- Preferable for the sweeper to be athletic, but critical that he/she is a superb tactician. Must be able to advise and support markers and be capable of anticipating future points of attack as man-to-man marking allows defensive shape to be pulled apart

- Sweeper needs to be a good header of the ball as quick, agile markers are often not tall. Must also be able to mark free players as well as cover space. Should be able to start the counterattack. Coaches may want to use the sweeper in other places on the field in order to develop that individual as a well-rounded player

2. Back three zonal (space) marking.

- Athleticism preferable, as there is a lot of ground to cover laterally by three players

- Zonal marking, however, can cover up for some deficiencies in athleticism

- As in all zonal marking, communication and tactical awareness are critical

- The central player should be a dominant personality with strong leadership qualities

- Need dominant players in the air among three players; this may be a tough system for women to play

- The central player should be a dominant header of the ball. He or she is almost always in a control area and called upon to head a flighted ball into the central corridor

3. Playing with only three in the back can limit attacking options.

- The three in back are asked to achieve penetration by passing only. Bringing the ball out of the back is limited. You do not want to lose it on the flank, as it places the group in a poor shape to win the ball back. Generally, try to penetrate through the middle with the five midfielders. If elect to work ball out of the back, use the weak side midfielder to create a fourth back. Holland brings a central midfield player back

- If a back three player penetrates through dribbling or moving forward into open spaces, a midfield player must assume the penetrating player's defensive responsibility

B. Forward Block

1. Two forwards, side-by-side, each responsible for his or her side of field;

2. One forward always stays high and serves as a target player (to occupy two defenders and ready to get on the end of counterattacks). The other forward forges underneath to narrow opponent defending shape and can serve as a wall for midfield players coming from behind. With this positioning, the player also can create a numerical advantage in the midfield third;

3. Tactically, the two forwards always stay 12-15 yards apart. They might stay central to concentrate the opponents' central covering system. They may go to a flank to pull apart the central covering system and make room for central attacks from the midfield. Usually needs two very technical players who constantly move and switch their positions. These players need to utilize quick flicks and 1-2 movements and usually exhibit a superb mutual understanding;

4. Two forwards can be selected based on special talents. Players with special gifts (i.e., exceptional speed, heading ability) and technique may be paired in order to emphasize and take advantage of these gifts.

C. Midfield Block

1. Flank midfield players are responsible to defend flank, with the usual defensive task to "take first one down" (the first and/or most advanced attacker on that flank is tracked by the flank midfield player).

- Usually asked to mark zonal when opponent flank player runs towards middle, he or she is passed on to players in the central zones

- May be detailed to only mark opposing flank player and not go in advance of that player when the ball is won

© Bernd Mai

2. Flank midfield player is responsible to attack from his or her flank.

- Player may be asked to achieve penetration up and down entire flank by passing, dribbling, and combining with forwards

- Player may be detailed to "anchor" his or her flank and only penetrate through passing vertically to forwards and central midfield players using space on flank in final third

3. Often a team "balances" the flanks by asking one side to anchor and the other to penetrate. Physical, technical and tactical qualities of players are taken into consideration if this tactic is invoked.

4. Flank players should be very athletic. Speed and anaerobic capacity are a necessary physical criteria as there is only one player to attack and defend the flank.

5. The three central midfield players are the essence of the 3-5-2 system. The rhythm, style and soccer mentality of the team are determined by the personality and playing characteristics of the three.

6. There are three standard tactical arrangements of the three central midfield players. The athlete's playing characteristics, the coach's conception of the game and his or her perception of the team are major factors in determining which arrangement is selected.

- One defensive midfielder (a holding midfielder) and two attacking midfielders. Here the two attacking midfielders must be good playmakers, be able to shoot from a distance and beat players both individually and collectively (1 v. 1 and 2 v. 1) (Diagram 2)
- Two defensive midfielders and one attacking midfielder. The lone midfielder is sometimes hard to defend against as he or she can play in the seams of the other team's alignments (Diagram 3)
- One attacking midfielder, one organizing midfielder and one defensive midfield player (Diagram 4)

The defensive midfielder is used to mark an opponent's attacking midfield player, screen the space in front of the markers (prevent the first ball out), or push up and complete a block of five zonal markers in the midfield. The strictest interpretation of the defensive midfield players' attacking function is that they only penetrate "with the ball."

If an organizing central midfield player is used, the player is usually a "special player" whose technical

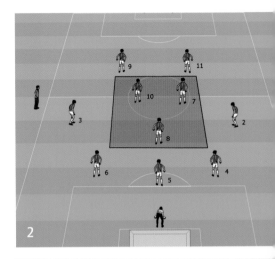

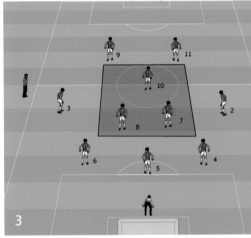

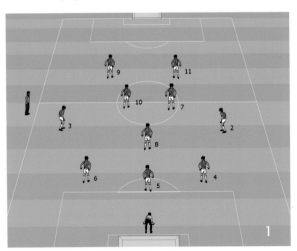

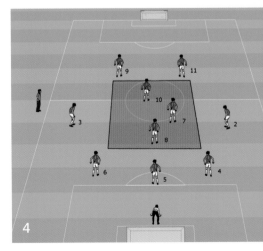

ability and vision allow him/her to dictate a team's rhythm. The individual can come back and get the ball from defenders and open the game with long passing, play short for possession or run with the ball at the opponents' defense.

The attacking midfielder is usually a special player as well. Whether with powerful running to the back of the opponent's defense, elusive dribbling and shooting from distance or combining with forwards, a team's style and methods are often dictated by this player.

It is up to the "genius of the coach" to organize and implement this engine room of the team. Often the coach will be specific regarding the central midfield player's function in the collective defending action while giving free rein to the group to express their individuality and special abilities.

D.  Strengths of the 3-5-2

1.  Inherent strength is its flexibility. Because of large numbers of players in the central corridor of the team, players can quickly move to support the attack, reinforce the defense and quickly attack from one flank or the other. Implicit in this statement is the need to have versatile players. They must be tactically flexible, not only possessing the ability to flow from attack to defense and vice versa, but also flexible in positional interchange. All players must be conversant with principles of play and exhibit a creative, mobile mentality. Most players in this system will play box-to-box and touchline-to-touchline.

2.  Specific strengths, which a team may exploit: Possibilities that may exist because of the structure and shape of a system are exploitable only to the extent that players can execute and press these variables to their advantage.

•   Outnumber opponents in the midfield area. Against other predominant systems, 4-4-2 and 3-4-3, the 3-5-2 has an extra player in the middle of the midfield. This system can be effective in the women's game versus a team such as North Carolina, which utilizes a 3-4-3 and tries to make the game in the opponents' defensive third. If they want to "press" an opponent in this manner, they can elect to bring a player forward from the midfield to create the third person to defend other team's backs

•   Tactical advantage on flank. Because of an extra central midfield player, the opponent may pull a player in from their flank, thus exposing their remaining flank player to a 1 v. 1 duel, which may be to the advantage of the 3-5-2 team

•   "Numbers up" in the central midfield area allows constant vertical running through and beyond the opponents' defending block. Central midfield players can alternate or, if one player has great anaerobic capacity, he or she may make constant runs forward. This will have immediate impact against teams which play flat in the back

•   It is easy for the central midfield group to combine with the forwards

•   The proximity of three central midfield players allows constant and close support for forwards as they may show for the ball

•   The one or two attacking midfield players can have total freedom to attack as the central corridor still has depth provided by the defensive central midfield player

E.  Weaknesses of 3-5-2

1.  While flexibility may be the strength of the 3-5-2 system, the lack of flexibility may be a weakness. Players who lack the ability or mentality to easily flow from attack to defense or who are uncomfortable with positional interchanges will make the imposition of this system a liability.

2.  Specific weaknesses, which an opponent may exploit.

•   Only three defenders compose the defending block

•   The three defenders leave exposed large spaces on the flanks behind the flank midfielders

- Space can be created anywhere, if the defending block is man marking. Active forwards will pull the defending shape apart at will
- Only one defender on each flank. Lack of athleticism or tactical naïveté may be exploited in individual duels or by combining and outnumbering on a flank. The team that is slow to push across or prepare for these situations may tactically have their flanks exposed to penetration by the opponent

F.  Possible Tactical Adjustments with the 3-5-2

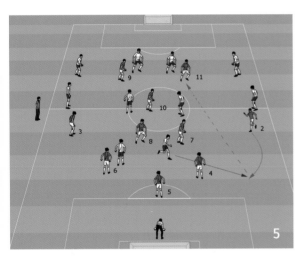

5

The coach, to meet the physical and/or technical tactical qualities of the players, can adjust all systems. Also, the tactical needs for a particular game may dictate a system permutation. The following are two examples of how the 3-5-2 can allow for this:

- The red team is playing with a 4-4-2 and the right flank player is in an area on the flank, but near the defending block. The left side forward for the red team is a special player with exceptional speed and his or her preferred style of play is sharp diagonal runs to the left flank. The coach of the 3-5-2 team has decided that his or her man-to-man marker needs help with the special forward, so he or she details the right flank player to play deep

on the right flank and "kill" the space that the forward wants to use. The right flank player holds a deep position and achieves penetration through vertical passing (Diagram 5)

- The red team plays with two attacking midfield players. The attacking central midfield player on the left side is an elusive dribbler and very effective at pushing out to the left and getting around the flank to serve

The coach of the 3-5-2 team asks the left flank player to accept a role of half a left back and half a left midfield player. The left flank in the attacking third is exploited by a 3-5-2 team's forwards and in particular the left central midfield player. The left flank player becomes a "distributor" from the flank as opposed to a penetrator (Diagram 6).

The following is a sample training session used to teach players their specific roles that are a vital to the success of the system.

## Part 2:

## Warm-Up:

A group of 24 played on a full field working on passing in groups of three. A passer played a short ball to a teammate, who played a wall pass back to the first player who would then "find" the third

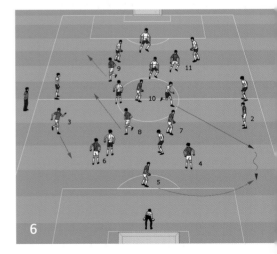

6

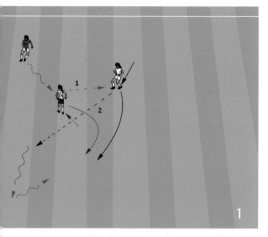

made an overlapping run. The ball was played to the third player who, in turn, was supported by an overlapping run. Once the sequence was completed the roles would be reversed until all three players had completed an overlap. The proper way to "show" for a pass and the timing/speed of the run were emphasized (Diagram 2).

The final phase of the warm-up involved the takeover. Here the player with the ball is defended by one of the trio and dribbles at the third player. Following the takeover, the roles change until all have played the three positions.

## Playing Out of the Back – 3 v 2:

On a field 60 x 75 yards, a ball is played by three midfielders to two attackers positioned behind a line of flat cone markers. They must try to combine with three passes to create a shot on goal (Diagram 3). once the shot is taken, the goalkeeper distributes the ball to one of the defenders who support the ball on the outside of the field. The two defenders try to force the play to the ball side of the field making the back with the ball play a long diagonal ball across the field to the third back. The third back plays to the central midfielder behind the cones at center field. The sequence now repeats itself.

player with a longer pass. The first player would run to support the ball. The sequence would then be repeated. On occasion the players would play a long ball to one of the two keepers in the field; run to the keeper to receive the ball back. Stretching was interspersed in this phase of warm-up.

Seeking to work on establishing a passing rhythm, the coach worked on passing combination play in threes. One player would dribble at a teammate and play the ball to feet. The second player would play a wall pass to the third player. The sequence would be repeated with the original passer becoming the next "wall" (Diagram 1).

The next sequence involved the overlap. The player with the ball played it to feet of a teammate and

The exercise is designed to emphasize the focus in the 3-5-2 of working the ball from the backs to the central midfielders for distribution. If the ball is played to one of the two outside midfielders and lost, then the shape of the three backs will be disrupted as they try to win the ball back.

## Playing out of the Back – 6 v 4:

Two midfield defenders now play against the three attacking midfielders on a large 75 x 75 yard field. The objective of the defending team is to take a shot within a prescribed number of passes i.e. three. Once the keeper distributes the ball to the outside back, the midfielder times a run and receives the ball. Emphasis is placed on the

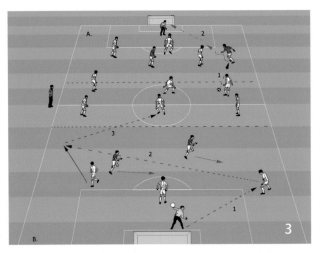

If the defenders win the ball, they attack. If the attacking team crosses the line with the ball, the coach restarts play with a ball to the defending team. The coach may want to make the game more realistic by "squeezing" the field by making it narrower – 44 to 60 yards.

### Full Field – 8 v 6:

On a full field, the defending team now adds a third defender against the three central midfielders of the attacking team, while the attacking team added its two outside midfielders who are unopposed making the game 8 v 6.

The objective for the eight is to work the ball out of the back (3 v 2) to one of the two "holding/playmaking" central midfielders (note the new alignment of three). The ball then is played to the outside midfielder, who dribbles to goal, supported by two central midfielders and his opposite outside midfielder. This creates a 3 v 2 attacking situation on goal with the three only able to score via a crossed ball. Play resumes with a goalkeeper distribution coming the other way or by a ball being played in from midfield by a spare player or coach. The defending team must try to score within four passes (Diagram 5).

back delivering the ball to the midfielder's feet. The midfielder either uses a 1-2 pass with the defender or turns and plays the ball to a free midfielder showing into space. The objective is to pass the line of cones with possession of the ball. While play is occurring with the attacking back the other two backs must stay compact centrally. The two defensive midfielders should play as one attacking and one defending.

Note the "two up-one back" alignment of midfielders. The set-up of the central midfielders is dependent on which of the three of the aforementioned alignments the coach utilizes (Diagram 4).

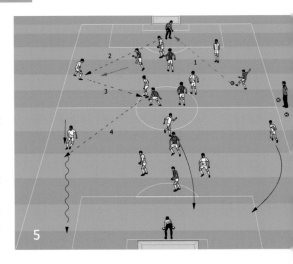

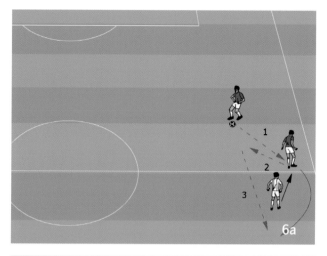

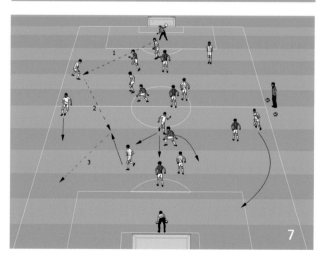

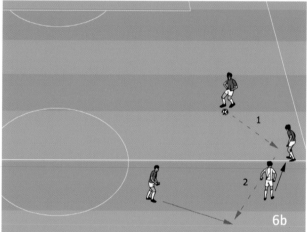

### Full Field - 10 v 8:

The coach now adds two strikers to the attacking team and two to the defenders, making the game 10 v 8. Again the objective is scoring via crossed balls with a central midfielder getting involved in the play.

Here the emphasis is on the two deep lying central midfielders trying to free themselves and change the point of attack.. Another coaching emphasis is for the third central midfielder to support the two strikers in attack.

Finally, the outside midfielders must stay on the touchline and work to create space for themselves on the perimeter of the field. If they are tightly marked, they can combine with their supporting midfielder for a "short-short-long" ball; if they are loosely marked, they can turn with the ball and combine with one of the central strikers (Diagram 6 a+b).

The outside backs must also look to deliver a long accurate ball to the feet of one of the central strikers. The strikers must be central. They do not run into wide spaces, killing space for the outside midfielders. The strikers then can combine with an outside midfielder to penetrate to goal (Diagram 7).

## Full Field – 11 v 11

Both teams start in the 3-5-2 formation. The emphasis is for the forwards to stretch the three defenders (a weakness in the 3-5-2) as wide as they can while not taking away the outside attacking space for the midfielders. The three central midfielders need to be playmakers using one-, two- and three-touch passing.

In Diagram 8 the backs are changing the point of attack to one another aided by support from the holding midfielder. A second change of the point of attack sees the back playing to an outside midfielder. Note the two central midfielders getting into the attack, one supporting the attacking outside midfielder and the second supporting the central strikers.

A second training game emphasized using the third central midfielder and adjusting to playing against a 4-4-2 system of play.

Diagram 9 shows that, as the outside midfielder attacks, there is numerical advantage in the central midfield for the 3-5-2 team. Depending on how the 4-4-2 team elects to combat that, there will be some good attacking opportunities for the 3-5-2 team.

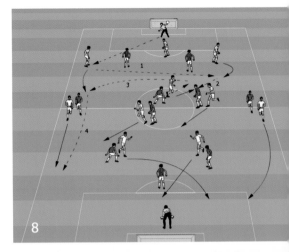

# Three in the Back

## Lauren Gregg

There has been an evolution in defensive systems utilized in the women's game. There is a much greater use of zones in the back, both internationally and in the college game.

These systems have replaced the more traditional assigned marking and sweeper systems. The system in which the Women's National Team won the '96 Olympic Games soccer title and our Youth National Team played when it secured the Nordic Cup championship was a three-man zone on a diagonal. The predominant international defensive system in the back is some form of a four-man zone. The Nordic teams are relatively similar, and they ardently use a four-man, flat zone system. So much so, that in Norway, they actually select players for their national team program who can play inside right back or outside left defense.

Collegiately in the U.S., there is still a great variety of defensive formations used in the back. However, here too, we see a trend toward the utilization of zonal defenses. For example, if we look back to the beginning of the 1996 fall season, both the University of North Carolina and the University of Notre Dame played with sweeper and marking defenders. This year watching UNC and Notre Dame play against each other, I noticed that both teams played with a three-man zone in the back. In fact, the 1997 Nordic Cup championship Under-20 U.S. team that summer was comprised mainly of players from each of those universities.

The U.S. Women's National Team evolved from a marking man-to-man with a sweeper to a zonal defense. The impetus for this change came, in part, from our 1995 World Cup loss and the overall improvement in the level of our international competition. After the 1995 World Cup, we realized we needed a system that kept its shape not only from a defensive standpoint, but from an offensive mentality.

By "shape" we mean the ability of the team to maintain player defensive positioning so that the individual performs functionally in relatively the same areas of the field throughout the match. Thus a right back in a zonal system of play will not be dragged out of position (for the most part) by chasing an attacking player all over the field because the individual is concerned with marking space, not a particular player. Thus when the ball is won, the right back will be allowed to become an attacker who will now link up with players she is familiar with in terms of playing characteristics, etc.

In fact (and this is illustrated in the diagrams), the pressurizing player in our zonal system of play always tries to direct or channel play toward our covering player in the central or interior part of the field. If we win the ball, we want to win it centrally. If attacking players are channeled to the width of the field, it tends to disperse defenders, thus changing the "shape" from the desired compactness.

In fact, our Women's National Team tries to engage our opponents in "even up" situations all over the field. The strategy is based on the fact in defending in our attacking third with three forwards we can then oppose the opponents' defenders 1 v. 1. With our players' athleticism at work, we feel we are successful using this strategy a good percentage of the time.

## Three-Man vs. Four-Man

At the beginning of the National Team's evolution in 1996, we experimented with a four-man zone. A four-man zone created a more defensive mindset. We wrestled with the fact that we were keeping an extra player on defense. In turn, this would make a system similar to that of the majority of the teams we would face. The beauty of our usual system is that everyone has to adjust to us especially when we play a three-man front line. With that in mind, we began investing in a three-man zone.

In order to play a three-man zone certain qualities are necessary in the players you choose to fill the roles.

First, there must be a dominant central defender. This player must have a good tactical understanding of the game, be confident in her decisions, be able to read service and be a good individual defender. (In a four-man zone the central defenders can share the role and are naturally positioned to cover for each other.)

It is important for the flank defenders to have speed, be good individual defenders and understand team defense — when and how to provide cover for the other two backs. All three must be willing to take on marking responsibilities. In addition, the role of a goalkeeper playing behind a zone is different from playing with a sweeper in front of her.

Our challenge, as I have noticed with many teams and players, was to convert marking defenders to zonal defenders. Initially, players feel lost, exposed and uncertain of their decisions. When marking, their decisions are simpler —

deny your assigned player the ball, and let the player have no impact on the game. From a coaching standpoint, individual defenders can be assessed based on how much influence the particular player had in the match. The objective in changing to zone has to be to translate your player's individual marking abilities into a system that requires a greater contribution to team defense and overall team defensive shape.

The difficulties for the individual defenders in the zone tend to center around the decisions of when to track runs, both back to the ball and into space. If a run back to the ball is tracked, there is the obvious space behind the player that becomes vulnerable to a second run. The central defender in the system must read service and be able to track the space behind the tracking defender.

Zones we face are very different with regard to how they treat runs. Some zones are very committed to their shape first. Norway, for example, is more willing to be pulled out of shape and maintain more of a marking mentality within the zonal concept.

*Diagram 1 – Here the balancing defender (3) through her diagonal positioning is able to track the penetrating run of red 2. Note the positioning of white 1 on the ball.*

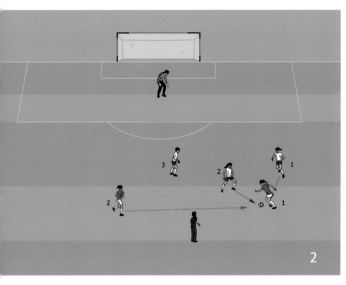

Diagram 2 – Here we see attacker 2 being "passed on", that is there is no tracking by defender 2 as the run is lateral. Defender 3 maintains her positioning allowing the three defensive players to maintain their original "shape."

we retreat until the point we can engage our goalkeeper as cover.

This was a recent lesson for us in Germany. Because of their tremendous transition, they got in on us several times. In the first match, we were caught stepping individually to close down the player on the ball. This forced them into quicker decisions. And because they were unilateral decisions, it broke our defense, in one instance resulting in a goal against us.

We play zone on a diagonal. Our weak side back provides balance for our defense. The critical factor is that we don't over-balance or else we give the opponent too much room for penetration.

The positioning of the balancing player also allows her to track runs in behind our central defender (Diagram 1). As a very general rule, we track runs behind the zone and pass on runs in front of the zone (Diagram 2).

It is important for the opposite-side defender to know when to step a player offside as well. Every penetrative run need not be tracked. Overall, we are not an offside trapping team. However, based upon the run, pressure on the service, etc., we will step players with opposite-side defender (Diagram 3).

In addition, this player must organize her flank midfielder. In a flat zone – whether it's a three-man or four-man – the goalkeeper provides cover higher on the field. In fact, if you get the opportunity to watch Norway play, you will note the very extended position of the keeper because of their flat, condensed defensive shape.

Another point of difference comes from how teams that play zones solve breakdowns (extra players in attack).

Because of the lack of cover and the amount of space covered by the three players, there are two basic ways in which breakdowns are handled.

When there is a breakdown, the defenders in the zone must immediately distinguish which is more important – the man on the ball or the space. There will be times when defenders should delay and choose to protect the space initially.

The critical factor is that whatever way you choose to play, all your defenders must be on the same page. For example, if an opponent gets in behind the midfield, the zone must either step together and compact or deny space to the offensive team or retreat as a unit. As a general rule, we retreat when a team gets in behind our midfield – for two reasons. First, it buys time and permits recovery of our other players. Second,

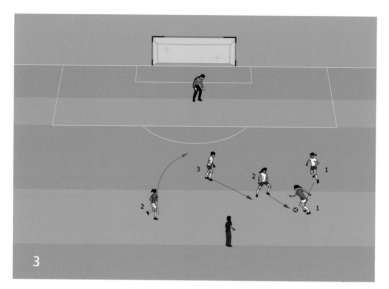

*Diagram 3- With pressure on the ball, defenders 2 and 3 "step up" to play the attackers offside. Note "high" position of the goalkeeper.*

The offensive roles of the players in a zone should also be noted. The beauty of the zone for us was that it kept us in a better overall attacking shape.

Our shape could absorb the mobility of a team like China. When we would regain possession of the ball we naturally would be in a better offensive position to attack. The zone allows a greater freedom offensively for flank midfielders, especially in a four-man zone. The space behind them is protected. For the U.S. Women's National Team this is important. We want to attack with our flank midfielders. The zone provides a greater freedom for them to do this.

Obviously, in a three-man zone it is important to have players who can handle the ball offensively as they are typically playing 3 v. 2, rather than the 4 v. 2 situations they would be facing in a four-man zone. This on-the-ball responsibility includes the goalkeeper. The keeper becomes a reload (support) option for the defenders and must possess the ability and confidence to play the ball with her feet.

Although the trend in the women's game has moved toward greater use of zonal defenses, each team must select the system that suits the players' profiles. Regardless of the defense you ultimately feel best suits your team, players should understand the principles of man-to-man as well as how to play a zone.

There will be instances throughout the match or in parts of the field in which each skill and knowledge will be put to use.

# The Four Main Moments of Soccer

## Jeff Tipping

This article deals with what the Dutch call the "four main moments" in a soccer game. It is interesting to note the evolution of the "four main moments" in the KNVB and Dutch soccer. Initially Dutch coaches looked at the game in terms of two phases (or moments):

* When your team has possession
* When the opponents have possession

It was clear that these two phases did not cover all that happens in a soccer game. Transition became a concern to the coaches. As coaches prepared their teams it was apparent that a lot of time in a game was spent in transition. Some could argue that the transition phase was longer than possession in most games and many coaches began to believe it was more important than possession. So coaches began to look at the game in three phases (moments):

* When your team has possession
* Transition
* When the opponent has possession

In the late 1990's the KNVB further developed the concept of transition. They introduced the importance of looking at transition in two different ways:

* When there is transition to possession by your team
* When there is transition to possession by your opponents

Coaches then began to consider the "four main moments" of a soccer game:

* Defending – when the opponent has the ball
* Transition to possession by your team
* Attacking – when your team has the ball
* Transition to possession by your opponent

The coach must consider the tactical and strategic ramifications of the four moments as he/she prepares the team. The team must know as a group how to respond to each situation.

## Defending – when the opponent has the ball

* How does the opposition play?
  * What formation do they use? (4-4-2, 3-4-3, etc.)
  * Which positions are strong? Which are weak?
  * What is the opponent trying to do? (Attack flanks, etc.)
* How does your team organize to defend?
* What formation does your team play?
* How does your team match up with the opponents?
* Should we play high pressure? Low pressure?

## Transition – possession by your team – counterattack

* Is the opposition organized? Is there attacking space?
* Is the opposition disorganized? Where is the space?
* On what part of the field have we gained possession?
* What are the tactical choices? Long pass? Run with ball?
* Who are the key players in our counterattack?

Every coach must have "rules of attack" to prevent the counterattack by the opponents. That may mean that a deep midfield screen holds the position or the fullbacks cannot attack, etc.

Every coach must have a plan for the team to control the counterattack. Frequently the key players in controlling the counterattack are the forwards. All the players must be trained to understand and read the transition moment. It is far more important for the players to be trained for transition than it is to train the legs. But, it is very important for the forwards to understand transition. In Italy, for example, forwards often are replaced after 60 minutes due to fatigue from chasing the backs and trying to pressure a lost ball to prevent the long pass. To prevent counterattacks, the defending team must have a plan and be prepared in the following ways. Your team must:

- Be structurally organized in the back
- Prevent the long pass
- Play the offside trap when necessary
- Press the ball immediately after losing it

The importance of the counterattack is apparent when coaches consider that 30 percent of the goals scored in the World Cup come on counterattacks. More and more teams are making counterattacks a main attacking method. Teams are particularly vulnerable to counterattacks after taking corner kicks or restarts when the backs go forward to become targets for the attacking team. The players summoned to play at the midline are usually not trained to play the counterattack and/or defending in the final third. The moment the ball turns over and transition begins is the most important test of a player's mentality. The typical moments for a counterattack include:

- After an interception of a pass
- After an interception by a tackle
- When the goalkeeper cuts out a cross
- After a stoppage by the referee
- After the team takes a corner kick, free kick etc.

The counterattack is becoming more and more of a weapon today in the game of soccer. It is an area that is often overlooked by coaches. In other words, it just happens on the field. The Dutch have taken the counterattack and examined it as the attacking team and the defending team. They spend time in training teaching their team(s) how to most effectively play this important part of the game.

## Attacking – when your team has the ball

- What formation does the team use?
- How shall we pass the ball? Long ball? Short ball?
- What are the tactical choices? Pass, dribble, etc.
- Is the team structurally prepared to defend the counterattack?

## Transition – possession by the opponents

- Is your team organized to defend the counter?
- Is your team disorganized?
- On which part of the field was the ball lost?
- What do the opponents do?
- Who are the key players, both for us and the opponents?

# Possession and Penetration

## Manny Sanchez

*The following article on a practice program is by Manny Sanchez, with variations suggested by Jeff Vennell of the NSCAA Academy staff.*

There are many areas that our players need improvement. We have technically sound players, but they are lacking in the tactical awareness and understanding needed to be able to be more successful at the regional and national levels. Saying this however does not mean our players are falling behind. Over the last few years our players have improved tremendously.

Tactically, our players need more work on their field vision, angles of support, mobility to create space individually and for teammates, first touch away from pressure and being able to relieve pressure with one pass while maintaining possession. They also need to continue to work on transition from attack to defense and defense to attack. Another noticeable area for improvement is maintaining possession and penetrating defenses when appropriate. Decisions that players make in these situations are a big part of the tactical component of the game.

The following training session will concentrate on possession and penetration. It is designed to improve the support of balls played in to target players and runs made by strikers to create opportunities for penetrating passes. Supporting angles play a major role in being able to maintain possession. Part of this is good team shape, proper spacing, good communication and mobility.

## Warm-up:

A. Inter-passing in groups of three emphasizing short-short-long rhythm.
- No restrictions
- Two-touch

B. Groups of five or six, number each player. Players must move and pass in appropriate order (i.e., #1 passes to #2, #2 to #3). Continue to emphasize the short-short-long passing sequence.
- Two-touch
- One-touch

Coaching points:
- Good angles of support
- First-touch in direction of supporting player
- Head up for good field vision

## Activity No. 1:

Set up grid 20 x 30 yards with a five-yard neutral zone at each end for the target players. Play 3 v. 2 plus 2 target players. Emphasize to the players to play to the target players as quickly as possible. When a team successfully passes a ball to a target player and receives the ball back to maintain possession, the team receives a point (Diagram 1).

The team receives an extra point if the target player is able to lay off a ball to the third player on

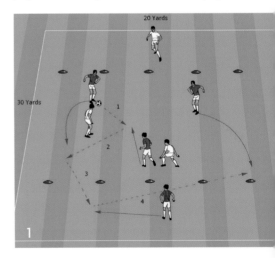

the team with possession. The team that scores on one end and maintains possession will now attack the other zone. Play approximately two minutes, keeping score, than change the players.

Coaching points:

- Look for good third attacker runs to get into position for a return pass from the target players
- Look for good angles of support from supporting players
- Watch that players are having heads up so that they can play penetrating passes to the target players when such opportunities are available
- Are the players playing into or away from pressure on the first-touch?
- Are players communicating?

Vennell's variations:

- Start with 3 v. 2 and then make one of the player a neutral player who plays with the team in possession of the ball (Diagram 2)
- As players improve in this exercise, eliminate the neutral player, playing 2 v. 2 in the middle zone
- Additional activity: In an area 15 x 30 yards, have two groups of four players. Start with 4 v. 2 in one zone. If defenders win the play, pass to two teammates in opposite zone and

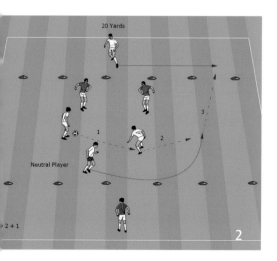

other team must have two members defend in second zone. Play two minutes with number of consecutive passes (established by coach) equating to a point. Play two minutes; bring on second group of eight players (Diagram 3)

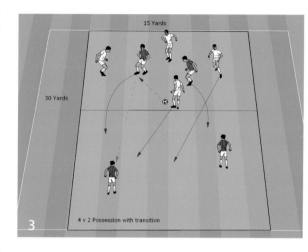

## Activity No. 2:

Set up a grid 30 x 40 yards. Play 4 v. 4 plus 2 target players and 2 neutral flank midfielders/wingers. Each team plays with a striker, two midfielders and a defender. Once again, emphasize to the players that the object of the game is to find the target player as soon as possible. Target players may show into the grid to receive the ball. The wide neutral players have only two-touches to find a supporting player and they are not allowed to pass the ball to the targets. A team scores by completing a pass to the target and receiving a return pass while maintaining possession. Now the team can attack the opposite end (Diagram 4).

Coaching points:

- Speed of play needs emphasis in order to play to targets
- Need to change point of attack (mobility)
- Watch everyone's angle of support
- Emphasis on decision-making, especially when changes of possession occur
- Communicate

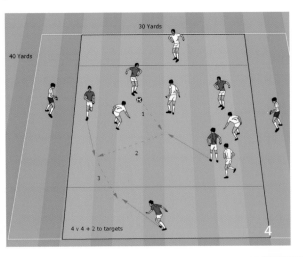

30 Yards

40 Yards

4 v 4 + 2 to targets

4

## Activity No. 3:

Set up slightly more than half the field with a full-sized goal. Play 6 v. 4 plus goalkeeper. Place 2 strikers against 2 defenders in attack and 4 midfielders against 2 defensive midfielders in the midfield. The coach starts the activity by passing the first ball into play. Forwards need to be very mobile to create space for the midfielders to penetrate. They also need to make bending runs and combine with midfielders to create 2 v. 1 situations.

Encourage and emphasize to the players to finish early and not to pass up finishing opportunities.

## Vennell's variation:

- In half field area play 6 (3 red, 3 blue) v. 6 (3 gray, 3 white). Start with keep away (you must pass to a color of a member of your team). When team achieves a given number of passes, other team does pushups (Diagram 5)
- Add goals and goalkeepers. Or add target players

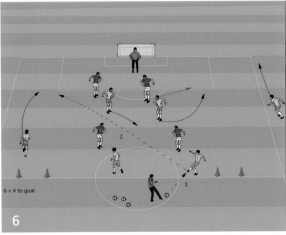

6 v 4 to goal

6

Make the training environment as realistic to match condition as possible, so the offside rule should be enforced. Make the players play at match speed. If play is too slow, place a time limit on finishing the attack (Diagram 6).

## Coaching points:

- Work on bending runs by strikers to get behind the defense
- Strikers can interchange position and make flank runs
- Strikers need to check back to the ball to create space for themselves and teammates

6 v 6 - Possession, then penetration

5

- Check that players are making runs into the right areas of the field
- Communication is essential

Vennell's variations:
- Add a third defensive midfielder to make choices more difficult for the four attacking midfielders
- Add two small goals at midfield for counterattack by defenders

## Activity No. 4:

Set up a three-quarter field with two regulation goals. Play 7 v. 7 plus two neutral flank midfielders/wingers. Mark off the attacking final thirds at both ends of the field with disks. The ball must be played in by one of the midfielders before the strikers or the defenders are allowed to enter the attacking third. All the players are allowed to play forward once the ball is played into the attacking third except the two neutral flank midfielders/wingers. The midfielders can penetrate with a penetrating pass to a striker running through or on the dribble (Diagram 7).

Coaching points:
- Bending runs are very important, so the strikers must not run into space too early
- Timing of the runs and passes needs to be precise. Note the support and runs by the attacking team
- Teams need to maintain good shape with emphasis on depth, balance and spacing in order to combat counterattacks
- The angles of support for the ball must be constantly adjusted
- Emphasis on speed of play
- Communication stressed

Vennell's variations:
- Can use this game to emphasize penetration and possession and mobility of play by eliminating the neutral players and inserting two regulation goals (with keepers) at midpoints on the touchlines

## Activity No. 5 – Match Condition:

Play either 8 v. 8 or 11 v. 11 and play an unrestricted match. Make corrections during the match based on the possession-penetration themes emphasized throughout the lead up exercises (angles of support, mobility of the second and third attackers, bending runs and overall speed of play). Examine if players are maintaining possession (first-touch), as well as how they penetrate from midfield. In making the corrections, have players rehearse the correct technique before allowing normal play. Try to allow for longer periods of play rather than constant stoppages

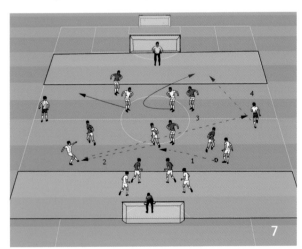

# Defending Not Hard But Smart

## Vince Ganzberg

Many teams like to play high-pressure defense, but often it is not smart. The whole idea behind "smart pressure" is to channel the ball into an area of the field where the team can win the ball back and then get started in the attack. With most high-level teams playing zonal defense, it is vital that the whole team, from the forwards to the backs, not get stretched and stay compact when defending. Here is a training session to teach the correct way to play high-pressure.

## Warm-up:

I wanted to get the players to think about defending in pairs, working together with a teammate to win the ball back. Not only winning the ball back, but working on forcing two players who have the ball into an area where the ball is either won by the defenders or played out of bounds. I got the idea from the movie "Gladiator," specifically the scene in which Maximus is chained to a fellow gladiator and they had to work together to win the battle. Maximus's superiority in winning battles was demonstrated tactically when they backed their opponent into a corner where there was no way out.

## The Warm-up Activity:

Everybody gets a partner. Half of the partners have a ball, the other half do not. The partners with a ball pass and move in the area and try to maintain possession of the ball. The partners without a ball try to win a ball from a pair that is possessing a ball. The only rule is that the defending pair must work together to either win a ball back or to try and force a pair with a ball to play it out of bounds. If a defending pair is successful winning a ball, then they possess the ball and the attacking

pair who just lost the ball must go try and work together to win it back. Depending on the size of your team, this activity could be done in a center circle or the penalty area (Diagram 1).

## First Activity: 4 v 2 +2

**Organization:** Play 4 v. 2 to two spaces – A 40 x 20 yard rectangle cut in half or two 20 x 20 yard areas.

There are two teams of four players. In one half, there are four attacking players versus two defenders. In the other half, two players who are with the defending team are awaiting a pass from the two defending teammates. When the two defenders win the ball, they play the ball to their two teammates in the other half.

The coach should work with the two defenders on understanding when and where to pressure. When the two defenders win the ball back, they should be facing their two awaiting teammates. The attacking team gets a point if they complete six passes, so it is vital that the two defensive players channel the ball to the front of the grid so they are facing their two teammates and can play quickly to them.

When the two defenders are successful at winning the ball back or forcing a bad pass from the attacking team, the play gets transferred into the other half of the grid. The former attacking team sends two of its players to win the ball and play it back to their two teammates. Award the defending team a point when the two defenders successfully win the ball back and play it into their teammates (Diagram 2).

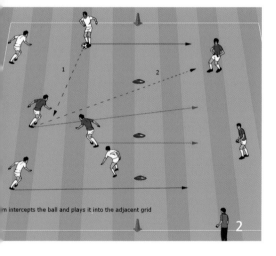

m intercepts the ball and plays it into the adjacent grid

## Second Activity: 10 v. 5 to 5

**Organization:** Approximately half to three quarters of a field cut in half.

Now the five defenders really direct the pressure into an area where they can play the ball to their teammates, who are waiting for them in the opposite grid. Communication is a must, as well as an understanding where to win the ball back and when to put pressure on the ball. When the ball is far away from their five teammates, they should work as a group to direct the ball to the front of the grid or closest to their five teammates, so when they win the ball they can play it to the

other half of the grid quickly and get into attack. When the ball is successfully played into the other grid, the former attacking team sends five across and the five former defenders come over to make it a 10 v. 5 situation. Points are scored in the same manner as the initial exercise (Diagram 3).

## Final Activity: 8 v. 8 to Large Goals

Two teams of eight players play in a 3-2-2 formation. As a coach, tell each team where you would like them to try to win the ball back. Have one team force the ball into the attacking teams left back and the other team force the ball into the right back. Award a point for each time they achieve this and win the ball back. Work with the two forwards in terms of their defending angle of approach in order to make play predictable for their teammates. They are the players who initiate the channeling of the ball, hopefully into an area where the team can quickly win the ball back.

## Conclusion:

This session may have to be repeated several times for your team to become collectively smarter defensively. If anything, it plants a seed in your player's minds that defending is as much mentally demanding as it is physically demanding.

# Zonal Defending: Making It Work

## Positioning of the back four is important to success

### Jack Detchon

**Z**onal defending is defending in such a way that you offer the attacking players areas to attack which good attackers would not normally take and deny them access to areas they would very much prefer.

All defenses tend to concentrate in the center of their penalty areas and deny attackers the chance to shoot at goal from central positions. They prefer to deflect shooting chances wide of, say, the line of the six-yard box.

The defenders will try to stop A6, A8 and A9 from shooting, but may be prepared to allow A11 and A10 to shoot from wider and further away (Diagram 1).

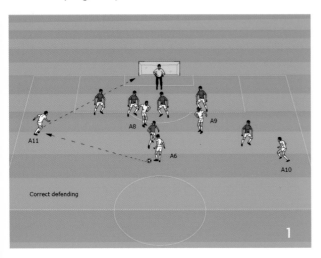

Correct defending

1

Similarly, zonal defending is designed to encourage attackers to play in front of defenders rather than behind and, if they do play behind the defenders, the defenders (including the goalkeeper) will be first to the ball.

Probably the simplest way to present zonal defending is to study players duties or jobs.

## First Defender's Job

This is the player who is (a) nearest the ball or (b) marking the player nearest the ball or (c) confronting the player with the ball.

If when the attacker receives the ball with his/her back to goal, the first defender's job is to stop the attacker from turning with the ball.

## Second Defender's Job

This is usually the nearest player to the pressurizing defender, whose job it is to cover or support the first defender, both physically and verbally.

## Third Defender's Job

This defender's job is to balance the defense by occupying vital or dangerous space. On occasion there may be more than one third defender.

If you now look at a complete back four, you can examine their marking positions vis-à-vis their jobs, i.e., first defender, second defender, and third defender. Although nowadays you rarely see four forwards employed as a front four, that opposition format will be used to clarify how zonal defending can cope with that degree of attack.

## Key Factors in Collective Defending

- The defense should be goal-side.
- The defender should be between attacker and goal. Defending "in to out" (Diagram 2)
- The defender's distance from the attacker should be that distance which the defenders can cover while the ball is traveling to another attacker. This is approximately one-third of the length of the pass.

In Diagram 2, each defender is (a) goal-side of his/her attacker, (b) between the attacker and the goal and the goal and (c) within a marking distance that is different from the other defenders since they are all different distances from the ball.

So D3 is close because A2 is near the ball, and D2 is the furthest away to balance the defense, because A11 is furthest away from the ball, perhaps 40 to 45 yards.

In Diagram 2, if A8 decides to switch the play, the pass probably will be to the feet of A11, since D2 occupies the space in front A11. However, if D2 doesn't take up this balancing position and instead marks A11 closely (Diagram 3), D2 is encouraging A8 to pay the ball over and behind the defense into what, for the defenders, is dangerous space.

If D2 maintains balancing position, A8 – in switching the play- will play to A11's feet. As the ball is moving between A8 and A11, D2 must cover the distance to A11 and decide:

- Can D2 intercept the pass?
- Can D2 tackle A11 as A11 receives the ball?
- Does D2 pressure A11 after A11 has received the ball?

D6, D5 and D3 change their positions – again as the ball is in transition from A8 to A11 (Diagram 4).

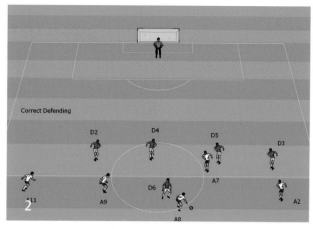

*Diagram 2 Distances and marking position of the back four*

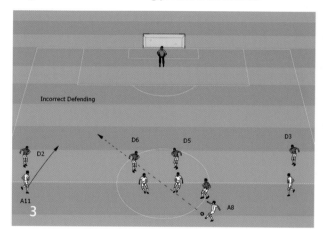

*Diagram 3 Lack of balance leaves dangerous space*

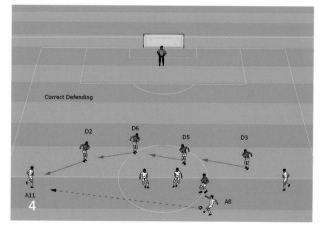

*Diagram 4 Good collective back four adjustment as play is switched*

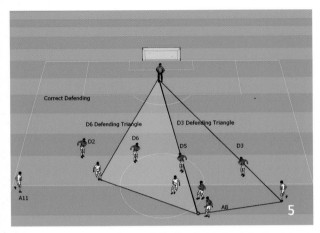

*Diagram 5 Marking inside the defending triangle*

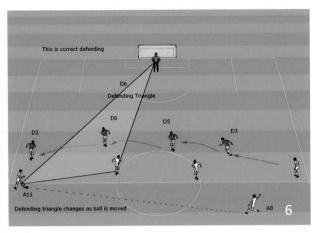

*Diagram 6 Defending triangle changes as ball is moved*

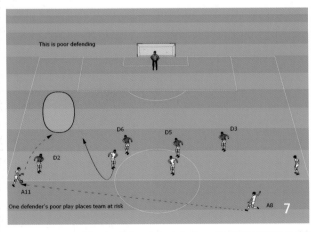

*Diagram 7 One defender's poor play places team at risk*

Now, D2 is the number one player pressuring the ball. D6 becomes the covering player. D5, and particularly D3, become balancing players.

## The marking triangle

It is wise on most occasions for the defender to be inside the marking triangle. This triangle is the one formed by drawing a line from the ball to the center of the goal, from the center of the goal to the defender's opponent, and from the opponent to the ball (Diagram 5).

D3 is in the D3 defending triangle. If D3 goes outside that triangle to the left, D3's position deteriorates considerably. Similarly, if D6's position is five yards to the right and outside that defending triangle, D6's position is poor. In Diagram 5, D6's position is good.

Note how D6's triangle changes as the ball is transferred to A11 (Diagram 6) and how D6 changes position because of it.

If D6 does not change marking position relative to A10, then D6 offers A10 the use of dangerous and advantageous space and the very good chance of A10 being first to any pass played into this space (Diagram 7).

Marking positions, therefore, in a zonal system, fulfill the main purposes, as seen from the diagrams in this section:

They allow a player to undertake the job of the number one defender, i.e., intercept, tackle or challenge the ball or the attacker with the ball. They allow the others to occupy important space and to encourage attackers to play into less important and therefore less dangerous space.

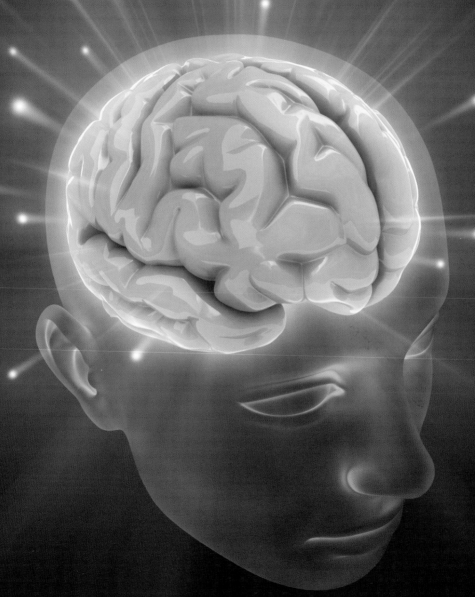

# Chapter 3:
# The Mental

# Weighing the Confidence Factor

## Mark Earles and Melissa A. Chase

*"We just have not been playing with confidence."*

As a coach, you likely will have heard or used a statement referring to low self-confidence to explain a team's poor level of performance. You probably also have been able to identify certain games when your team has been playing with a lot of confidence, resulting in superior levels of performance. With this being the case, it is clear that the confidence of your team is an important psychological factor that can have a profound effect on performance levels. You also may find that when your team is playing with a high level of confidence there are more positive interactions and greater satisfaction among players.

Coaches have long recognized the relationship between team confidence and performance in soccer, and, more recently, researchers in the field of sport psychology have investigated this relationship. Specifically, we know that teams, which have a high level of confidence, have a higher level of persistence, put forth more effort, and outperform those teams with lower levels of confidence.

## What Exactly is Team Confidence?

There have been numerous articles published about how to enhance an individual's level of confidence. It is important to recognize that there is a difference between individual or self-confidence and team confidence.

Self-confidence is an individual's belief that he or she can successfully perform a specific activity or task. For example, an individual may have a lot of self-confidence in his or her ability to dribble past an opponent in a one-on-one situation, but less confidence in his or her ability to make the right pass to a teammate to score.

Team confidence reflects the fact that teams often have collective beliefs about their ability as a team. This describes players' judgments about the team's performance capabilities, what challenges and goals they pursue as a team, how much effort they exert during practices and games and the team's willingness to persist when they are not playing well or failing to win games.

Team confidence is not a summation of all the players' self-confidence, because beliefs about your own ability and the ability of the team could be quite different. For example, you may have an all-star goalkeeper who is very confident in his or her own skills. However, his or her confidence in the rest of the team is low because he or she believes that the team does not have the ability to be successful.

Although coaches may think that simply increasing the individual confidence levels of each team member would enhance a team's confidence, research has shown that strategies to enhance team confidence need to be more specific, as there are numerous interactions between players. If a team consists of a group of players who all are pursuing their own self-interests, they will not have the ability to work together, which also is required for success. This is why team confidence is an important concept and should not be overlooked by coaches.

## What Information Sources Influence Team Confidence?

The sources of information that players use to form team confidence can be grouped into four different categories:

- Past performance accomplishments
- Persuasive information
- Social comparisons
- Physiological information

Athletes may select one or two of these sources or use a combination of all four.

**Past performance accomplishments** refer to how well the team has played in previous games and training sessions or how much they have improved. If the team perceives successful experiences in games or practices, then team levels will be higher. These successful experiences are not solely determined by whether the team wins. Perceived failure experiences will lower team confidence levels. Again, these are not necessarily determined by losing a game. These past performance accomplishments are believed to be the most influential source in raising confidence levels.

**Persuasive information** refers to the way in which team confidence is enhanced through comments by significant others. This includes encouragement, expectations and evaluative feedback from coaches. Other sources of persuasive information can come from spectators, the media and teammates. For example, teams that can see and hear the support of spectators are likely to have higher confidence and expectations for success than if they are playing in front of a hostile crowd. Similarly, if the media constantly criticizes performances, players may start to doubt their own abilities to be successful.

**Social comparisons** are sources of confidence that teams gain through comparing their ability with the ability of other teams. If a team is playing a weaker opponent, such as a team from a smaller conference, then team confidence is likely to be high. For example, confidence also would be expected to be high if the team had made favorable comparisons with an opponent about their ability to run their offense and score

goals. In contrast, if a team is playing a stronger opponent, and they believe that their own ability is lower than the opponent's ability, then team confidence may be lower.

Modeling also is a form of social comparison that can influence team confidence. Watching another team perform a skill, then modeling your behavior after them, can increase your team's confidence.

**Physiological information** also provides team confidence information to players. This is gained through judgments about the physical and mental states and well-being of a team such as fitness level, fatigue, and levels of tension, anxiety, or fear with regard to an upcoming game against a particular opponent. Specifically, if a team has played numerous games in a short period of time, then team confidence may be lower than usual due to the effects of fatigue. Team confidence also will be lower if players are not mentally prepared when playing a certain team.

## Guidelines for Improving Your Team's Confidence

Before trying to enhance your team's level of confidence, it would be beneficial to understand which sources of information your team uses the most to develop confidence beliefs. For example, it would be useful for you to know that your team relies mostly on persuasive information (in the form of comments from the coaches) to develop their level of confidence. If this is the case, then you, as the coach, must realize the impact your words have on the team's confidence.

One way you can gain understanding is to consider how your team responds in terms of their confidence after game/practice performances (past performance accomplishments), after you give them feedback in practices and games (persuasive information) and after playing other teams (social comparisons). These responses both are on physical and emotional (physiological state/condition) level. In trying to understand the interactions that influence team confidence, it also may be useful to ask some of the more experienced players what makes the team feel more confident about them.

As a coach, it also is important that you understand that your team's confidence may vary throughout the season. However, by considering these guidelines, you may be able to incorporate a number of these specific strategies that will enhance your team's confidence as the season progresses.

## How to Improve Confidence

Team confidence is derived from any one or a combination of the sources we have described. Using these sources as a guideline, here are suggestions that may be used to enhance the confidence of your team.

- **Provide players with successful experiences in practice:** For most athletes, we believe that practice performance is a more important source of team confidence than game performance. There are two main reasons for this. First, the players themselves can determine practice performance and success, as opposed to potential uncontrollable game events. Second, teams have many more practice sessions than games over the course of a season, providing more opportunities from which to draw past performance information that helps form confidence levels.

You should reward team effort, improvement and learning of, say, set plays or a particular style of play, and persistence. These variables are much more under your team's control. If your team is not successful in a practice, your response should be to work on specific aspects more rather than focusing on an unsuccessful outcome.

Successful practice experiences are especially important prior to games. Instead of trying to improve team tactics immediately prior to a game or late in the week for an upcoming weekend game, you could have your team perform favorite drills and match-related exercises that are usually successful. This will leave them with a higher level of confidence entering games.

- **Reward and emphasize successful performances rather than winning:** Team confidence increases after perceived successes and decreases after perceived failures. By emphasizing and rewarding controllable factors within your team, such as effort, persistence and their own performances, it is possible for your team to still perceive some success and certainly improvement, even if they lose a game. For example, after losing, you could tell your team that you were very happy with the way in which they quickly supported each other and the amount of scoring opportunities they created.

The outcome of a game often is uncontrollable because of factors such as weather, officials or opponent's plays. Emphasizing losing as only a failure will lower team confidence. If there is an aspect of play that your team needs to improve upon, then you could address this while not emphasizing the loss. For example, you could suggest "although we did a good job of marking in our defensive third we need to do a better job of picking up runners from midfield."

- **Attribute success and failure in an appropriate way:** The reasons coaches and players provide to explain success and failure have a large impact upon future team confidence beliefs. After playing well during a game, most coaches acknowledge their team's performance in a group setting, which helps in raising team confidence. However, the explanations for success should focus on ability and effort attributes. Specifically, if your team defeats a difficult opponent or plays well, emphasize that the result was due to the team's high level of effort and its overall ability. Avoid attributing success to luck in comments such as "we were lucky to win this one today" and "you did not deserve to win the game," as this will not increase future team confidence.

The reasons or excuses coaches provide after playing poorly or losing should be attributed to the team's lack of ability, and players should be encouraged to respond with increased effort in upcoming practices and games. Avoid attributing failure to lack of ability or performances that will never improve.

- **Encourage your team:** Team confidence can be enhanced by encouragement given by significant others. In pre- game team talks and practices, coaches should encourage the team with positive information, such as "I know you have the ability to play well today," "I'm really pleased with the way you are playing" or "Your effort in practice is going to really pay off in our upcoming games." If players are not playing well, they can be encouraged by using statements such as "We're not making enough diagonal runs in the attacking third of the field, which I know you can do because we have done this in practice."

When talking to parents, ask them to support and encourage the team, so that they can help improve the team' s confidence and performances.

Encouragement between your players can also help in raising team confidence. This may include remarks in games such as "Come on, we can do it" and "well played."

- **Use yourself and more experienced players as a model for confidence:** Team confidence can be enhanced by seeing confident role models within the team. Showing the confidence you, as the coach, have in your team will increase their confidence. This can be achieved in your coaching behavior by understanding that you can influence the players' attitudes and skill level, demonstrating your belief in their abilities by what you say and how you carry yourself and by setting high but realistic goals for the team. Coaches also should explain to the experienced players and team captains the importance of these factors. Observing this, raising the level of team confidence, then will influence the entire team

- **Keep your team focused:** A team that lacks focus, is fatigued or is fearful of an upcoming opponent may have a decreased level of team confidence. To keep teams focused on the upcoming game, coaches should be calm when talking to the team and not try to over-arouse them. Also, emphasize the way in which you want them to play rather than who they are playing. To avoid fatigue, coaches should try to avoid scheduling a number of games in a short period of time. If this is unavoidable and you recognize that the team is tired, then you might give them a day off from practice or use the time for game analysis

- **Make appropriate comparisons with other teams:** Team confidence can be enhanced by making appropriate comparisons of strengths and weaknesses with opponents. For example, you might make your team aware of the strengths of an opposing team's offensive skills, but you still are able to raise your team's confidence for the game by telling them that they have the defensive ability to be effective in minimizing this offensive threat. You also may point out any weak areas in your opponent's team, such as a goalkeeper who does not like to come off the goal line for high crossed balls or a dislike of being put under quick pressure

By having an understanding of the team's level of confidence and using these suggestions to enhance their confidence, coaches should find that over time their team plays with a higher level of persistence and effort in adversity. Team performances should also be higher, and as a consequence, you will notice that there is more satisfaction among players. Coaches will then be more likely to say that "we have been playing with a lot of confidence and are really on top of our game."

*Editor's note: Mark Earles earned his MA at Miami University and serves as the youth coach for Norwich City Football Club and Norfolk County Football Association in England. Melissa A. Chase is an assistant professor in the Department of Physical Education, Health and Sports Studies at Miami University in Oxford, Ohio.*

# Developing Consistency

### Steve Boutcher, Ph.D.

*Competition can devastate even the best athlete's performance. The missed open net, the fumbled ball by the keeper that leads to a goal, the wrong tactical decision such as whether to dive in on the tackle or delay an opponent are soccer examples of athletes succumbing to the demands of intense competition. However, many athletes do compete successfully under enormous competitive demands. How do these athletes consistently maintain high standards of performance? How do they regulate their emotions and avoid thoughts of failure? How do they maintain their focus of attention?*

**A**thletes who consistently deliver in clutch situations tend to rely upon *performance routines.* For example, basketball players and archers may have a performance routine for establishing their stance and shooting position, whereas golfers may waggle the club asset number of times before executing a shot. Soccer keepers go through set warm-up routines to prepare them to meet the demands of the game. These athletes may also go through a preplanned sequence of imagery, relaxation, and other mental strategies as part of their performance routine. These routines could be used before or after skill performance, or while waiting on the sidelines.

Research evidence for the existence of performance routines has come from a number of different sports including golf, archery, riflery, basketball, baseball, and weightlifting. Our own research has demonstrated that professional golfers' pre-shot behaviors are remarkably consistent over many hours of play. Professional golfers repeatedly take the same amount of time and the same number of practice swings and glances at the target before playing each shot. Furthermore, the overall results of these studies suggest that these routines can enhance performance.

## How Routines Develop Consistency

The effectiveness of performance routines has been demonstrated in at least three areas: *First, routines may enable athletes to concentrate more efficiently.* By focusing on certain cues it is possible that distractions (e.g., crowd noise) are less likely to influence performance. *Second, routines may help prevent "warm-up decrement."* Research has shown that there is often a drop in performance after a brief rest until one can get warmed up or back in the groove. Routines can serve the purpose of "keeping you warm" during these periods of time. *Third, routines may also prevent athletes from thinking about the details or mechanics of well learned skills that are better performed automatically.*

Recent investigations in sport have attempted to explore the mechanisms underlying the performance routine. A number of studies have examined cardiovascular and brain wave patterns. For example, cardiac deceleration has been found with shooters. Researchers have demonstrated that elite rifle shooters reduce their heart rate just prior to the trigger pull. Similar effects have been found with archers and golfers. Attention states during the pre-performance routine have also been assessed through monitoring left- and right-brain wave activity of elite shooters while shooting. Results indicated that seconds before pulling the trigger shooters exhibited more activity in their right hemisphere compared to their left. This suggests that elite marksmen may possess such a high degree of attention focus that they can effectively reduce conscious mental activities of the left hemisphere, thus reducing thoughts unnecessary to performance of the task.

Terry Orlick maintains that routines or psychological plans hold one's focus away from negative self-talk. An effective routine can therefore "make the body respond just as you would like it to respond, and much more consistently."

## Ritual versus Routine

There is an important difference between a routine and a ritual. Rituals include wearing certain clothes, using lucky symbols, or repeating the same behaviors or thoughts solely because of superstition. This is compared to the well-developed performance routine that can be adapted to varying conditions and different situations. Rituals tend to control the athlete, whereas a well developed performance routine is controlled by the athlete.

## Laying the Foundation

The development of effective performance routines is based on previously acquired psychological skills. Psychological skills such as imagery, relaxation, attention control and coping strategies all serve to create a foundation from which to build a routine that serves its purpose. The development of such skills will not be described here but it is emphasized that the athlete must progress through a series of stages in order to acquire the mental skills necessary to develop an effective individualized routine.

Individualized performance routines focus specifically on establishing optimal psychological and physiological states immediately before, during, and after skill performance. Athletes' reactions after performance of a skill and when waiting during competition are also important determinants of overall performance. The following sections offer suggestions for developing consistency through the use of performance routines at various stages.

## Pre-Performance Routines

The main components of pre-performance routines are attention control, physical and mental control, and behavioral consistency. Thus, athletes need to have the ability to focus their thoughts on task relevant cues, they need to be able to control their psychological and physiological states, and they need to be able to acquire an appropriate routine set of behavioral actions. Consequently, the challenge for the athlete is to find the most efficient routine and to repeat this routine before every performance.

Pre-performance routines will vary in content for athletes in the same sport. For instance, in golf there are clear differences regarding the speed of pre-performance routines of the faster, more spontaneous golfers compared to their more methodical, slower counterparts. Similarly, pre-performance routines will vary between sports. Thus, a pitcher's routine when standing on the mound preparing to pitch will have different attention and behavioral components than those of a springboard diver preparing to dive. Skill level will also influence the type and nature of the routine. If the skill is still being acquired, and not performed automatically, then a less complex, abbreviated routine may be more appropriate.

Pre-performance routines can be divided into either *self-paced or reactive categories*. During self-paced routines the athlete will initiate movement, whereas in reactive routines, the athlete is waiting to react to an environmental cue (i.e., the goalkeeper will react to the cues of the coach warming him up). An example of a self-paced routine would be a penalty shot in soccer or serving in tennis.

## Self-Paced Routines

Self-paced pre-performance routines consist of a series of both mental and physical steps, as indicated by the soccer and golf examples below. Each component of the routine is also enhanced by general mental skills previously acquired by the athlete. Relaxation, imagery, and breathing techniques could be used to develop the "setting" response and then specific relaxations cues could be transferred to the routine. For example, a setting response in a routine could be achieved through the use of a combination of techniques such as a cue word like "cool" coupled with breathing technique.

The imagery component of the routine would be developed in a similar manner. Initially, the effectiveness of imagery for each individual athlete needs to be assessed. Soccer players before taking a penalty shot can use imagery and see the ball hitting the upper 90 before making their attempt. Imagery may help to avoid focusing on irrelevant task information and provide a way to activate the appropriate set. Research examining the influence of imagery on gymnastics, tennis, and badminton performance has suggested that imaging immediately before execution may enhance skill performance.

The kinesthetic coupling component is concerned with establishing the feel of the upcoming shot. This component seems to be especially relevant during chipping and putting as elite golfers tend to rehearse far more when performing these kinds of shots. Thus, this component will entail rehearsing the correct action and attempting to establish the correct "feel" of the actual performance.

The next state is the set-up. In most accuracy sports the alignment of the body to the target is of crucial importance. Thus, a routine which directs attention to the stance, grip, posture, alignment, ball position, and so forth, is a vital component. A quick mental checklist, supplemented by kinesthetic cues could be performed as part of the routine.

The golfer is now ready to swing the club. Initiation of the swing is often preceded by a "waggle" which comprises small movements of the hands and club. Waggles usually consist of a forward press of the hands in the address position

preceded by a number of small movements of the club away from the ball.

During the swing, which should be automatic and reflexive, a common technique used by golfers is to focus attention on a swing *thought* such as "tempo." Thus, timing the backswing to "tem" and the downswing to "po" focuses attention on the overall rhythm and timing of the shot rather than on specifics of the swing.

Clearly, athletes in other sports will require different components in comparison to golfers. The basic principle that applies, however, is that the pre-performance routine establishes a rhythm and a focus of attention that simultaneously prepares the body and mind for the ensuing skill. It should be emphasized that although the routine is aimed at establishing consistency the routine itself should by flexible. Thus, athletes who have an imagery component in their routine may have three or four different images that could be used if the one they are using does not appear to be effective for that particular situation.

In attempting to develop an effective pre-performance routine for your sport you must first establish a sequence of mental steps and behavioral actions similar to those outlined in the golf example. The content and structure will be highly individual and will vary for different sports. The refining and fine-tuning of each component will be a continuous process. Once a routine has been developed, its effectiveness can be assessed through videotaping and time analysis. For most sports the preliminary work should occur in practice settings (on the practice range, at the swimming pool), but will eventually be monitored and observed during competition. Once a routine has been established, distraction strategies can be used to test the consistency and attention efficiency of the routine. For instance, loud music could be played during the routine and its resulting effect assessed on video and through discussion with the athlete after performance. Eventually, other irrelevant competition cues such as camera clicks, crowd noises, crowd movement, and so forth, can be simulated. Vicarious experiential techniques can also be used to create competition-like environments. For example, a competitive situation in the Olympics could be created through imagery, by structuring the environment to simulate the competitive setting, and by playing video tapes of world class athletes who will be competing in the actual competition. The challenge for athletes will be to focus attention away from distractive thoughts and concentrate on their own individualized pre-performance routine.

## Reactive Routines

The major difference between self-paced and reactive routines is that in the reactive situation *environmental* cues will play a more important role. Thus, the separate components may be similar to the self-paced routine but there will be a greater emphasis on responding to vital environmental cues. Vision training for athletes in sports such as baseball and tennis is a vital component of the reactive routine. For example, for the hitter in baseball, focusing on the placement of the ball in the pitchers' hand before the pitch could be an early cue in the reactive situation.

## Post-Performance Routines

How the athlete reacts, thinks, and feels after executing a skill (the post-performance routine) is another area where routines can be utilized. There is a tendency for athletes to focus on negative aspects immediately after unsuccessful performances. Thus, a poor golf shot or a bad pitch can carry over and affect subsequent performance. The post-performance routine attempts to stop this negative transfer. Components of this routine may include emotional release, post-performance analysis, kinesthetic rehearsal of the correct skill, coping strategies, and mind clearing techniques. Emotional release refers to

an emotional catharsis immediately following performance. Some athletes may need to release emotions through verbal or behavioral responses; however, other athletes may not feel the need to vent emotions. The analysis component might include a review of the performed skill to monitor any form or technique flaws. Kinesthetic rehearsal might involve performing the correct action to reinforce the feel of the skill. *Coping strategies* might include a relaxation technique such as the setting cues used at the start of the pre-performance routine. Thus, if the athlete perceived he/she is over-aroused, a quick, efficient coping strategy can be employed to re-establish optimal physiological arousal levels. Finally, mind clearing techniques to eradicate all thoughts about performance of the last skill can be employed. The athlete may use a technique such as centering to clear the mind and prepare the body for the next skill. Centering involves focusing thoughts on cues such as breathing to clear the mind in preparation for the next performance.

The following is an example of a post-performance routine for a missed foul shot in basketball:

- Emotional release; exhale a long breath and remind self the last shot is history and now the important thing is the next shot
- Analysis: "I missed the foul shot because I didn't not extend fingers through the ball to the basket"
- Physically rehearse the free throw minus the ball – extend fingers through imaginary ball to the basket
- Mind clearing; take a long breath and use a quick centering or relaxation technique
- Use a pre-performance routine for the next shot

# Evaluating and Extending Routines

## Evaluating Performance Routines

There are a number of ways that athletes and coaches can assess the effectiveness of their performance routines. For instance, the routine can be videotaped and examined for consistency over repeated performances in different situations (e.g., practices, matches). The athlete can also monitor his/her own routine to assess how useful it was in avoiding distractions and keeping attention focused on the task at hand. For example, the athlete could rate the overall effectiveness of the routine on a 1 to 10 scale for distraction, mind clearing, and emotional control. With further development of the routines, each component can be evaluated, modified, and/or fine-tuned. Ultimately, the routine would allow for flexibility in each of the components.

## Before the Competition

Pre-competition routines have two aspects: the first deals with preparation leading up to an athletic event (e.g., activity, sleeping, and nutritional patterns), whereas the second is concerned with preparation immediately before performing (e.g., warm-up, controlling arousal, and pre-performance thoughts) Many athletes have reported experiencing a variety of problems during the days prior to an important athletic event: For example, disruption in eating and sleeping habits, excessive worrying, and increased muscular tensions levels have all been associated with the build up to competition. Thus, it is important that the athlete be able to prepare adequately before competition. As each athlete may have different preparation strategies the challenge is to select the most efficient preparation strategy for that particular athlete given the unique characteristics of the athletes' sports. Thus, a preparation routine could be developed that guides the athlete through a series of steps during

the days before competitions. The routine could consist of certain exercise activities, particular nutrition habits, and previously developed stress management techniques.

The period right before performance can be crucial for athletes. It is here that athletes may experience the pre-match nerves often associated with performing in competitive situations. Thus, a routine could be developed to handle the minutes leading up to the match or game. Much has been written regarding self-regulation during these important minutes right before the match. For instance, strategies used in this period by athletes have included relaxation, breathing, coping, and positive affirmations. Athletes typically will find some of the techniques more useful than others. Again the challenge for athletes and coaches is to develop a routine before competition that uses the most suitable techniques and strategies for the athletes' particular sport. One interesting technique suggested by David-Kauss is the "readying spot." This should be a place that you can be totally alone for at least 20 minutes so that you can give 100 percent attention to your performance. It is a place and time that you can use to get yourself into a specific frame of mind.

## Interruptions and Stoppages in Play

The between-performance routine is pertinent for athletes engaged in sports that take many hours to complete are characterized by periods of inactivity. Thus, football players and basketball players sitting on the bench, golfers waiting for their next shot, and weather delays in tennis will challenge the athlete's ability to maintain optimal psychological and physiological readiness. This waiting during performance may induce a warm-up decrement and may also give the athlete additional time to worry about losing or performing badly. The between-play routine then is a strategy to use the time between performing effectively. Components of the between-play routine may take the form of attention distraction techniques, and psychological and physiological preparation strategies. Attention distraction techniques could include imaging a personal scene or successful past performances. For example, the golfer waiting for an upcoming shot could imagine a private scene such as walking through an alpine meadow or along a sandy beach. Other distraction strategies could be talking to fellow competitors and spectators, looking at the the scenery, and listening to music. Preparation strategies may include a physical warm-up, stretching, and use of setting cues as discussed earlier.

## Media

Interacting with the media can be more stressful for many athletes, than actually competing. However, handling interviews can follow the same principles already discussed. Athletes should be well prepared before the interview. Terry Orlick maintains that dealing with the media can be positive if the athlete develops a media place. One of the most important components of this plan is to understand the agenda before you do the interview. To assist in determining this, part of the routine may be interacting with the reporter before the interview to find out what kinds of questions they will be asking. During the interaction you could suggest topics or areas for the reporter to consider. Armed with this information you can organize your thoughts so that you know that you want to say. You may also develop a plan for listening to the questions offered by the interviewer as well as a plan for responding to question, particularly probing questions. Finally you may want to role-play the interview with a teammate, coach or sport psychologist to simulate the actual interview session. The key point is to have a plan that you have practiced so that when you are in front of the camera or microphone you can give an effective interview.

Performance routines can be great allies. David Kauss maintains that they build the foundation of discipline and self-control. Moreover, having a routine that "readies" you for the challenges of competition can generalize to other areas of your life. Remember, routines are not rituals, they are systematic patterns of thinking, feeling and behavior that you control. In building your routines start simply. Focus on building consistency in your actions. Once this consistency is established add cognitive and emotional components. Begin using your routines in low stress, practice situations. As their effectiveness increases, you will find that the use of the routine becomes automatic, a part of your game. As is the case with any mental skill, regular practice is essential. The more you employ routines, the more automatic and effective they will become. Be patient and above all find what works for you so that you can let go and trust yourself.

# It's a Mental Game

### Albert Gamarra, MS and R. Keeth Matheny

Imagine a season filled with ups and downs, dramas and conflicts. At the culmination of this long season, you find your team tied in overtime with nine seconds left on the clock and just 12 yards away from the greatest season in your team's (club's) history. You've been awarded a penalty kick and as your player readies outside of the box, both teams are now on one knee holding hands and praying. Your 17-year-old captain stands over the ball with an air of confidence, waiting to shoot.

*"Don't worry, coach," the captain says. "I can make this in my sleep. I've been practicing this moment in my mind for years."*

Her face reflects concentration, but there's a slight smile as she strides confidently to the spot. She goes through the same pre-kick routine you have seen literally thousands of times in practice (not including the countless weekend and off-season kicks). She nods deliberately to the referee for the whistle and focuses slowly on the flow of a comfortable swing. You hold your breath as the ball sails perfectly into the upper 90 and into the net, thankful for the emphasis you placed on developing your players' mental toughness.

Coaches can play a crucial role in the development of this and other related mental skills. Most coaches are well aware of the importance of the mental side of soccer. However, few coaches emphasize the development of mental skills, mainly because they are not familiar with techniques for developing those skills. A lack of techniques for mastering the mental side of soccer can significantly block your players' chances of excellence.

As the gap between the elite teams at all levels and their less talented competitors grows smaller, more focus on technical and mental training is becoming apparent. Excellence results from physical technique and mental skills. Technique comes from quality instruction and quality practice.

Mental skills, like physical ones, are trained over time with practice. Just as a coach uses practice and coaching points to develop a physical profile of greatness, a mental trainer uses mental practice and coaching points to develop a mental profile of greatness. Provided the physical strength and technical skills are there, the mental profile becomes the determinant of success. A mental profile of greatness has emerged through my discussion with successful players and coaches. The main characteristics in this profile:

- Commitment
- High quality practice
- Imagery/mental practice
- Owning the zone
- Confidence

> *The quality of a man's life is a full measure of that man's personal commitment to excellence.*
>
> *Vince Lombardi, former NFL coach*

## Commitment

As with every athlete, great soccer players develop through hard work and good practice. And like every athlete, they must have a high level of commitment to becoming a champion. Coaches can do a great deal to raise an athlete's commitment level. Have the athlete visualize the ultimate goal he/she is trying to achieve, then work backwards to where he/she is now. Ask the player to list the skills of great players, then lead the discussion toward skills from this article and other materials you have obtained while coaching. Then have the player rate his/her current ability levels in the top 10 skills you both have rated as most important.

> *Practice without improvement is meaningless.*
>
> *Chuck Knox, former NFL coach*

throw-in, shot or pass). The player always should know what he/she is working on with every shot. Never do meaningless repetition and avoid just going through the motions. Ten good focused kicks are better than 100 going-through-the-motion shots. Make sure that your players stay focused during practice and that they don't start a shot until they are focused on what they are doing.

After identifying these, set specific goals for each skill and a plan of action for attaining these goals. This will serve as a contract between you and the athlete. The athlete will feel ownership in the training and it will focus and increase his/her commitment level. Post the skills and goals and refer to them regularly. Make sure to give progress reports and frequent feedback.

## High Quality Practice

Practice does not make perfect; practice makes permanent. Perfect practice makes perfect.

A player who respects the game will work on the quality of effort in practice every day. High quality practice begins with having a daily mission, working on a specific goal. An example might be working on keeping the head down while following through on a shot.

However, this goal must be specific and measurable. So a good example would be: "Today I am going to kiss my knee on 9 of 10 practice shots." The player should be encouraged to state this mission to some teammates and coaches so they will hold him/her accountable.

Have a purpose not only for each day of practice but also for each act during practice (i.e., each

A second skill of high quality practice is awareness. Awareness is concentrating on the feel and the technique to the point that your player knows what is right and wrong in every shot. Encourage the player to concentrate on the process – the swing, the feel – and let the outcome take care of itself.

A final skill in high quality practice is pressure. As a coach you must seek ways to put pressure on their practice shots and you must encourage them to add their own pressure. Try challenges, players rushing kicks and even players yelling or distracting each other. Some coaches even have a team sprint session riding on whether the player makes a shot. This technique is good if used appropriately and in moderation. Simply getting the athlete to make a commitment to high quality practice will help immensely.

## Imagery/Mental Practice

From darts to archery to pistol shooting, imagery has been proven to be a very successful tool in enhancing performance. Imagery can have two important uses for players: (a) enhancing performance and (b) mental practice. Imagery can enhance performance by "triggering" the mental blueprints for the skill. These blueprints are the stored versions of the physical skills. Athletes can use imagery in the split seconds before each shot to "prime" this blueprint. Imagery also can be used for mental practice. Players have very limited practice stamina. They can only do so much physical practice each day. Mental practice enables them to gain unlimited additional practice and thus, a significant advantage.

Most of our players already have had some exposure to imagery through camps, clinics or books. Imagery is a skill like any other, and you must practice it and work on the fundamentals to make it most effective. The fundamentals of imagery are vividness and controllability. Vividness is the clarity or sharpness of the image, like the contrast, tint and color settings on a television. Controllability is the degree to which the athlete has control over his/her images. Players must constantly work on these two fundamentals in their imagery. Here is a list of basic tips for good imagery:

- **Multiply:** Elaborate images to include as many stimuli and senses (sights, smells, feelings and sounds) as possible

- **Internalize:** See the actions from within rather than as an observer

- **Success:** It is self-created imagery, so make sure it is extremely positive and amazingly successful

- **Specific:** Encourage use of imagery to practice in the settings of the next performance and to practice overcoming difficult situations. (i.e. game-winning penalty kicks, free kicks, 1 v. 1 defense or offense, etc.)

Having introduced your players to imagery, start giving them imagery homework regularly. Include kicks from all angles and distances, and in pressure situations. Have them include future opponents poor officiating, negative fans, etc. Imagery is a great way to dramatically increase your players' performance.

## Owning the Zone

Many athletes refer to their best performances as being "in a zone." This zone is their ideal frame of mind and excitement level for performance. Owning the zone is controlling yourself enough to always be in the zone for performance. Here are the steps for owning the zone:

- **Awareness:** The player must first know the exact feelings associated with the zone. How excited are they? How focused are they? What are they saying to themselves? How did they prepare for the game? Have the player keep a journal of these answers for each performance and practice. Then relate the answers with how well they played. Simply look at the answers for each individual player's excitement level, focus, preparation, and self-talk during his/her best performances. This information is the definition of their zone

- **Pregame routine:** Use the answer to what kind of preparation gets them to their zone in order to build a pre-game routine. For example, if going for a short jog while listening to their favorite music leads to their best performances, then have them make that a permanent part of their pre-game routine

- **Pre-shot routine:** A pre-shot routine will give the kicker a set of thoughts and behaviors that he always does before shooting. This will enable them to ready his\her mind and make his entire performance automatic. Personalize each routine, but be sure to include the elements of release, focus, image, and trust. Release is a deep breath and smile to clear the mind. Focus is a concentrated effort to bring all the attention to the present moment and on to a small target (e.g., a patch on the ball). Image is imaging a successful shot just prior to shooting, in order to prime one's mental blueprint. Trust is letting the body do the motion on automatic pilot

- **Control what you can:** Look back at every player's journal. Help the players avoid the thoughts and behaviors that lead to their poor performances and keep their focus only on the thoughts and behaviors that lead to their best performances.

## Confidence

Confidence stems partially from the skills we have already discussed. If your athletes are putting in the quality practice, using imagery and mental practice, and are in control of their zone, then they will be confident. Confidence is so crucial though, it is worth the time to work on additional sources for confidence. Here are three simple additional sources.

> *Whether you believe you can or believe you can't, you are right*
>
> Henry Ford

- **Mental highlight film:** Always encourage your players to constantly relive their best performances and to forget their poor performances. Of course before simply forgetting the poor performances, we want the players to learn from them. The key is to remember only long enough to learn and then to forget.

- **Positive feedback:** Both the coach and the players must strive to say positive things about the players' performance. Negative comments will take a heavy toll on a player's confidence if he/she is not almost drowned in positive feedback.

- **Walk the walk:** Body language can have a significant impact on confidence. If your player can look, walk, talk and think confidently, he/she eventually will become more confident. Encourage the player to walk the walk.

Share the material in this article with your players and coaches. Use the materials you are comfortable teaching and expect a learning process. You can help your players develop much more quickly if you can get them to work on the mental skills in the off season. During the off season encourage your players to seek help in developing mental skills by attending camps that emphasize the mental part of soccer or by working with a qualified mental trainer.

*Editor's note: Albert Gamarra has been involved with youth soccer as a player and coach for 22 years. His playing years were spent in Miami with the Florida Youth Soccer Association. After completing his high school career at Miami Killian Senior High as an all-state selection, he moved to Gainesville, Fla., to attend the University of Florida. He received a bachelor's degree in psychology and a master's degree in sport psychology.*

*He began his coaching career in Gainesville, assisting with youth teams and the Bucholz High School. team In 1994 he moved to Tucson, Ariz., and continued his coaching, assisting at Sahuaro High School. In Tucson he has made numerous presentations on the mental aspects of soccer. Gamarra credits his high level of soccer knowledge to his father, and also his former coach and mentor Dennis Hackett.*

## References

Ravizza, K. & Hanson, T. (1994) *Heads up baseball: Playing the game one pitch at a time*. Masters Press.

Vealey, R. S. & Walter, S. M. (1992) In J. M. Williams (ed.) *Applied sport psychology: Personal growth to peak performance*. (p. 200-219), Mayfield.

Williams, J. M. & Krane, V. (1992) In J. M. Williams (ed.) *Applied sport psychology: Personal growth to peak performance*. (p. 200-219), Mayfield.

# Relaxing Under Pressure

## Dr. Keith A. Wilson

On July 10, 1999, the Rose Bowl hosted a pivotal event in the history of women's sports. Over 90,000 fans crowded into the Rose Bowl to see the U.S. Women's National Team play China for the World Cup. It was a very tough match that the United States eventually won by penalty kicks after a scoreless game and overtime.

As my family and I sat in the Rose Bowl that day enjoying this spectacular event, I noticed another game within a game. I focused a lot on Michelle Akers. My eyes kept focusing on her: 1) because of her stature as a soccer player; 2) because I knew her story of enduring chronic fatigue syndrome while playing world class soccer and 3) because I met her in person at an NSCAA meeting several years ago.

Akers dominated the midfield. She was simply everywhere. She was a physical presence. But one had to wonder how long she could go on. How long would her body allow her to play with such intensity? You could see her fight through exhaustion and keep going. You could see she was fighting the mental and physical battle of her athletic life.

In the *Sports Illustrated* article in which the entire team was named "Sportswomen of the Year," part of Akers' mental battle is chronicled:

*For the entire second half Akers was delirious. She was oblivious to the crowd noise. The only thing she was aware of was the pounding in her head and the words going through it with every step she took: Only 20 more minutes. Don't quit. Only 19 more minutes. Track that ball. Don't look at the clock. Win this head ball. Only 16 more minutes. Only 15 more minutes. Win this tackle. Get lost in the game. Don't quit. Don't quit. Do not quit.*

This is one of the most incredible examples of a world-class athlete who created such mental toughness through her personal and professional crisis that she was able to will her body to play world-class soccer on a day when the chronic fatigue syndrome had zapped her body of strength. Yet Akers believed her mental toughness would allow her to play, and play very well, in the most important American women's soccer game in history.

Her example leads us to the question: How do the rest of us build belief and confidence in our mental skills?

We may not face the challenges of Michelle Akers, but each of us faces the possibility of caving in and collapsing under pressure. We want to believe our mental skills will pull us through a difficult athletic challenge. But often we face the reality that we have not prepared our mental toughness skills to the level we need for success under duress.

Most soccer players have known the heartbreak of choking when their team was counting on them. They put the ball right at the goalkeeper during a penalty kick even though they had perfectly executed 100 penalty kicks in practice the week before. Or they may have made a silly mental error that caused a turnover and gave the opposite team an open shot at the goal.

The biggest factor in choking during a game is when a player is not relaxed under pressure. All coaches know that soccer players perform best when they are relaxed and the muscles are not working against themselves due to undue anxiety or tension. Bill Beswick, a sport psychologist from England, believes this is one of the most important skills soccer players need to learn and master. Often a soccer coach will yell to the players to relax but this is as ineffective as yelling to the player, "Jump higher."

## Dynamic Relaxation

If the coach has not provided the tools to learn to jump higher, then comments like these are useless. If the soccer coach does not teach the athlete relaxation tools to use under pressure, then yelling "relax" is useless as well. In fact it may create more performance anxiety because the athlete does not know how to interpret the coach's statement.

Performance hypnosis is one of the most effective ways of teaching soccer players how to relax under pressure. Hypnosis is often defined as an altered state of consciousness, a trance. In a trance state a person is focused and is able to block out distractions and stay relaxed. Most often hypnosis takes place in a clinician's office where the goal is to provide relaxation as a counter skill to debilitating anxiety. Medically, hypnosis can help a

person become absorbed (focused); it can also help to dissociate away from pain. This is very helpful in dealing with the pain of a chronic illness such as cancer or even the intense pain of childbirth.

Usually hypnosis is learned in a clinical setting. The typical scenario is that of a patient lying on a couch with the lights dimmed, learning to block out distractions. This form of clinical hypnosis is difficult to transfer to something as active as sport performance. One can't take the couch and light dimmer switch out to the soccer pitch.

To denote a more active style of hypnosis, this author has coined the phrase performance hypnosis. Performance hypnosis uses the category of hypnosis known as alert trance. Performance hypnosis utilizes the properties of clinical hypnosis but makes the power of focus available while one is in an active state. Learning performance hypnosis can help provide one of the keys to entering the zone of optimal performance. Performance hypnosis can help the soccer player maintain dynamic relaxation during an entire soccer match.

© Piksel / Dreamstime.com

In order to create the power of performance hypnosis, the soccer player must first learn how to obtain the state of dynamic relaxation. This is best done in the traditional way of learning to use and reinforce the following steps:

1. Using relaxation induction.
2. Using fractionation as a deepening procedure.
3. Moving down the path to the performance relaxation zone.
4. Using visualization to experience a place of total relaxation (beaches or mountain scenes are the most popular).
5. Using autogenics to build belief that one can change how the body feels (creating the feeling of heaviness and lightness).
6. Using post hypnotic suggestion to teach rapid induction procedures so one can return to the performance relaxation zone (eye roll and rhythmic breathing).

This procedure is first taught in an office or classroom setting so the athlete can develop confidence in the establishment of the state of dynamic relaxation. It can be taught to individuals or as a team exercise. The procedure is put on audiotape so the athlete can practice it during the week to continue to build confidence in her ability to reach the state of dynamic relaxation.

## Distractions Minimized

When one uses performance hypnosis to enhance the possibility of entering the zone of optimal performance, mental distractions can be minimized. The athlete is able to do a quick hypnotic induction and return to a higher level of focus. Two important principles of performance hypnosis are useful in this instance.

First, the performance hypnosis intervention must be something that is quick and powerful to refocus the athlete. For the soccer player who is selected to take a PK either in the flow of the game or in a shootout, performance hypnosis can help the player be prepared to be relaxed and ready to take a confident penalty kick. She can do a quick "eye roll induction," a technique for entering into a hypnotic state and take herself into the Performance Relaxation Zone. She can spend 15-30 seconds there and experience herself returning to the state of dynamic relaxation. When she is ready to take the PK she can physically feel the difference in her body. It is relaxed and the mind is sharp and she is ready to perform at the level she has practiced for this important PK.

This technique can be used throughout the game during the natural stoppages of the game. The more players work at staying focused and playing at optimal intensity level, the less likely they are to be negatively affected by distractions of the game. These could be external distractions like trash talking of players, parents' comments or a questionable call by the referee. The ongoing refocusing will also help the player not to get distracted internally where she may be thinking too hard about the play ahead.

Performance hypnosis works on the field in a quick way to contain internal and external distractions because the player has established a foundation of dynamic relaxation by her practice and mastery of the skill off the field. Performance hypnosis is first learned in the office or classroom and then practiced with an audio tape every day to become very comfortable in the performance relaxation zone.

Second, the player works on several quick inductions so that they are natural tools to select from when the situation calls for mental refocusing. The soccer player is confident she can use a quick induction to get to a relaxed state because she has done it thousands of times and knows it works. She has built a powerful belief that he can relax under intense pressure. She has been able to feel the physical difference of being in the state of dynamic relaxation thousands of times in practice and game situations. Consequently, she believes she can do it under the pressure of performance.

The second important hypnotic principle at work is called fractionation. Fractionation is the hypnotic principle that states if a person is in a heightened state of trance (absorption) and is interrupted, but then allowed to return to the trance state, the depth of the trance will be even more powerful. This is a great principle to understand in athletic performance because there are so many challenges in the game, which will try to pull the athlete out of the zone of optimal performance.

If the athlete knows what to do to continually return to a higher level of focus then she is more likely to stay in the more efficient state of high-level absorption. Understanding this principle can help the player be mentally sharper at the end of the contest than she was at the beginning. This may be part of the principle at work when a player continues to get better and better as the game moves into the later stages of the match. This is a great advantage when the player is fending off physical exhaustion and game pressure in the 85th minute of the match.

## Contact a Professional

When you or your team are ready to add performance hypnosis to your performance tool bag, where should you turn to receive this training? Although there are two choices, only one would be recommended. One choice is the stage hypnotist or lay hypnotist who has taken a short course in hypnosis but has no professional mental health background. The danger with this type of trainer is they know some techniques but are not well versed in the intricacies of human behavior. Consequently, their performance interventions will be very shallow and you may even end up barking like a dog! Needless to say, players would not benefit from such training and could be harmed.

The recommended choice is a professional who is certified in clinical hypnosis by a professional organization like the American Society for Clinical Hypnosis. In order to reach the certification level, the practitioner must be at least a master's level health care provider and complete required annual continuing education. The training received by ASCH is focused on integrating hypnosis into their professional, clinical practice. The athlete also would want a professional who is experienced in sport psychology. One way to affirm this is to check if the professional is a member of the Association for the Advancement of Applied Sport Psychology. This would provide the best of all worlds, as the athlete would learn performance hypnosis from a professional who knows the power of the mind as well as the intricacies of the sports world.

Performance hypnosis is a powerful tool. When performance hypnosis is learned well, the soccer player learns to contain anxiety and mental distractions even during extreme levels of pressure. Performance hypnosis can indeed enable the player to perform at the highest level she has trained.

*Editor's note: Keith Wilson is a performance consultant and psychotherapist in El Paso, Texas. He can be reached at Wilson@ TheWinningMind.com*

# Youth Soccer Coach Wanted:
## Only those with patience and perseverance need apply

### Gary R. Allen
### Virginia Youth Soccer Association Director of Coaching Education

*Following are excerpts from an article in The Scientific American, July 24, 2006, by Phillip E. Ross, entitled "The Expert Mind." The article focused upon studies of the mental processes of chess grandmasters and clues to how people become experts in other fields as well. These excerpts can help us address some important points concerning the development of young soccer players in America.*

Simon coined a psychological 'law of his own' the 10-year rule, which states that it takes approximately a decade of heavy labor to master any field.

The 10-year rule, or 10,000 hours rule, can be applied as easily to soccer as to chess. Each soccer game involves a myriad of decisions, technical and physical challenges in an ever-changing environment, among and against other players of varying abilities, and in different stages of physical exhaustion. More than any other team sport, the game takes on the characteristics of those playing it, and requires development in all of the areas: mental, physical, technical and social.

Kids develop at different rates in all of these areas. Both the game and the players themselves are complex. To help them fully develop their potential as players, we must allow them to unlock in numerous stages the many aspects of the game. As philosophers and numerous experts studying human development throughout many generations have discovered, experiencing, doing, is necessary for perceptual change to occur (Jean Jacques Rousseau—1712-1778), and learning and growth and development owe their efficiency to slow and inefficient experiencing that has gone on before (Dr. John Lawther).

It is the "slow and inefficient experiencing" that is captured by the 10-year rule concept. When one combines this truth with the complexity (continual decisions in a constantly changing environment) of a soccer game, it becomes apparent that we must allow and provide players time and opportunity to experiment over a long period of time, rather than seeking to accelerate their play by focusing primarily on the outcome of their games.

Teachers in sports, music and other fields tend to believe that talent matters and they know it when they see it. In fact, they appear to be confusing ability with precocity.

Sports history is rife with stories of the experts overlooking players who later, by sheer dint of their own will, became great athletes. In basketball, Michael Jordan was dropped from his high school basketball team as a sophomore. In soccer, Johan Cruyff did not draw attention until after his teen years. In fact, across the board, those trying to predict who will be the future stars have a dismal record. For example, studies in England have shown that less than eight percent of the players picked by the experts to play professional soccer, even at age 18, ever made the grade as day-to-day professional players. With this kind of record, it is important that we recognize that we must pour our time, resources and efforts into a much larger pool of players, and not restrict our focus to those we think have "talent" at the early ages.

The various stages of technical, mental, physical and social development do not necessarily coincide within one individual, let alone in a team of individuals. Thus, while certain physically precocious 12- or 13-year-olds might be able to outrun others and win games because of their speed, it would be a mistake to attempt to predict future success in the sport based upon this one aspect and stage of development. Worse, it would be foolish to try to define what successful soccer players look like, or try to select "elite" players, based upon their ability to win games because of their precocious development in one or a few areas.

Yet, this is precisely what we do in the United States. Instead of allowing more players to play in environments that require more varied ways than just speed or size to solve game-like problems, we tend to select out those players we deem to be "elite" at too young an age, and then reinforce the use of the precocious attributes they may possess, by putting them on teams with other players who also may have one or a few precocious attributes.

What the 10-year rule should teach us is that more, rather than selected fewer, young players should be exposed to training and playing together. They should be encouraged through smaller field sizes and smaller numbers per side to develop more varied ways to solve the problems the game presents, as well as to develop better technical ability by touching the ball more in game-like situations.

Ericsson argues that what matters is not experience per se but 'effortful study,' which entails continually tackling challenges that lie just beyond one's competence. It is interesting to note that time spent playing chess, even in tournaments, appears to contribute less than such study to a player's progress; the main training value of such games is to point up weaknesses for future study.

This confirms the point that it is primarily through training that players learn, not in match or tournament play. Yet, how many youth coaches, as a "training tool" across the country, load up

their schedules with pre-season and mid-season tournaments and multiple scrimmages.

Players must be given plenty of opportunities to experiment and fail, to creatively solve problems in ways that are uniquely suited to their temperaments and abilities. They can only do this to a very limited extent in games. The consequences of a failed experiment in a game cause most players to do only what they think will succeed. If they do experiment and fail, there is a great likelihood that they will be sitting on the bench and not playing.

As coaches and parents, we must allow time and opportunity for this experimentation to take place. We cannot be guided by wins and losses that really only provide a snapshot at a particular moment, and do not constitute purposeful training. Games thus are not the ends in themselves for younger players; they mainly show the weaknesses at that moment, and provide a guide as to what is needed in training. It is the training environment that should constitute most of exposure players have to the game – training and free play, without the specter of winning or losing affecting a season-long record. Consequently, a much larger percentage of our time should be spent in the training environment, rather than loading up the season with extra tournaments and scrimmages.

In today's youth soccer, there is virtually no "non-adult" organized free play. Kids don't play pick-up soccer the way many of us played various pick up sports in the neighborhood growing up. We may not realize it, but these types of games provide an integral ingredient to the development of top-class athletes. One of the things most of us forget about the neighborhood games we played growing up is that they were, indeed, competitive. Competing to win each day was extremely important, but once the day was over, tomorrow was another day, with a new chance to compete, but without the accumulation of a record and standings in a division. This is predominantly what the 10-year environment must be: opportunities to experiment, to succeed, to fail, to play and to compete.

Another key aspect to the freedom to experiment present in the neighborhood pick up games that we lack in organized youth soccer today is the challenge of playing with and against many different levels and types of players. As kids, when we picked up teams we did not just take the best five and play against the worst five. It wouldn't have been any fun. Instead, we always tried to create even teams, and if one team was winning handily, we would have mid-game drafts to create more even teams. This gave each of us the opportunity to play with and against different players all the time, and we had to adjust, both individually and collectively, as to how we solved the problems of the game depending on who was on our team and against whom we were playing.

This ability to adjust and change the rhythm of play is something we lack in soccer played in the US. This development is all but lost in youth soccer today because the adults controlling youth soccer currently do exactly the opposite from kids playing pick up games. We try to put all the "best" players on one team so that we can win the division, etc. It is the result, not the development which is paramount.

One of the key aspects to effective training is to continually provide players with different types of challenges that are just beyond their grasp. Because of the varied and free-flowing nature of the game of soccer, doing so in an efficient way requires constant innovation, but also a huge amount of time on the ball in game-like situations for the players. It is mainly through inefficient experimentation that players learn intrinsically and efficiently, and develop the instincts for the game that are activated once they are engaged in full play.

They had to work things out for themselves, as did Bach, Mozart and Beethoven, and if they fall below today's masters in technique, they tower above them in creative power. The same comparison can be made between Newton and the typical newly minted Ph.D. in physics.

Of major interest for all soccer fans, and really fans of any sport, is to watch an incredibly talented player solve problems in ways no one else has tried before. Highlight reels are loaded with heretofore-unseen feats.

It is interesting to note that some of the greatest players of all time: Pele, Maradona, Cruyff, Platini, Bobby Charlton, etc. were not especially tall players, but each of them was electrifying to watch. Yet, because we tend to focus on the results of games, and selecting future stars out so early, our attention most often turns not to the player with a spark of something unique, but to the physical attributes of the precocious "early bloomers." While this may seem to reinforce collective efficiency at a given time, because of the nature of development, it ends up placing a premium on being bigger, faster and stronger, and eschewing the creative methods that less physically precocious athletes use to solve the problems of the game. In addition to bypassing many future potential stars, this focus also causes the "selected" players, in these very crucial years of their development, to learn to be successful by using a very rudimentary, direct style of play.

Soccer is a game played on a relatively large field. Arguments for years have centered on trying to make the field and the numbers per side smaller. Unfortunately, even though strides have been made in these areas, fields generally tend to be too large for younger players. This often results in foot-races to balls driven into spaces that are mostly won by the bigger, stronger and faster players. Thus, in the formative years when they could be put in smaller environments that require them to solve problems by developing many different tools, these players are rewarded for relying almost exclusively on their precocious attributes. Thus, they learn to be efficient, direct players, but don't develop the creativity to work out different problems of the game for themselves.

*Motivation appears to be a more important factor than innate ability in the development of expertise.*

This statement is immensely important, because it affects both the type of players we develop, as well as whom we develop. First, as to the type of players we develop, by placing such importance on the physically precocious player, we motivate those players to perpetuate the physical and direct style and method of play. The premium placed on winning games and having successful seasons actually diminishes any motivation for players to experiment, or try to solve a problem through guile or indirect and crafty play, because of the penalty for failure.

Two crucial aspects of the game at the higher levels are patience and concentration. Because success based upon physical prowess often results in promoting direct play, players up through the mid-teen years often have never developed the patience or the concentration to hold possession of the ball beyond three or four passes, and certainly do not have the foresight to use the ball to draw opponents into certain parts of the field so that they can exploit the spaces they create. This sort of patience, concentration, guile, and using the ball as the ultimate decoy are not even considerations for most teenaged players. Most of it is due directly to what has been the reason they have been "selected" and the continual motivation throughout their earlier years: success through physical, direct and efficient play

The second issue of motivation is "who" is motivated to continue to play. It is well-known that in youth sports generally, approximately 70 percent of all athletes at age 12 stop playing sports altogether

by age 13. Why? Most of it comes back to intrinsic motivation. Players entering their teen years are like all teenagers, they are beginning to search for their identities, and they also start to realize that they do have choices about how to spend their time. Why is there such a rise in "extreme" sports in this country? Could it be that these sports provide teens with a way to express themselves and solve problems in unique ways, without the constant prodding from adults to do things in certain, prescribed ways?

Another fact, of which many are unaware, is that almost 75 percent of physically precocious athletes only develop into mediocre athletes. By focusing all of our "special" attention at ages 9-14 primarily on these players, we are missing many players, who, though they are not precocious, could ultimately be the great athletes when they mature. Yet, currently, we provide them with very little motivation to continue, focusing most off our attention on those we deem to be "serious" players.

A 13-year-old searching for affirmation as he or she begins to go through tremendous changes physically, mentally and emotionally, is generally not going to be motivated to continue in an area where he or she may not be successful because he or she has not grown enough yet, or may have grown too much too quickly and is temporarily awkward. Yet, instead of focusing on providing intrinsic motivation for more and more young teens to play, we adults do just the opposite, seek to select out those we perceive to be "elite" for success.

*A 1999 study of professional soccer players from several countries showed that they were much more likely than the general population to have been born at a time of year that would have dictated their enrollment in youth soccer leagues at ages older than the average. In their early years, these children would have enjoyed a substantial advantage in size and strength when playing soccer with their teammates.*

The study mentioned above showed that the vast majority of successful players were born in the first half of the year. Since we place such a premium on physical prowess between the ages of 9 and 14, this makes sense. It is at these ages that there is the greatest diversity in development. For a 14-year-old, six months can make a huge difference in physical development. Every parent can relate to the fact that at these ages they have to constantly buy larger clothes and shoes. Most kids born in the second half of the calendar year, therefore, are at a distinct disadvantage having to compete with players born in the first half of the year.

Our current push to select Olympic Development Program players at younger ages exacerbates this problem. While we are legitimately searching for ways to increase our ultimate level of play, our efforts in this instance hurt us more than helps us. We have decided that the solution lies in finding and identifying players at younger and younger ages. There is an Under-14 national team, for which players must be chosen from Under-12 regional teams. Thus, at the very ages when we should be expanding the pool of players for development, we are shrinking it, based upon the faulty premise that we can identify the future stars at 13 years old.

The issues for youth soccer development in this country are huge, but not insurmountable. To be sure, the solutions will require nothing less than a paradigm shift. All of the modern organization and viewpoints notwithstanding, the nature of how kids learn has not changed. If we truly want to develop players who can play on a world level and a society that enjoys the game as much as the rest of the world, we have to recognize, embrace and utilize these truths. Otherwise, we will perpetually be pushing the rock up the same hill, only to have it roll back down again.

© Craig Bohnert

# The Perils of Criticism:
## Positive Reinforcement can do more than Negative Feedback

### Craig Fisher, Ph. D.

When you consider all the barriers that athletes face in their search for success and then think of all the ways coaches assist athletes in reaching their goals, there is something that just does not fit: That is the major form of giving feedback to athletes.

Negative feedback, commonly and accurately called criticism, far outstrips positive reinforcement as many coaches' major communication style. Add a sarcastic flavor to the criticism and what you have is one of the prime factors destroying athletes' self-confidence. The real tragedy is that no coach intends to be destructive and would surely argue that this is not the case. Let me suggest that you withhold judgment on this matter until I have completed my essay on the perils of criticism.

- Does being criticized ever leave you angry, resentful, belittled or feeling rejected?
- Do you sense you ever make others feel this way, even unintentionally?
- Do you ever hesitate to offer helpful correction for fear of offending someone?
- Have you ever heard an athlete claim, "Coach is on me"? In your days as an athlete, did you ever say that?
- Right now, can you recall three times in your life when you really appreciated being criticized?

These questions begin to put a different slant on criticism, I hope, because you can see the picture from the myopic view of the giver of criticism.

Criticism was originally conceived as a neutral, objective appraisal of ideas and actions. To criticize meant that you communicated in a way that enabled others to use the information to their advantage and benefit. Criticism, then, was a tool to enhance personal growth and relationships. Does your experience match this description? Or might it be valuable to consider just how criticism works?

Sid Simon, prominent growth therapist, suggests that people are connected by thin gossamer threads along which communication passes; when a person (the giver) sends along some critical comment such as, "How many times do I have to tell you," the barbed arrow is acknowledged by the receiver who immediately sends back an equally caustic reply. "What gives you the right to talk to me that way?"

The reply might be verbal or nonverbal, depending on the equality of power in the relationship. The athlete typically would not throw verbal darts at the coach following critical feedback, but the nonverbal signs can be just as obvious. The important point is this: The receiver of the criticism loses a little chunk of self-confidence because of the negative message and immediately responds by sending an equally harmful reply. Not surprisingly, criticism begets criticism and soon threads are so stretched or torn that communication ceases. But consider who loses the most in this exchange of criticism.

It is well known that success tends to beget success, whereas failure tends to beget failure. Equally well known is the adage that sugar attracts more flies than vinegar. The cost to the receiver of criticism, basically negative feedback, is a loss of self-confidence, the opposite of what the coach intended.

But this is only the beginning of the criticism cycle. When the athlete's self-confidence is threatened, a protective strategy (albeit subconscious) is to send the return message to the coach to "right the ship." Overtly or covertly, the coach is bound to receive emotional backlash, either in the form of anger or silence. The critical coach ends up the big loser because he or she is labeled a critical person who may see how such an innocent and maybe non-thinking comment gets blown out of proportion (from at least the coach's perspective). The intention is to be helpful but the criticism achieves just the opposite result.

Why is criticism so destructive? First, criticism tends to close paths of communication, not open them. Coach criticism is tended to be a one-way street; no acknowledgment is called for, only the idyllic hope that the athlete will internalize all that the criticism entails and be grateful. Interestingly, it is the coach who labels the criticism constructive because "after all, that's my job and I want my athletes to achieve their potential." Need I belabor the point by asking you to consider if the majority of athletes see constant streams of criticism as helpful. Very few athletes believe that constructive is that beneficial?

Second, as stated earlier, coach criticism is usually followed by the particular athlete's self-justified emotional response (shouting back, denial, silence, moodiness). If you think about your past experiences, my guess is that you have seen all of these responses. Adding this emotional layer to the failure experience prevents athletes from being able to sort out what might be helpful to them.

Third, most criticism offers no suggestions for improvement. Where is it written that athletes tend to perform better when they are told what they are doing wrong?

Where did we learn that highlighting athlete's errors results in performance changes? Or, if it does sometimes, is it the best approach? Are we so naïve that we believe athletes will thank us for our reasoned criticism and vow to be better next time? What little I know about the complexity of human motivation and behavior change suggests that athletes tend to be motivated more with positive reinforcement (i.e., praise, recognition) than punishing criticism.

Last, criticism overlooks the larger performance picture. In reality, most athletes do more things right than wrong, but coaches often tend to focus on the errors. If we get extremely critical, we can even begin to criticize the random and inconsequential errors always present in imperfect performances. We end up criticizing and trying to correct mistakes that rarely repeat themselves in the same week or month.

Is it possible to recast performance feedback in positive rather negative directions? More specifically, is it not possible to reinforce performance when it is correct or approximates correctness instead of constantly pointing out what is wrong?

Why is criticism used so much? With all the obvious drawbacks of a critical communication style, why would reasoned individuals continue the practice? It clearly is not because it has been well thought out and systematically planned. And maybe that is what makes it so unfortunate.

We are slaves to the power of models unless we recognize and learn to break the cycle. Everyone has heard it prophesized: We will teach as we were taught, coach others as we were coached and raise our children as our parents raised us. What have we experienced and what behaviors do we now model? For a large number of us the answer is criticism.

I am not suggesting that any of us intentionally set out to destroy our athletes' self-confidence and place unnecessary emotional hurdles in their paths, but nonetheless that is the reality. Coaches have their athletes' best interest in mind when they direct critical comments their way. That is what makes the outcome so unfortunate; we mean to help but often we hinder.

On a more castigating note, there is a certain inherent cheapness to criticism. It is possible to use perfection as your frame of reference and judge each of your athletes against the standard. The reality is that there is no perfect performance; therefore every performance that you observe affords the opportunity for your critical comments. I refer to this as cheap shot coaching because almost anybody can do it; it takes no talent at all. If, indeed, you sense you must always offer some feedback, then you will always have material for your evaluation. But, then, that is the mark of the mentally lazy coach, one who cannot see the big picture of emerging performance glitch.

I suppose by this point you have decided either that my arguments have some validity or that I am out of touch with reality and know nothing about coach-athlete communication; because, after all constructive criticism is the backbone of sport skill improvement. For those of you who are going to continue to use criticism, hopefully not as unthinkingly as before, I offer some guidelines.

Periodically, you need to remind yourself of the main purpose of your criticism – to get athletes' attention and motivate them to change their behavior. Criticism then, being as sensitizing as it is, needs to pass some particular tests. To be effective, criticism needs to be filtered before and as it is given.

© Craig Bohnert

Following our suggestions to you as coaches you consider the application of criticism in the coaching process:

- **Is the timing right?** Is the athlete in emotional shape to hear the criticism? Athletes who are frustrated with their lack of success are not good consumers of negative feedback; they have enough negative thought of their own to process.

- **Do your athletes need more praise?** Positives are more powerful agents of behavior change than negatives.

- **Is your criticism novel?** Or is it the "same old, same old" harangue? The latter is ineffective because you have heard yourself say too often, "How many times do I have to tell you that?"

- **Are you positive that the athlete can make the change?** Is the behavior primarily under the particular athlete's control or are others involved (e.g., a bad pass needs both a passer and a receiver's participation). Does the athlete have the skills and confidence to make the change? Is the performance error due to inadequate skill or a lack of effort? The latter is perhaps correctable; the former demands time on task. Do not dismiss the significance of self-confidence because it lies at the heart of behavior change. Only self-confident athletes will be able to internalize performance feedback if it is layered with a negative evaluation.

- **Is your criticism clear enough to be acted upon?** Does the athlete know what needs to be changed? Nothing is more frustrating than being criticized and not knowing what to do to make the criticism go away.

- **Criticism often forecloses the possibility of improvement because the coach critic does not listen to athletes' response.** You must process how the information is being received to assess its effectiveness (e.g., frowning brow, gritting teeth, no effort made to change). Be quick to recognize any changes made in response to your criticism.

- **No hit-and-run behavior is going to work.** Unless you are prepared to be systematic with your criticism and commit yourself to the length of time it takes to change old behavior and consolidate new behavior, it's very doubtful your criticism will be effective.

# Winners are Different

**Following is written by Doug Williamson, Assistant Director of Coaching of the NSCAA, on the presentation of Bill Beswick at the 2001 NSCAA Convention in Indianapolis.**

Bill Beswick, team psychologist for Manchester United, discussed some of the characteristics of elite soccer players and some of the unique challenges faced by such competitors and coaches. Although the vast majority of coaches in attendance will never work with players of the caliber of David Beckham, there were jewels of instruction and inspiration for coaches of all age levels.

athletes in the sports of basketball and hockey. Gallup concluded that seldom did the elite NBA and NHL players demonstrate all of the talents indicative of success in those leagues, but they did possess a larger share of those talents than even the mediocre players who managed to earn spots on professional teams in those two sports.

**Why players achieve:**
- Intense desire to win
- Desire to be the best, to achieve mastery
- A need for stimulation, especially the spur of intense competition
- Emotional need for success – a strong ego drive

**How players achieve:**
- Capacity for focused concentration
- Ability to respond positively to intense pressure
- Capacity to confront opposition aggressively
- Courage to deal with pain
- Consistent desire to improve
- Coachability – ability to learn and adapt
- Intelligence – learn to play smart as well as hard

Beswick reminded coaches that because of the many factors that go into the composition of an elite soccer player, we should not label any youngster as "talented" before age 12. His rationale is twofold: first, it is next to impossible to gauge accurately if a young player possesses the attributes that characterize an elite player before age 12, and second, labeling a player "talented" or "elite" generates a host of potential psychological problems and dangers, including:

- Insecurity and instability
- Loss of identity

Quoting Jim Riordan, a sport psychologist from Columbus, Ohio, Beswick reminded the audience that "a top player is an ordinary person with extraordinary talent." He went on to describe the characteristics of the elite players with whom he has worked. He divided the psychological traits of such players into two categories: why players achieve elite status and how they do so.

The characteristics Beswick listed resemble some of the attributes that The Gallup Organization discerned in the early 1990s as being distinctive of the most successful American professional

- Constantly changing self-esteem
- Loss of self-belief/confidence
- Stress
- Performance fears
- Over-arousal/aggression/violence
- Escapism through alcohol and substance abuse
- Burnout
- Depression and withdrawal

The list is one more reminder to coaches, parents and youth club administrators of the inherent problems associated with and the counter-developmental nature of attempting to identify elite players at too young an age. In addition to possibly "burying" some players with elite potential before they are 8 years old, we place psychological burdens on children who do not have the cognitive, psychological or physical strength to shoulder such a load.

According to Beswick, once talented players are identified, it is crucial to find coaches with the ability to shepherd them throughout their early teen years. These coaches should understand the personality changes that such players will undergo and be able to guide them through those modifications in behavior without a psychological meltdown. Here are some of the changes Beswick identifies as elite players move from "initiation" to the "development" to the "perfection" phases:

Beswick singled out parents as the most influential people in a young player's life. The attitude they

bring to the table in the growth and development of the elite player is critical.

Beswick described Eric Harrison, who coached the players who form the nucleus of the Manchester United elite when they were 12, 13 and 14 years old, as one of the most outstanding mentors of our time.

"The culture (at Manchester United) is what Eric Harrison coached them in at age 12," he said.

Beswick contends that the key to coaching elite players is to teach them how to thrive under the pressure of being elite players.

"Top-level players must self-manage," stressed Beswick, who added that coaches must find ways to give elite players responsibility for their own progress. How to do that? Beswick offered guidelines for coaches in four areas:

Motivate
- Understand that at the elite level it's all about winning
- Sell them the vision, the reason why (beginning with today's practice)
- Make each player part of the journey to success (a whole squad is needed to win a league title)
- Help each player set personal goals
- Find players' sense of self-worth and help them achieve it
- Understand the "whole player" and potential stress points
- Emphasize finding intrinsic, rather than extrinsic, rewards

Communicate (sell, not yell)
- Never be in awe of superstars
- Increase communication, decrease anxiety (better to give bad news early than to let it linger)
- Respect each player – listen, build trust
- One-to-one communication is critical
- Be wary of criticism or praise – help players self-evaluate and self-reference
- Understand each player's ethnic and cultural background
- Give honest feedback on performance

Prepare
- Coach smart, not hard; sell your expertise and personality
- Don't limit players, let them surprise you
- Allow players to do what they do best
- Under coaching is a skill ("Let them play a bit")
- Attention to detail is vital
- Balance work and rest
- Beware of player burnout (irritability, lateness, etc.)
- Boredom is the enemy – offer variety, challenge and enjoyment in practice

Solve problems
- Limit stressful situations
- Be proactive in dealing with problems
- Focus on what can be controlled
- Change negatives into positives
- Use peer pressure where possible
- Teach players emotional intelligence
- Build a resource team to help the elite player
- Remember that injuries are devastating

Beswick attempted to heighten coaches' awareness that all players are not the same. He said that even though we must create and maintain a cohesive team, at the same time we must recognize and treat each player as an individual. Nowhere is this more important than in dealing with elite players.

Beswick's lecture raises anew the thought that it would be exceptionally helpful to coaches of national teams, professional squads and other high level clubs to be able to identify, sometimes in adolescence, those players who have the psychological "talents" to succeed at the elite level. The research methodology exists to identify which of these talents are most important to soccer players and to develop an instrument to identify the presence of those talents in individuals. The Gallup Organization has pioneered such research and used it effectively in guiding NBA and NHL franchises.

If Beswick's thesis that "winners are different" is true, one wonders why the best soccer teams in the world have resisted doing as much to identify the players' psychological talents as they have to identify their physical talents. Perhaps with the developing credibility of sages like Beswick, coaches and general managers will begin to examine more closely the psychological makeup of those players they hope will lead their teams to glory.

# Women: It's OK to Compete
## There often is a conflict when they go head-to-head in practice

### Anson Dorrance with Tim Nash/University of North Carolina

One of the major factors in the development of our players over the course of time is that we create a wonderful training intensity. And the toughest challenge in developing female players is getting them to compete against friends in practice.

They don't struggle when they are competing against other teams. But when they compete against their friends in practice, there's usually a lessening of intensity.

Women have a superior understanding that their relationships are more important than the game itself. Men never struggle with that. Men never take competing with best friends personally, but women do.

I think the way in which girls are socialized exaggerates the difference between males and females. When they are growing up, girls are not encouraged to compete as much as boys. But I also think head-to-head physical confrontation with friends and teammates is not where girls are naturally comfortable.

I think if you socialized a boy against competing, he would not be socialized easily, and if you socialized a girl toward competing, it would also not be easy. That is basically what we try to do at North Carolina. We take young women who do not feel comfortable in those directly competitive arenas and throw them into a fierce competitive pool, and they sort of beat it into each other that it's OK to compete.

There was an interview done by one of our alumni magazines about the program, and the writer really did a good job. This idea of competing intrigued her, and she really got to the core of this issue. She interviewed a lot of the girls on the team, and the girls told her that the difficulty they had coming in here as freshman was that they all wanted to be a part of this great program, but they also wanted to be accepted personally. So they come into our preseason with incredibly mixed emotions: They want to be the best they can be on the field, but they don't want to alienate anyone.

They have this internal war going on between wanting to prove they are great soccer players and the social agenda of wanting to be accepted by the group they are joining. So when they go into direct confrontation with a veteran, it's almost like they feel they have to acquiesce-no matter how good they are-just because they want to be accepted by the veteran.

Of course, I am standing next to them saying, "I saw you play in high school and this is not what I saw." Now they are getting mixed messages. The freshman is getting the message from her socialization and her gender about trying to bond with everyone, and she is getting a message from me and her teammates who are beating her to death that it's OK to pound your teammates. That's the way it's done here.

It's a very difficult period for them. In fact, almost every player's freshman year here is very difficult. Not just from a soccer perspective, but from a social perspective. Things they have been taught all their lives are brought into question, and it's a very difficult adjustment period.

The greatest example of this in terms of teaching young women to win is Carla Overbeck. We do a log of one versus one here. It's a direct one-on-one competition and over the course of the season each girl plays against everyone else on the team. It's like an ongoing 1 v. 1 tournament among all the members on the team.

In Carla's freshman year, she didn't win a game. Not one game. Her freshman year was an emotional catharsis for her because we really needed her to play, really needed her to win for us because she was our starting sweeper-back. She was under a lot of pressure.

It was a very difficult transformation for Carla to go from where she was as a freshman to where she finally was as a senior. Her senior year, she did not lose a single 1 v. 1 game. By then you would not recognize her. In fact, Carla's competitive fury was so developed by the time she was a senior, she would tell me from the field, "Anson, you gotta sub so-and-so. She's killing us." She would not tolerate any lack of effort from anyone in front of her. She would scream at me to substitute any player on the field who did not give everything she had.

Now for the United States National Team, she is one the most competitive people and one of their greatest leaders. But if you saw her as a freshman, she was really nice girl, wanting to be a part of everything. And now, if you watch her in a National Team training session, she is aggressively encouraging, directing and leading every session in which she's involved. There is a competitive anger in her, and she developed it here. I know she did because I watched it happen.

If we are playing a 4 v. 4 tournament in practice at UNC, and two veterans are on a team with two younger kids, there's going to be times when the younger kids are going to feel like easing off a bit, like it's not important. When this happens, the veterans will get on them immediately. All of a sudden, the freshman understand that if they are not pushing at 100 percent, they are letting the veterans down. The veterans' body language and tone will tell them "If you give up and we lose, I lose. That's unacceptable."

Then eventually-or right away with some-intensity comes to be taken as the norm. We try to create

training environments that are incredibly intense. And by recording everything, it gives the players permission to compete. It tells these women it's OK to be the best. It's OK to win. And we think this competition has a hardening effect on the women on our team. A mistake many male coaches make when they are trying to make the transition from coaching men to coaching women is they try to motivate with the intensity of their own personality.

In my experience, aggressive, loud, in-your-face fury does not motivate women. I know because I tried it my first few years with the team. So we substituted this "competitive cauldron," this "keeping score," to create the intense environment we knew was critical for top player development. In fact, we named one of our early clinics "Keeping Score: Training the Female Psychological Dimension." That clinic is still one of the more popular ones that we do.

I had a long meeting with Tracy Noonan after the 1994 season. We were talking about how beneficial the season was for the goalkeepers. Rarely have we created a competitive atmosphere in goal, but we've always succeeded in creating it for field players. In 1994, for the first time in our history, we had two goalkeepers-Tracy Noonan and Shelly Finger-who we allowed to compete on the same level, even in games. During the season, we rotated who started and who played in the second half. It was all a competition to see who would play in the NCAA tournament. So there was a competitive cauldron in goal.

Tracy and I were talking about how we thought it was similar to the way Briana Scurry and Skye Eddy were developed. In 1993, Skye Eddy transferred from UMass to George Mason and took them to the national championship final, and Briana Scurry might be the best goalkeeper in the world today. How were those two wonderful keepers developed? It happened at UMass in a competitive cauldron where every practice was critical to see who would play that weekend.

We discovered that the competition made Noonan and Finger each so much better. We rotated them every game. Not alternating games but basically every half. I'm convinced that's the way to develop high-caliber keepers. But it's better to have the starting job up for grabs every day. I'm convinced of that now. But I'm not convinced that you should let that keeper play the whole game.

For years, I've been trying to figure out a way to develop my goalkeepers the same way my field players are developed. I know how my field players develop-there is no mercy paid on them in practice. Everything is win-lose all the time. Playing time is based on objective evaluations, and so there is a competitive fury in practice. That has never existed in goal before.

What was lacking in goal? We'd go with one keeper for the majority of the season, and that would shatter the confidence of the other one. It also would not give the reserve a chance to play in games, which is critical for growth.

More importantly, it would give the starter a kind of complacency, but also a kind of fear-the fear that if she ever made any mistakes, the roles would be reversed. Obviously, if the roles were reversed, the starter would become the reserve, and now her confidence is totally shattered. The reserve is now thrust into the starting position without much playing experience. Her confidence is probably not built to the extent that she really feels she can do the job.

The ideal way to develop them, in my opinion, is to do exactly what we did with Noonan and Finger-split games in half but alternate who starts. Now, both goalkeepers are getting up for every game. They're competing with each other in practices. The regular season just develops them for the NCAA tournament, but each keeper still has to compete to preserve her status. We're convinced that having a competitive cauldron in goal is the way to go. Noonan, when called upon in the 1994 finals, was absolutely brilliant.

I've seen goalkeepers come to college as tremendous keepers, but end up very average.

Why? They have no competition in practice. They have a complacency that stunts their growth. Coaches will try to shake things up by benching the starter after a poor performance. But the starter knows she's better then the other goalkeeper. If she didn't, she wouldn't be complacent.

So good teams at the collegiate level, or at any competitive level, will benefit from having two comparable keepers, two very good keepers. And every game should be split in half. One goalkeeper doesn't win the starting job for good, which permits them to genuinely compete in practice because they know they are going to play. Save the one keeper for the do-or-die tournament. Your goalkeeping will certainly benefit, as will your chemistry in goal, if handled properly. With Noonan and Finger, we told them, "We think you're very close. Both of you have earned the opportunity to play."

In 1993, I made a mistake in goal. In the preseason, I thought Finger was playing better than Noonan, and I rewarded Shelly by starting her two out of every three games. Noonan was an excellent goalkeeper, but playing only one out of every three games did not permit her to feel like she was effective. The luck of the draw also gave Noonan many of the tough games, ballooning her goals-against average.

When that was added to her relative lack of playing time, it did little for her confidence. In the off-season, she did a lot of work on her own, and she absolutely killed herself in the weight room, unlike any player we've ever had. Before the 1994 season, I thought Noonan was better. But Finger was close enough to compete. I didn't want to make the same mistake again, so they split games in half. They didn't have to win the position for each game. That would create unbelievable pressure. Now you've created that competitive cauldron in practice for everyone, goalkeepers and field players.

# Mental Toughness:
# Developing Self-Awareness

## Erika Carlson

Mental Toughness: Some have it. Some don't. If you believe this, stop reading now.

However, if you believe that mental toughness is teachable and you want to learn how to help develop it in your players, read on.

The concept of mental toughness, even the psychological pillar as a whole, often seems more elusive than the other three pillars of soccer development (tactical, technical and physical). The most common reason for this is that coaches were not directly taught mental skills when they were players. Additionally, most have limited practical knowledge on how to coach the mental aspects of the game. Therefore, it was the case that some players were more mentally tough than others, just as some players are more physically talented than others. Times are changing. Sport psychology slowly is making its way into the world of soccer, right down to the youth level, and mental toughness can be developed, just like technical skills. There are practical and simple ways for coaches to enhance the mental toughness of their players. Let's begin by examining the definition of mental toughness.

Jones et al. (2002) provide a useful definition of mental toughness:

*Mental toughness is having the natural or developed psychological edge that enables you to:*
- *Cope better than your opponents with demands; competitive, training and lifestyle*
- *Be more consistent and better than opponents are remaining; determined, focused, confident, resilient, composed under pressure*

Developing mental toughness provides coaches some unique challenges. One of the first challenges is getting athletes to learn from themselves as they progress. Self-awareness is the foundation of learning and development. Athletes need to develop awareness of what they are thinking about and feeling emotionally (mental and emotional awareness) and also what they are feeling physically (kinesthetic awareness). It often is the case that athletes develop this through both trial and error and feedback from coaches.

There is an additional way to increase self-awareness. Reflective practice is a relatively simple but incredibly effective process that allows athletes to exploit all playing experiences for their benefit. This writing task aids players in enhancing both their kinesthetic and mental and emotional awareness during both training and competing.

This process can be incorporated into training by coaches, and many will find it useful to practice what they preach and commit to doing self-reflection exercises for themselves. The reflective process is best explained by Gibbs' (1998) six-staged model of reflective practice.

Following training and games, players need to answer the following questions. Reflections should consider technical performance, tactical performance, physical performance and psychological performance.

1. Describe Your Experience: What happened in the practice, training or game situation?
2. Thoughts and Feelings:
   a What thoughts, emotions, physical feeling affected my performance both positive and negative? (excitement, nervousness, strong focus/lack of focus, anger/frustration)

b   How did my coach, teammates, opponents, equipment affect my performance both positively and negatively? (What was said, how did I respond, was I able to recover)

3. Evaluation: What was good about this performance (training, practice, game)?
4. Analysis (Adjustments): What should I do differently in the future?
5. Conclusion: What did I learn from this experience?
6. Action Plan: Set performance goals for the next soccer session.

Following training, practice or games, a small investment in time (10-15 minute) will help to create awareness within the athlete about what happened, what was going on, how it felt, the result it had and adjustments that need to be made. While players may have this information "swimming around" in their heads, the process

of writing it down systematically will clarify and confirm the athletic experience. This in turn will allow the athlete to move ahead with the next training or competition more focused.

For example: Susie, a 15-year old center midfielder, needed help to deal with all the negativity she was experiencing during games. She was tremendously hard on herself when she made a mistake and was known to yell out "Sorry!" to her teammates when she made a mistake.

Susie was introduced to the reflective process, which was used both as a tool for to assess what exactly was going on internally with Susie's self-talk and as a tool for Susie to become more aware of what was going on. In our work, we began to refer to Susie's self-talk as the "little voice." She would speak in third person about the little voice. "The little voice would not shut up today!"

Her reflections revealed that the little voice was very active and very negative following mistakes. In order to recover from a mistake, Susie felt compelled to do something "right" to make up for it, like get possession back, make a good pass or score a goal. At times it could take several minutes for something "right" to happen. While waiting to redeem herself, Susie would punish herself internally the whole time, playing angrily and erratically, yelling at herself "You know better than that!" I can't believe the coach hasn't taken me out yet!"

Susie began to write her complete reflections following each training session and game. She returned the following week and was asked to read what she had written in her reflections. As she read it out loud, her body language shifted and a look of amazement came over her face. She looked up and said, "I sure am wasting a lot of time on my mistakes! All I can think about is that stupid mistake I made!"

It was clear that she was very distracted after she made mistakes. Susie agreed and suggested, "Yeah, I sure am! I really need to get back into the game, even after mistakes!" The important question was "What should you be thinking about during that time?"

Susie thought and replied, "The game, the ball, my position, communication... whatever my job is at the moment!" Awareness has been achieved!

From this point, Susie was given a plan to include a cue word to get her refocused following mistakes or anytime she found herself focusing on "the little voice" instead of the appropriate task. The reflective process allowed Susie to look at herself more objectively and recognize her own patterns. With this self-awareness she can then move on to making appropriate adjustments to help improve her focus when needed. Susie proceeded to play more consistently, dealing with adversity in game situations better, remaining focused for the whole game and overall became more mentally tough.

Notice that Susie did all of the work herself. She took the time to write up the reflections, she read it out loud and she made all the connections. This was her process. All that was needed of the coach was a list of reflective questions to give your athletes and some accountability to ensure the reflections are completed. Have players keep spiral notebooks in their gear bags and commit 10 minutes at the end of practice for players to reflect on their practice performance. Like other skills, reflecting takes some practice before players are good at it. Encourage players to communicate questions, positive insights or confusion that they may have as a result of reflecting.

This process allows players to be more independent and take more responsibility for their own development as players. It also opens the door for communication between player and coach. (As a coach you also may find that you have players that may require more specialized training from a sport psychology consultant.)

As Susie showed us, the self-awareness that she gained from the reflective practice allowed her to make adjustments to cope better with mistakes and play more consistently focused, confident and resilient. She's got it. She proved that mental toughness is teachable through self-awareness.

# The Right Ways to Motivate

### Andy Roxburgh

What does the professional coach have to cope with when players are earning their living playing the game? Here are 11 aspects of coaching at the professional level.

## 1. Child's Play

*"Train up a child in the way he should grow and when he is old he will not depart from it." (Proverbs)*

The aim with youngsters is to inculcate a love of the game, a desire to master the ball and a positive mentality. The romance of the game must go hand-in-hand with soccer technique and tactics. Extrinsic motivation (i.e. cups, medals, etc.) is inappropriate with the children who are under 12 years of age; enjoyment and commitment are the prerequisites.

## 2. High Hopes

The research work done by Rosenthal and Jacobson in the education field is, it would suggest, equally relevant to other businesses. They advocate the "self-fulfilling prophecy" thesis, which suggests that the quality of performance is often in direct relation to the level of expectation, which the teacher/coach has of the person. If the football coach believes in the ability of the player and radiates confidence to him/her, faith in his/her ability, and high hopes for the future then, assuming he/she has some talent, the player will strive to achieve the standards expected of him/her.

The same principle applies when working with professionals. The way the coach relates to a player will influence that player's motivational level. Failure on the part of the coach to communicate with a player will create ill-feeling and damage the relationship. The coach should grasp every opportunity to offer the player positive reinforcement and constructive feedback.

## 3. Leadership

*"As for the best leaders, the people do not notice their existence. The next best, the people honor and praise. The next, the people fear, and the next the people hate. When the best leader's work is done, the people say, 'we did it ourselves.'" (Lao-Tzu)*

In leadership, consideration must be given to the following:
- Do people know what to call the leader? First name terms suggest confidence
- When the leader delegates, does the staff member know the leader's needs and does the staff member have the confidence to handle the situation?
- Does the leader invest time and effort in everyone attached to the organization? Subordinates take precedence over superiors if the coach is to do the job successfully
- Does the leader have an effective intelligence network? Remember, knowledge is power

The leadership style of many successful coaches suggests that neither a strongly authoritarian approach nor a fully player-centered one should be used. Effective coaches seem to be able to vary their style to meet the needs of the situation.

Causes of failure in leadership:
- Inappropriate management style
- Fear
- Inability to organize details
- Weak personality
- Unwillingness to perform basic tasks

- Seeking rewards for knowledge rather than action
- Lack of imagination
- Anti-social behavior
- Indecision
- Evading responsibility
- Lack of diplomacy
- Poor personal control
- Negative thinking
- Cheating
- Hasty over-reaction
- Inconsistency
- Unfairness
- Lack of humility

## 4. Organization

Good organization is vital if people are to perform at an optimum level. Priority consideration must be given to the work, which has to be completed, the nature of the people involved, the environment in which the job has to be carried out, the time allocation, the support services available and the objective to be achieved. The aim is to produce a structure, which allows efficiency and creativity. The following must be considered in relation to good organization:

- Tell people in advance what you want in order to avoid chaos and confusion
- Set standards, i.e. dress, time-keeping. The use of the broken record technique is recommended in this context
- Pay attention to small details *("Man does not trip over mountain, man trips over stone."* Chinese proverb)
- Remove all agitations from the operation

The key words in creating an efficient organization are flow and balance. For things to flow smoothly the people need to know what is required of them and the environment must be carefully structured. Creativity may be enhanced when a balance prevails between discipline and freedom, seriousness and enjoyment.

## 5. Harmony

In order to create harmony within the group, the following suggestions should be considered:

- Identify leadership within the group. Select a captain who is good at superficial relationships and who is more interested in the cause than his/her own ego
- Eliminate disruptive influences immediately
- Don't allow cliques to form
- Create an atmosphere of comradeship, friendly rivalry and enjoyment
- Make players aware of the need for mutual support and personal sacrifices
- Highlight the role and the value of the backup players
- Get the group to focus on collective goals and common causes in order to produce a strong squad commitment
- Encourage positive communication within the group
- Create a pleasant working and living environment
- Instill a pride in the players in relation to themselves and the squad
- Challenge all negative influence immediately, i.e., put losing into perspective, take an objective view of public criticism, control player's fear of failing, etc.

## 6. Incentives

The game can provide a number of rewards. They can be classified as follows:

- Symbolic – Praise, status, recognition
- Material –Money, cups, medals
- Psychological – Sense of belonging, sense of achievement, knowledge of improvement. The desirable of these rewards are the psychological ones

## 7. Discipline – Punishment and/or the threat of punishment

Although positive reinforcement is preferable, punishment, when employed properly, can be effective with some players in some instances.

To be effective, punishment must be used infrequently, be severe when employed, be specific, be applied consistently and be handled with as little emotion as possible.

In the professional game, fear is used a great deal in order to motivate players.

## 8. Rehearsals

Rehearsal for a match can involve mental rehearsal by the coach and the player. Mental rehearsal is valuable for preparing the body and the mind for action.

- It should, if possible, take place in the performance environment
- The whole event/move/skill should be viewed in its entirety
- Match speed should be employed
- The imagined action must be successful
- Emphasis should be placed on how it feels
- Team talks should be short and to the point
- Don't embarrass players
- Maintain a positive attitude in talks
- Leave on a high note
- In pre-match training, satisfy players' competitive urge by using small games and skill contests; set training targets
- Expose the players to problems which they may encounter during match days, e.g. give one team two goals of a start; the other must try to fight back in a given time

- Give the players the opportunity to make suggestions about the best way of solving a playing problem
- Stimulate the imagination by encouraging creative play when possible
- Warm-ups are important because they set the tone of the session
- Make sure that the training environment has visual impact

## 10. Match play

A number of factors can influence the motivational strategies for a particular match. These include:

- The previous result. If a loss, the effect must be minimized; if a win, the effect may need to be controlled

## 9. Player power

Each player must be viewed as an individual and treated accordingly. Some need a push; some need a pull. The coach's repertoire must include the ability to plead, cajole, threaten, shock and inspire. It is vitally important to find the key to each player – his/her motives, ambition and personality. The following are some examples of the underlying principles when dealing with players:

| Difficult Player | Coach |
|---|---|
| Opposed to everything | Well-informed |
| Fault finders | Good performer |
| | Good preparation |

| Egocentric Player | Coach |
|---|---|
| Show-off | Must have no doubt about his power |
| Usually intelligent | Smarter than the player |
| Wants recognition | Be prepared to take risks |
| | No animosity |

| Reserved Type | Coach |
|---|---|
| Pleasant | Should not make unrealistic demands |
| Well-liked | Try to get the other players to respect him |
| Shy | Make him help the coach |
| Reliable | |

- The technical, physical and mental state of the team
- The importance of the game
- The physical surroundings for the match
- The number of people in attendance (including the television audience)
- The standard of the opposition (if it is a good team, focus on the weaknesses)
- The critic's view (players read newspapers)
- The conditions, e.g. the weather, state of the pitch, etc.
- The local environment where the game will be played
- The match officials

It is the coach's responsibility to judge the particular situation and to decide which factors should be:

- Played down (the state of the ground)
- Used as a cause (antagonistic press comments)
- Highlighted (tough match officials and therefore the need for discipline)
- Assessed objectively (the opposition)

## 11. Adversity

In football, where uncertainty prevails, the coach must be ready to deal with trauma, especially the unpredictable. Shrewdly anticipating the problems and having answers at the ready can avoid many difficulties. However, there is always the possibility of the unexpected crisis and the coach then needs to display the necessary self-assurance, composure, intelligence, energy and resilience to survive the storm.

Remember, winners in life cannot be losers! The "fire-fighting" coach will benefit from:

- Advisers – objective and trustworthy
- Supportive colleagues and followers
- Up-to-date facts rather than opinions
- Previous experience of critical situations
- Diplomatic acumen

- Knowing the costs involved in different types of strategy
- Championing the common cause rather than self-preservation. When dealing with crises there are two key factors to be considered:
  - What decisions should be made
  - How will the arguments be presented

The decision-making process must take into account the club/association, the coach, the group, outside pressures, sources of information, traditional responses and possible innovative action.

Players are taught to see the situation early, anticipate the outcome, but be prepared to change the decision at the last minute, if necessary. Once committed, there is no going back. Likewise in coaching/management.

Troubled times require bravery. The following quotation offers some inspiration:

*"Far better it is to dream mighty things, to win glorious triumphs, even though checkered by failure, than to take rank with those poor spirit who neither enjoy much nor suffer much because they live in the gray twilight that knows not victory or defeat."*

Janssen, J. (1999). *Championship team building: what every coach needs to know to build a motivated, committed, and cohesive team.* Tucson, AZ: *Winning The Mental Game.*
Ravizza, K., & Hanson, T. (1995). *Heads-up baseball.* Chicago, IL: Masters Press.
Vernacchia, R. A. (2003). *Inner strength: the mental dynamics of athletic performance.* Palo Alto, CA: Warde Publishers.

# Building Morale? Egos Must Go!

## Positive attitude and respect for coach and teammates are important

### Tim Schum

The following question was asked of selected coaches of the NSCAA: "How do you develop the proper morale and spirit of cooperation among your players?"

Our starting point this month is with our resident sports psychologist, Mel Lorback of West Chester State (Pa.). Lorback's synopsis of the development of proper morale and spirit of cooperation among the players is that morale is the transfer of ego identification from the individual to a group which in turn manifests itself as mass emotional commitment. The essential ingredients of morale are a unity of purpose and spiritual cohesion. Group motivation and like motivation on an individual level include at least the following:

- **Identification:** The athlete must identify with the sport and the group
- **Incorporation:** The player must add admired aspects of others to his own behavior
- **Emotional commitment:** The person actually becomes the model he/she hopes to be; he/she finds attractive the adoption of a role or roles within the group

The survey of respondent coaches to our NSCAA survey in this area of the psychology of coaching reveals that many coaches target the three aspects of the problem emphasized by Lorback.

**Jerry Yeagley's** (Indiana University) overall approach is to work on attitude with certain rules underlying its development on his Indiana University team. The end result of such an approach would be a team with a united approach to its objectives. Yeagley's comments:
*We strive to have each player develop a positive attitude toward his teammates and coaches, the opponents, the laws of the game and the officials who enforce these laws and, most important, toward himself as a worthy member of a worthy team.*

*Only positive constructive comments are allowed between players. Negative comments and gestures quickly destroy player relationships and tear down team morale. Likewise, the players may direct only positive comments toward an official. Giving the proper respect to the laws of the game and the officials will pay dividends in the long run. If a team cannot win within the framework of the rules, then victory is worthless. Opponents are to be respected and any intentional physical or verbal abuse is not allowed. There is no need for a "kill your enemy" approach because a player needs to address his full attention to his role as a player on his own team. If a player allows himself to become intimidated by the opposition, he loses concentration and becomes a much less effective team member.*

*Each player must feel good about himself and see himself as a worthy team member. He must be willing to work in order to achieve as an individual and a team. Following are some questions each player is asked when he tries out for the team:*
- *What is your objective in soccer?*
- *Are you willing to pay the price to find out how good you can be?*

*If you are not willing to follow good personal health habits, such as not smoking, and if you are not willing to train and keep fit during the off-season, then don't plan to be a great soccer player. However, if you desire to be the best and you are willing to work for excellence, then you have the right attitude to become a great player. If every* player trains and performs to the best of his ability, then the team will be at its best and this is the ultimate anyone could hope for regardless of the record. Be proud; don't settle for less. Here lies the challenge, are you willing to accept it now?

**Tom Griffith** of Dartmouth emphasized the same points as Coach Yeagley with the reminder that "If one player messes up, regardless of who it is, we all suffer. We all win or we all lose."

**Mike Berticelli**, NSCAA Coach of the Year in the South in 1981 at North Carolina-Greensboro, emphasizes the word "respect":
Morale and spirit of cooperation come from respect – respect for the coach and for each other as players. The respect of a coach only comes from the players' awareness of the coach's sincere dedication to the team, its success, and the honest development of players as people. Players' respect of each other is also earned by performance and dedication. We as coaches set the team's guidelines for practice, performance, and dedication. Dedication and performance result in success and success breeds morale and spirit.

**Al Miller** of the Tampa Bay Rowdies also dealt with the question by listing mutual respect as the first element in good team spirit. He then zeroed in on things a coach must be sensitive to during the season:
- Control all elements that impinge on the team, i.e. fans, booster clubs, administration of school or club
- Be prepared to deal with a crisis or problem, but best of all to be very observant and act and react to potential problems and head them off
- The coach must be in control of himself at all times, including such elements as speech, behavior, decision-making, and even in such things as his dress

**Bill Hughes** of Roberts Wesleyan (N.Y.), a former NSCAA All-America player now turned coach, lays everything at the foot of the coach:

The nuts and bolts of any sports program begin with the coach. The effort that he or she puts into the program will be reflected in both the attitude and spirit of their players.

**Walter Bahr** of Penn State emphasizes the role of the coach and continuity:
Morale and spirit are expected and are passed on from player to player and from year to year. Tradition and reputation of the school and coach are also factors.

**John McGettigan** (Penn State) has leaned heavily on captains to carry on in terms of creating the right atmosphere on the team. He notes:
It is the major job of the captains of the team to develop morale and spirit. If possible, I select individuals to be captains who have experienced success with my team the previous soccer season. I would like to clarify the word success: Success does not necessarily mean winning: To me, it means getting the most out of the talent you have on hand.
These individuals, the captains, have seen the worth and value of the preparation procedures and therefore can visualize what you, the coach, are trying to accomplish. They have experienced where you, the coach, are going and how you prepare the team to get there.
If the leaders of your group accept and have developed a respect for you and your program, it will become contagious to the rest of your team and morale and spirit will not be a problem.

**Joe Bean** of Wheaton College also believes that the captains are important:
I give responsibility to the captains to serve as sounding boards and develop a real open line of communication from players to the coach. It has worked well for us.

**Ron Newman** of the San Diego Sockers talks about pride in his game, his team, his school and professionally, his city, as important ingredients in good team morale, as does North Babylon's John Eden. Eden emphasizes pride and responsibility:

*The team is told before the season, constantly during the season and after the season that they represent the school, the community and their parents. If they, the players, cannot do this properly then they will not play for this team. They are told that winning is important, but winning is only important if it is accomplished within the proper spirit of the game. The proper spirit of the game includes sportsmanship and cooperation among the entire team. We do not make any exceptions here regardless of the ability of the player.*

**Ray Buss** of Fleetwood High School (Pa.) feels that guidelines must be established to provide for a common ground that everyone must follow for the well being of all concerned. His further comments:

*Our fundamental drills and practice sessions are mostly competitive in nature, yet enjoyable and fun, which perhaps leads to good team morale and working towards a goal of cooperation on the field of play.*

**Billy Charlton** of the U.S. Army takes the approach (as with Buss) that practice sessions play a role in the morale of a team:

*Morale is a mental condition within an individual player and within an entire team. Since morale involves individual and team confidence, enthusiasm and willingness to endure hardship, the development of it can easily be integrated into the types of drills and practice sessions directed by the coach. A good spirit of cooperation among players usually accompanies good morale.*

**Klaas de Boer,** formerly of the Los Angeles Aztecs, differs somewhat with Charlton. He emphasizes the role of communication in establishing good team morale.

*Presumption that proper morale and spirit of cooperation are prerequisites for success is not necessarily true, although it is a big help. The 1981 Aztecs were very successful on the field (19-13). despite internal conflicts and tension, brought on primarily by communication and cultural differences. When the team was winning*

there were no problems, but after a loss some of the conflicts would surface. Teams with a variety of nationalities or particularly teams with two distinct groups almost invariably incur these problems. The key to developing morale and cooperation is communication. The coach and team must have commonly agreed-upon goals. This is best accomplished through team and individual meetings with players. A coach must appeal to the player's pride and sense of responsibility and instill in the players a sense of mutual respect and cooperation.*

**Gary Avedekian** of Centerville (Ohio) High School believes the coach must strive to be logical and progressive with individuals in terms of teaching, in order to move players and the team forward:

*We maintain morale and cooperation by trying not to lose our sense of humor. We try to stay analytical, not angry. We assign individual tasks, such as vacuuming the locker room, and we always get at least one meal together a week. We try to help individuals identify their deficiencies, and we give analysis and develop corrective training programs. As the individual gets better, he is rewarded and the team benefits, The total benefit is victory and that's always good for morale, Hard work for the sake of hard work will not be beneficial. Unless the players see its relevance and it brings obvious results, hard work is meaningless. Appropriate hard work stiffens their resolve to win.*

**Jeff Vennell** of Kenyon College also likes the role of correction of performance, stating:

*Try to build confidence from doing things correctly and avoid labels, using performance criteria instead.*

**Gordon Jago**, long-time professional coach, picked up on the Avedekian "victory" comment with some cautions:

*Success is the easiest way to obtain a good spirit, but it is important to see that players accept a team concept, for individuals cannot be totally responsible for success. Bring all problems out* into the open and attempt to get players to accept constructive criticism.

**Howard Goldman** of Marist College (N.Y.) picked up on the themes of other coaches but added his own emphases. He encourages his team to do things other than soccer off the field, i.e. play intramural softball together, hold team parties, etc. He also continually reminds the team of how the group must function, including the need for the team to have fun and enjoy its soccer. Lastly he believes that certain team traditions unique to the soccer team need to be maintained each year as a means of uniting the group (hosting indoor tournaments, annual team dinner, etc.).

**John Cossaboon** of the North Texas Youth State Soccer Association:
*Favoritism is something the coach tries to avoid if he expects to develop good morale among his players. Proper morale and spirit of cooperation can only exist if all players feel they are being dealt with in a fair and equal manner. Players can handle their playing and non-playing roles much more easily if they feel that there is a genuine concern for their development, from the coach.*

*Players can accept their deficiencies if the coach presents them in a proper way. They can't accept inconsistent treatment based on current ability level. I can't think of a single greater contributor to team friction than "favorite treatment."*

**Bob Guelker** of SIU-Edwardsville believes that equality of treatment of players is important. The coach must treat everyone with dignity, not have double standards and must show that he cares for his players.

**Richard Broad's** (George Mason, D.C.) comment pertained to role-playing. He believes that it is important for every player to have a role defined for him in order for good team morale to be present.

**Hank Steinbrecher's** analysis of the match itself is interesting and involves morale:
*Sport is a cooperative venture not a competitive venture. The ultimate contest is between groups to demonstrate cooperation. Those teams that cooperate the most will win. The competitive essence in soccer is which team demonstrates the highest degree of cooperative spirit. Thus team play is the ultimate goal. This cannot be done without a bond between players, a sense of brotherhood.*

© Noonie./Dreamstime.com

# Where Are We Going and How Do We Get There?
## Make Your Goals Count This Season

### Ed Kingston, M.S. Boston University

If done the right way, goal-setting can often give a season a purpose and define a team's legacy. Common goals can bring a team together; realistic goals can increase individual and team effort; and specific, measurable goals can provide that spark that drives a team to reach their potential (Gould, 2006). Investing the time and effort to set goals the right way can provide a team a clear roadmap from where they are at the beginning of a season to where they want to be at the end of a season (Cook, 1996).

None of this should be groundbreaking news for many coaches – in fact, most teams set goals at the start of their seasons. Unfortunately, many teams will fail to reach their goals during their season, not from a lack of talent or quality coaching, but from setting goals the wrong way. Too often, teams seem to follow the "set-it-and-forget-it" principle of goal setting – players set goals at the beginning of the season only to forget them by the middle of the season. Don't let your team's goals hanging in the locker room become monuments to your team's good intentions. The key to setting goals the right way is keeping your team's goals connected with your team's performance on the field.

## Setting Team Goals the Wrong Way

Here are a few common mistakes coaches and players make when they set team goals for the season:

**Goals are unrealistically high or too easy to reach.** Effective goal-setting is always a delicate balance between your team's ambitions, their talent, and their potential. Unreachable goals can sap a team's motivation and energy throughout the season. Likewise, easily reached goals will do little to motivate players to work hard. Effective, realistic goals should stretch your team without breaking them (Ravizza & Hanson, 1995).

**Goals are too general.** Teams and athletes often set goals without thinking about how they would measure their progress towards these goals (Ravizza & Hanson, 1995). Players might want "to get better throughout the season" or "play together as a team," and these are good goals to work towards, but teams and players often stop there. Consequently, they have a tough time later in the season recognizing if they met their goal or not. For every goal your team sets this season, they have to ask themselves, "How will we know if we met this goal?" Straightforward and specific goals will help your players answer this question.

**No ownership by the players in the goal-setting process.** Many well-meaning coaches often devise team goals and dominate the goal-setting process at the start of the season. Consequently, players won't feel like their goals belong to them. In effect, players would be renting their goals from their coaches. Players want to own their goals. You take care of something you own. You attend to it because you recognize its value. It's no different with goal-setting. Players are more likely to attend to and work hard towards reaching their goals if they believe those goals belong to them.

**Focus is on the outcome and not the performance.** Outcome goals give us a sense of direction, but they don't help us focus on the present or the task at hand (Vernacchia, 2003). When setting team goals, teams ask themselves, "Where are we going?" Unfortunately, most teams never ask themselves the next, more important question: "How do we get there?" Answering the latter question will enable a team to identify the steps needed to take to reach specific goals for the season.

## Setting Team Goals the Right Way

Setting goals the right way is an investment of time and energy that can reap rewards in the form team accountability, respect, and trust (Janssen, 1999). At the start of any season, time always seems to be in short supply. Coaches can be tempted to short-change the goal-setting process. Resist this temptation. To be effective, a team may need more than one quick goal-setting meeting to hammer out where they are going as a team and the best way for them to get there. Once player selections are finalized, coaches should set aside time for the team to meet to discuss their goals for the season. The coach can determine how to structure goal-setting meetings and provide basic goal-setting information, but it's important that captains and players have ownership (Gould, 2006). Once your team is assembled it's time map out a goal strategy.

**Start with a Realistic Dream.** Your team's motivation to work towards a goal will be dependent on a combination of their ability, skill, and desire to put the work in to reach that goal (Janssen, 1999). Your team should ask themselves what they *could* achieve if everything came together during the season, but more importantly, what would they want to achieve. In *Championship Team Building* (1999), Jeff Janssen recommended that teams balance the *"could achieve"* and the *"want to achieve"* in order to increase motivation and minimize frustration over the course of the season. Your team's dream goal has to be set high enough so that your team will want to stretch to reach it, but

realistic enough so that your team stays focused on their goals without giving up. Above all, your team has to believe they can and are capable of reaching their goals for the season.

**Create a Game Plan For Your Team Goals.** Reaching one's goals require more than just desire and belief. It also requires a plan – a set of steps to get a team from where they are to where they want to go. Can you imagine walking up to Chelsea manager, Jose Mourinho, after winning his second straight Premiership title and asking, "How did you get here?" And he said, "I don't know. We just showed up every game and started kicking a ball around and now we've won it twice." Chances are Mourinho and his players had developed and practiced a well thought out game plan before they ever stepped on a pitch. Your team needs a game plan if they want to reach their goal(s) for the season. This requires that your team break down your long-term goal, that realistic dream goal discussed above, into smaller outcome goals for the season. Short-term goals identify the specific steps your team needs to take to reach its long-term goals. Each outcome moves you closer to your final destination. Like a roadmap, it keeps your team moving in the right direction (Cook, 1996).

Let's break down a conference championship in college soccer:
**Outcome Goals for the Season**
Dream Goal: Win Conference Championship

Qualify for conference tournament
Undefeated at French(home) Field
Win 7 of 9 conference games
Have at least +10 GD by season's end
Take advantage of set piece opportunities
Limit soft goal opportunities by opponents

**Focus on the W.I.N. (What's Important Now?)** Once your team has a set of outcome goals for the season their focus needs to shift from "Where are we going?" to "How do we get there?"

This requires breaking each outcome goal into smaller, more manageable performance goals. Performance goals focus on how the team can be successful each game. Players have more opportunities to meet success when their coaches emphasize the "how" instead of the "what" of competitive performance (Gould, 2006).

**Now let's identify the performance goals for some of the outcome goals we listed earlier:**
Win Conference Championship
Qualify for conference tournament
Undefeated at French(home) Field
Win 7 of 9 conference games

Outcome Goal: Have at least +10 GD by season's end
Performance Goals: Put 70% of shots on frame. Final pass success – 50% good service to beat back line or keeper. Limit opponents to three shots or fewer

Outcome Goal: Take advantage of set piece opportunities
Performance Goals: Accuracy – 70% dead ball service within shooting range. Earn a shot on goal, corner kick or goal 40% of time.

Outcome Goal: Limit soft goal opportunities for opponents
Performance Goals: Limit balls played behind our back line to one per game. Win 60% more loose and air balls than opponent.

These performance goals should be written out and placed in an area where players can be reminded of them everyday. As sport psychologist Ralph Vernacchia reminds athletes to do with their goals, "Think 'em and ink 'em, view 'em and do 'em, believe 'em and achieve 'em." (Vernacchia, 2003).

Coaches and players can work together to further break down each performance goal into specific techniques and skills necessary to put 70% of shots on frame or limit the number of balls played behind the back line, etc. These smaller goals are called process goals. Process goals, specific techniques and skills, keep your team's focus in the present moment and give your team a chance to reach its performance goals for each game (Vernacchia, 2003). Process goals allow players to focus on the very things they need to do at the very moment they need to do them.

From charting their success at meeting each outcome goal and its corresponding performance goals, a coaching staff can outline specific process goals to focus on in training throughout the year. Simultaneously, individual players can look at the team's goal chart hanging in the locker room and create daily goals for themselves to focus on in training throughout the week (see chart below). Most importantly, a wall chart gives up-to-date evaluation and feedback on how close the team is to achieving its goals (Gould, 2006).

Of course, we don't know what the season will bring and there are a lot of variables we don't control (injuries, quality of opposition, etc). Be sure to revisit your goals throughout the season and adjust your outcome and performance goals to keep them realistic and achievable (Gould, 2006). With a little effort, your team's goals can stop being a forgotten "wish list" and start being a valuable part of your team's success throughout the season.

*Ed Kingston holds a Master's Degree in Sport Psychology from Western Washington University and is currently a doctoral student in Sport Psychology at Boston University. He has consulted with club, high school, and college soccer teams. He is currently a sport psychology consultant with Boston University Men's Soccer.*

Table 1. Example Team Goal Chart for 2006

| OUTCOME GOAL | PROCESS GOAL | OPPONENTS | | | | | | |
|---|---|---|---|---|---|---|---|---|
| | | SFU | UM | UMBC | BU | UNH | SBU | UV |
| | | | | | | | | |
| | Put 70% of | X | X | X | X | X | X | X |
| | shots on frame | | | | | | | |
| Have at least | | | | | | | | |
| (+) 10 GD | Final pass success | X | | X | X | X | X | X |
| | 50% or better | | | | | | | |
| | | | | | | | | |
| | 3 shots or fewer | | | X | X | | X | X |
| | by opponents | | | | | | | |
| | | | | | | | | |
| Take | 70% or better service | X | X | X | X | X | X | X |
| advantage | within shooting range | | | | | | | |
| of set piece | | | | | | | | |
| opportunities | Earn shot, corner, or | X | | X | X | | X | X |
| | goal - 40% of time | | | | | | | |
| | | | | | | | | |
| Limit soft goal | Limit balls played behind | | | X | | | X | X |
| opportunities | back to 1 per game | | | | | | | |
| by opponent | | | | | | | | |
| | Win 60% or more of | X | | X | X | | X | X |
| | loose & air balls | | | | | | | |
| WIN !! | | W | L | W | W | T | T | W |

## References

Cook, D. L. (1996). The composition of confidence. In R. A. Vernacchia, R. T. McGuire, & D. L. Cook, Coaching mental excellence: "It does matter whether you win or lose...", (pp. 81-89). Portola Valley, CA: Warde Publishers.

Gould, D. (2006). Goal setting for peak performance. In J. M. Williams (Ed.) Applied Sport Psychology: Personal growth to peak performance, (5th ed., pp. 240-259). Mountain View, CA: Mayfield Publishing Co.

# Chapter 4: Fitness and Nutrition

# Get Serious about Warm-Ups

## Steven Smith and Lee Schopp

Warming up players for the demands of practice and games is a vital role of every soccer coach. Often this task is relegated to the players and captains without thought to the implications for the practice session.

When coaches understand the purposes behind a correct warm-up, they will better prepare the athletes to compete in a safer, healthier fashion. There are three vital areas that are positively changed through proper warm-up.

Many coaches tend to do with the players what their coaches did with them. This typical pattern has led to unhealthy or even unsafe practices in warm-ups. Understanding the purposes of a warm-up may help change the approach to best benefit the athletes and prepare them for both practice and game sessions.

The purpose of warming up can be divided into three overlapping categories. Coaches are responsible to prepare the athletes in each of these three commonly recognized domains: Attitudinally, Bodily, and Cognitively (ABC's).

---

### The ABC's of Thematic Warm-ups

Attitude – The effective domain related to mental preparation
Body – The Physiological changes necessary for full participation
Cognitive – The player's (increasing) knowledge of the game

---

## Attitudinal Changes

Many coaches receive the athletes after long, demanding days in school or work. The players have faced many other pressures, which they may tend to bring to the game or practice session with them. A wise coach will recognize this and address it through the warm-up.

A gradual increase in the demands of mental concentration will help the athletes begin to change focus from outside pressures to the demands of the game. This gradual increase in the demands and intensity of the task will enable the transition. The typical stretch and play approach will not allow players to shift their focus.

Another vital attitude that a good warm-up addresses is the feeling of preparedness. Whether it is a practice or game setting, the warm-up must help the athletes believe that they are ready for the task at hand. Once again, this is best accomplished as described below, with a gradual approach and intentional focus.

## Body Changes

There are many changes that take place physiologically with a proper warm-up. Research has shown that changes occur in heart rate; muscle temperature and muscle flexibility as there is an increase in energy output during initial movement.

Gradually increasing the length and flexibility of the muscle groups to be used also is possible through stretching activities. Such changes will assist the athlete in performing optimally for practice and competition and reduce the chances for injury during intense ballistic movement.

## Cognitive Changes

It is vitally important that we relate warm-up activities to what we will be teaching that day. Too often the warm-up is not linked to the topic

---

## Typical Incorrect or Unsafe Warm-up Styles

· Players arrive and stretch on their own
· Coaches lead stretching before physical activity
· Players or captains lead stretching prior to coach's arrival
· Little or no increasing demands of each task
· Activities unrelated to the theme of the day

---

of emphasis for the training session. For many coaches, the warm-up doesn't relate to increasing the athletes' knowledge of the game or particular training session.

An excellent warm-up will demand that the athlete become cognitively involved in the session. Therefore, all warm-ups should be linked strongly with the theme of the day. This becomes an ideal time for the coach to give feedback to the individual player on technical and tactical aspects of the game that are being emphasized during the warm-up activities.

### Practice Warm-ups

The warm-up for a practice session is one of the most integral parts of a training session. Often, the focus of the players and the flow of the warm-up will dictate whether the session will be effective or not. It is reasonable to state that the first 20 to 30 minutes of practice will determine the success of the training session.

For example, a training session emphasizing passing and receiving through the middle third of the field could look like this:

- Passing with a partner in open space, one half of the field
- Stretch two muscle groups
- Passing with a partner in limited space with other players in same space (35 x 45 grid)
- Stretch two muscle groups
- Passing with a partner while an individual (or two) in opposite colors attempt to knock the ball out of the grid
- Stretch two muscle groups
- Passing with a partner while two players (joined by holding a towel) attempt to tag one of the players without the ball at their foot. Once tagged, the towel is exchanged with the tagged group and the "taggers" become passers and receivers
- Final stretch determined by individual player.

Each of these activities becomes increasingly more demanding on the attitude, body, and cognitive abilities of the players. The ball activities are consistently alternated with stretching of specific muscle groups. Early in the season, the coach should lead these stretches and emphasize gradual lengthening techniques and no ballistic (bouncing) stretches.

The progression leads to a main series of teaching that will have the players ready to apply the concepts in a functional tactical training session to solve the problems of moving through the middle third of the field. If done correctly, it will be difficult to determine when the warm-up ends and when the main series begins.

A training session emphasizing beating defenders one on one in the front third may look something like this:
- Various Coerver activities in limited space.
- Stretching two muscle groups
- Dribbling in limited space: All players in a grid, each with a ball, dribbling without touching another player or leaving the space.
- Stretching two muscle groups

- Dribbling in limited space with pressure: All players in a grid, each with a ball, dribbling while one player (without a ball) attempts to knock out the other players' balls
- Stretching two muscle groups
- Dribble knock out: All players in a grid or circle, each with a ball, dribbling for possession while trying to knock other players' balls out of the grid
- Final stretch determined by individual players

These activities become increasingly more demanding for the players in maintaining control of the ball while being aware of the presence of teammates and defenders. They can lead to an increase in the demands of the tasks in each of the domains of preparation (ABC's). As in the earlier example, if done with increasing intensity, the activities lead to a seamless progression into the main series of beating defenders one on one.

By the conclusion of the warm-up session, it should be obvious to all that the players already are engaged in the training process. Correct preparation will allow players to be more purposeful and successful during practice because they have warmed up and already practiced what the coaching staff will later ask them to perfect in more game-like settings.

*Editor's note: Steve Smith is the coach at Hope College. He holds an NSCAA Advanced National Diploma and also serves as the Director of Hope Soccer Camp. Smith also is Associate Professor of Kinesiology at Hope College and holds a Ph.D. in motor development.*
*Lee Schopp is a two-time NSCAA All-America at Hope College and is the assistant coach and head goalkeeper coach at his alma mater. He holds a USSF "C" license and also serves as assistant director of Hope Soccer Camp. Schopp has a master's degree in educational leadership and also is an elementary teacher in the West Ottawa Schools in Holland, Mich.*

# Warm-Up – When, Why and How

## Dr. Don Kirkendall

Elmar Bolowich, the former men's soccer coach at the University of North Carolina, passed along an observation to me a while back. When he would go watch high school and club teams play, he thought they did a pretty poor job of warming up for matches.

The general purpose of warm-up is to get the body ready for exercise. The body doesn't just jump up from rest to competition; it has to slowly raise the body's function to a higher level. Warm-up too slowly and players aren't prepared for the high level of competition. Warm-up too rapidly and lactic acid production has to be eliminated before productive play can begin. Preparation for play is physical as well as psychological. Proper warm-up seems to help muscles be more resistant to injury. In addition, the metabolic processes for generating energy function more effectively at temperatures slightly higher than body temperature. Thus, the warm muscle produces energy quicker, more efficiently and resists injury better than a "cold" muscle.

Warm-up usually is a combination of general or specific activities. General warm-up activities include calisthenics, stretching and general "loosening up" activities unrelated to the upcoming exercise. Some people like warm showers or massage as a general warm-up. Specific warm-up includes performing the upcoming exercise at a reduced intensity. Lots of teams use selected small-sided games as specific warm-up. Remember to increase the intensity of specific warm-up as kickoff approaches.

The benefits of warm-up can be both psychological and physical. The mental preparation for so many contests gets the athletes a feel for how they think they will perform. Some jumping during warm-up might let the athletes know if they think they will be jumping high to challenge for headers. Shooting lets them know if their shot is "on" that day. Confidence going into the match comes, in part, from warm-up activities done accurately and precisely; specific activities done poorly may leave a player thinking "Oh, no. My left foot is really off today."

While the psychological side of warm-up may be difficult to prove, the physical side of warm-up is well studied. Warm-up helps the body prepare for activity in five physiological ways:

1. Speed of both muscle action and relaxation is increased
2. Movements by a warm muscle are more efficient
3. Oxygen moves through warm muscles more quickly and efficiently
4. Nerve transmission and muscle metabolism are improved
5. There is increased blood flow through the warm muscles (specific to the muscles warmed up)

The warm-up activities usually begin as general activities, then move to the more specific exercises. Don't do so much so intensely that players get fatigued. A good all-purpose guideline is that once you have broken a sweat from the warm-up, then the body is probably prepared to play. Those exercises I presented in the May-June issue of Soccer Journal on the F-MARC 11 for injury prevention (performed after breaking that sweat) would be classified as general activities. The sidebar lists a series of activities, including the F-MARC 11 that one might try. It takes some time, but it is effective for both performance and injury prevention.

It is best to organize warm-up so that the match starts fairly soon after the warm-up because

## Sample Warm-Up exercises

Here are some sample exercises for general warm-up I've picked up from watching various teams and from fitness experts like Vern Gambetta and Mark Verstegen. The exercises of the F-MARC11 are italicized to show how these would be inserted in a general warm-up. This routine would take about 20 minutes before training or a match.

### Activity

- General light jogging
- Jog - sideline to sideline
- Shuttle, - start one direction leading with the right leg, stop at midfield, return leading off with the left leg
- Backward running
- Calf Stretching – (30 sec each leg) two players on opposite sides of the ball, with a straight leg and heel on the ground, put the ball of the foot on the ball to stretch the calf
- Standing thigh stretch – (30 sec each leg) Stand on one leg, grab the other ankle behind the back and stretch the thigh. Use a partner for balance.
- Figure four hamstring stretch – (30 sec each leg) While seated, the other leg is bent and the foot touches the knee of the leg being stretched
- Inner thigh stretch – (30 sec each leg) Seated, spread legs, lean forward trying to put the chest on the ground
- Hip flexor stretch – (30 sec each leg) In a forward lunge position, back knee on the ground, lean forward stretching the hip muscles
- *Bench – core strengthening*
- *Sideways bench – core strengthening*
- Walking lunges – (3 sets of 10 reps) Push off with the right foot and lunge with the left, drop right knee to the ground. Keep control, you should be able to see the toes of the lead foot
- *Cross country skiing – strengthening leg muscles*
- *Russian hamstrings – strengthening the hamstrings*
- *Single toe raises – (30 reps each) On one leg, no support, slowly rise up on toes, then slowly lower*
- *Chest passing in a single leg stance – Improvement of coordination and balance; strengthening the leg muscles*
- *Forward bend in single leg stance – Improvement in coordination and balance strengthening the leg muscles*
- *Figure 8's in a single leg stance – Improvement in coordination and balance; strengthening the leg muscles*
- *Jumps over a line –Improvement in jumping power and technique*
- *Zig Zag shuffle – Improvement in coordination, agility, jumping*
- Phantom headers – (20 reps) Pause between jumps, bent knees to take off and land. Land on the balls of your feet
- Scissors jumps – (20 reps) Forcefully push off with the right leg, draw left leg up high and land on the balls of the feet with bent knee. Maintain control when landing.
- Shuttle run forward and backward – Cruise or sprint between cones set about 10-20 yards apart
- *Bounding – improvement of coordination, jumping power and technique*

the benefits are lost quickly during rest. If the body temperature, and especially the muscle temperature, returns to resting levels, warm-up needs to start all over again.

When to stretch? A warm muscle responds better to stretching better than a cold muscle. So a reasonable thought might be to perform a general warm-up until you break a sweat, stretch and then do a brief general warm-up again followed by more extensive specific activities with gradually increasing intensity. The trainer's line is: "You warm-up to stretch, you don't stretch to warm-up."

## Halftime Warm-Up

The halftime clock is counting down the last one to two minutes and neither team is back on the field. Finally, the players slowly gather, touch a ball a couple times and the referee blows the whistle to begin second-half play. The quality of play in the first 10 to 15 minutes is not very cohesive. Running is not as strong, touches are less than ideal and decisions seem a bit off. But soon the match settles down and play looks more organized. You all know what I am talking about. You've experienced it.

I bet many coaches just accept this first 10 to 15 minutes as a period to be endured, to be survived. Dr. Jens Bangsbo, the Danish physiologist now the No. 2 coach at Juventus FC, has looked at this phenomenon. He noticed that the running volume in the first 15 minutes of the second half is reduced compared with any other 15-minute period except the last (when players are getting tired). As a part of a larger project, his research team recorded body and muscle temperatures of players after warm-up, every 15 minutes of a match, after the first half and after halftime. During halftime the temperatures returned to nearly normal and the temperatures didn't return to match levels until the 15-minute period of the second half. Bangsbo's group also had a team take 5 to 10 minutes out of halftime to warm-up

for the second half. The temperatures were back to match levels before the second-half whistle. The team that warmed up had more overall running, more intense running, more ball touches and more attacks in the first 15 minutes of the second half than the team that didn't warm-up.

The coaches of most teams I see take every last second of halftime to talk with their players and then arrive just before the referee is ready to start the second half. Those players end up spending the first 15 minutes of the second half warming up for the last 30 minutes of the game.

So what does Bangsbo suggest? Be brief and efficient in your halftime comments. Realistically, you probably only have two or three points you want to make anyway. How many different ways do you have to say it? Make your points and get them back on the field to warm-up for the second half by doing soccer-specific activities. Have you ever seen a college basketball team just walk out for the second-half tip-off? Of course not, so why should soccer players? If the other team doesn't do warm-up, it will be at a distinct disadvantage, vulnerable to attack and you should make this point to your players; "We're warmed-up. They aren't. They will be a step behind you for the next few minutes, so now it's our time to attack." You can bet Juventus warms up for the second half, as do many of the big time teams.

# Fitness Training: How Much and How Hard?

### Jeremy Boone & Vern Gambetta

Here are answers to frequent questions concerning fitness training for soccer.

## When is it Appropriate to Begin Formal Speed Training?

A common mistake many coaches make when beginning formal speed training is to prepare their players for a track meet and not for the game of soccer. Speed training for soccer should always have a game-like emphasis. Typically, younger players between the ages of 7-9 should focus on free play. Variations of games such as tag are a wonderful way to work on speed and improve gross motor skills. Coaching considerations prior to implementing any type of formal training include the ability of the player to handle formal instruction and the player's physical maturity level. Starting at an early age, soccer technique should be developed concurrent with speed training. Once these skills have been mastered, **players need to learn to distribute their efforts** relative to the technical and tactical demands of the game, incorporating short explosive bursts with varied changes of direction.

## Should I Include Distance Running in Training Sessions to Improve My Team's Endurance?

Practical experience and research have shown that slow steady distance running detracts from speed and explosiveness. It's the 88th minute of the game and the score is 1 to 1. Your players should not only be able to run, but continue to run fast. This is accomplished by incorporating fartleks and interval runs into your training. For example, have your players perform a 30/30 run. This is a 30-second jog followed by a 30-second run at 70% of maximal effort. Start with a 10-minute run and work up to 18 minutes. Carefully consider the conditioning that also occurs in small-sided games. This can be manipulated by changing variables such as the number of players, size of field, duration of play, ball supply and touch restriction. Unfortunately having only 2-3 practices per week is insufficient to get your players fit. Additional fitness work that is relative to the demands of soccer and properly planned into the overall training cycle will help to ensure a fitter and faster team.

## When is it Appropriate to Begin Formal Strength Training for a Young Player?

Strength is one of the biggest deficiencies in players we work with at all levels of soccer. As with speed training, the athlete's emotional development and level of physical maturity are important in determining if the athlete can learn the routines and handle formal training. Although research has shown that pre-pubescent athletes may be able to Integrate each component throughout the entire practice. It all starts with a proper warm-up. This is the time to work on balance, coordination, speed work, and high quality touches on the ball. The objective is to work up to game effort speed, therefore, warm-up to play, don't play to warm-up. From this point forward, the entire practice session should mimic the game. This requires a well–constructed training plan that flows from one component to the next with a smooth transition. For example, when performing team drills, the length of the lines affects the work to rest ratio. Players should never stand around for more than 30-40 seconds at a time. Transition right into a small-sided game after finishing the last team drill. We look at the whole practice as a water break. Have your players bring their own water bottle so that whenever they need a break, they quickly take it and get immediately back in to practice.

## What Can I Do to Help Prevent Fatigue when My Team Plays Two Games in One Day?

Your players are only as good as their ability to recover. Factors such as hydration and a pre- and post-game nutrition plan are always important. Be aware of environmental conditions such as altitude changes, time zone changes, and the weather. The warm-up before the first game will be more extensive while the warm-up before the second game should be much shorter in duration. Many teams will go through a long warm-up before their second game and end up coming out flat. This may be attributed to the players becoming fatigued from the long second warm-up. Include a cool down after each game lasting around 10-15 minutes incorporating light jogging and dynamic flexibility. End the cool down with a short static stretching routine to help the muscles return to resting length.

*Editor's note: The SoccerFit™ team helps individual coaches, teams and youth clubs improve their training and conditioning programs. For any comments, questions or further information please contact Jeremy@carolinaadi.com or vgambetta@ aol.com*

# Strategies to Get Your Team Soccer Fit

## Jeremy Boone and Verne Gambetta

Today's typical youth team will train two times a week as a team and play one or two games on a weekend or in a tournament. However, in order to develop the complete player, this is less than ideal from a skill and tactical development perspective and is equally undesirable from a physical preparation perspective.

Just as soccer skill development demands attention more than two days a week, proper physical preparation demands attention at least four days a week, preferably five days a week. The immediate question that comes to mind is where will the time come from?

Realistically speaking, proper planning, combined with built-in accountability of your players, will allow you to train some component of soccer specific fitness every day. The following strategies for developing in-season fitness are based upon our experience working with various youth clubs around the country.

On the days of team practice look for opportunities to include components within training. For example, you need to warm-up every day specific to the session's objectives. This is a great time to attend to speed and coordination development. Integrating footwork drills such as an ABC Speed ladder or short fitness modules throughout a practice will also bring valuable results.

A frequent comment from youth coaches is that they do not have time to address physical training during their practice time. However, through observation of several youth teams over a three-month period, results were somewhat startling. There was never less than 15 minutes of "dead time" in an average 90-minute to two-hour practice. More often it was 20 minutes.

"Dead time" is defined as time standing with no movement, usually waiting in a long line to do a drill or standing in a group listening to the coach talk. This is time that could be productively used for physical development. In the typical week, 15 to 20 minutes of dead time per practice adds up to 30 to 40 minutes a week, which extends to more than two hours a month. Given a team that trains 10 months a year, at least 20 hours are lost to dead time in a training year.

Use this time productively by:
- **Being organized** – Thoroughly plan practice, not just for the day and the week but at least a month at a time
- **Being intense** – The game is intense, therefore training to play should be intense
- **Being specific to the game** – The majority of the movements are quick bursts of stopping and starting. Training should reflect this. The purpose is to improve speed of play and decision-making
- **Assigning homework** – Written workouts should be given to the players to complete on the non-team training days (This should only be done above the U-12 level)

With these thoughts in mind we need to rethink the approach to fitness training for soccer at all levels. It is imperative to work on some component of fitness for soccer each training day, from the youth level on up to the professional level.

In the preceding article, we presented a framework for incorporating fitness into a training session for your team. Part II will provide a soccer-conditioning spectrum to be used as a conditioning tool within that framework.

### What type of conditioning is best?

The physical demands of the game are somewhat contradictory because they are at opposite ends of the spectrum – speed on one end, aerobic endurance on the other. There is no question that a significant aerobic base is necessary to be a good player. The problem is how to achieve this aerobic fitness base without compromising speed or explosiveness. Slow continuous running or jogging will not build the aerobic base needed to play without compromising speed and explosiveness. It might be helpful to think of the base as the sum total of all the work done. This is why the term Work Capacity base is preferred rather than aerobic base.

The aerobic base is a component of work capacity. This base is built through varied intensity interval workouts, circuit training, and various combinations of games with varied numbers of players, touches, availability of balls, and size of field. Some work can be done with the ball and some without. As the technical proficiency of the players improves, then it is productive to do more fitness work with the ball.

The following is a continuum of soccer fitness training. The continuum begins with the highest intensity demand component, speed, and works down to the lowest intensity, aerobic work. It is important to place all these workouts within the context of actual soccer practice. Always take into consideration the total workload because training is cumulative. A simple rule of thumb is to remember that one workout cannot make an athlete, but one workout can break an athlete.

### Speed 95 –100%
All out sprints and acceleration work. This is an example of a Ball Acceleration Module (Length of acceleration should be 10 meters)
- One Touch & Go (instep)
- Feint & Go (Outside of Foot)
- Turn & Go (Sole of Foot)
- Juggle & Go
- Out of Air & Go

### Speed Endurance 90 – 95%
- 30 meters with 30 sec recovery in sets of 4 or 5 reps – 3 minutes between sets

### Intensive Tempo 80 –90%
(Mixed Aerobic/Anaerobic Work)
- 30 sec walk/ 30 sec jog/ 30 sec run
- Whistle Fartlek 6 – 10 minutes with & without the ball
- Short/Short/Long (Two short touches followed by a long touch) 30 –40 seconds active recovery dribbling the ball
- 10 Second Bursts with the ball – With 25 –30 seconds recovery dribbling ball

### Extensive Tempo 70 –80%
(Aerobic Interval Work)
- 30 sec run/ 30 sec jog @ 75% x 9 –12
- 2 or 3 minutes runs x 2 –3 @ 70%

### Continuous Tempo <70%
(Low intensity aerobic work)
- 20 – 30 minute runs. Use this primarily for recovery sessions

The majority of youth club teams practice twice a week with games on the weekend. However, a minimum of four days per week of planned training is required to see any benefit in improved fitness levels. The following is a model one-week training template for the in-season that you can use with your team. Refer to the soccer-conditioning spectrum when designing your team's conditioning.

Make fitness a priority and you will see the results in improved quality of training as well as game performance!

*The SoccerFit™ team helps individual coaches, teams, and youth clubs improve their training and conditioning programs. For any comments, questions or further information please contact Jeremy@carolinaadi.com or vgambetta@aol.com.*

A typical week of a youth club practice

| | Mon. | Tue. | Wed. | Thurs. | Fri. | Sat. | Sun. |
|---|---|---|---|---|---|---|---|
| | Active Recovery- Continuous Tempo | Speed Practice | Speed Endurance | Speed Practice | | Game | Game |

# Soccer Circuit Training

## Jeremy Boone
## Athlete by Design

What comes to mind when you hear the words "strength training"? Most athletes respond immediately with answers such as "going to the gym," "using machines" or "lifting heavy weights." Even more common is the thought that strength training for soccer means always performing three to four sets of 12 to 16 repetitions of each exercise. While this may be effective, there is another way to train that can help you get stronger, faster and fitter at the same time.

## A Tried and True Method

I began using circuit training consistently in the mid- to late-1990's with all of my soccer athletes. This was in response to training time constraints imposed by teams' coaches. Many of them feared that "time away from practicing soccer-specific skill was time wasted." Implementing the concept of circuit training was the solution. Not only could I now develop all components of athleticism, but I also could include soccer-specific skill where appropriate (more on that later).

There are numerous benefits of using circuit training in your workout program. Circuit training:
Improves strength
- Improves stamina
- Improves sports skill
- Is time efficient
- Can be done anywhere
- Doesn't require expensive equipment
- Is FUN!
- Helps decrease body fat
- Helps increase lean body weight

## What Is Circuit Training?

Circuit training can be used to help get athletes in shape and get them stronger at the same time. This method of training involves performing a series of exercises designed to improve strength, fitness, speed and other athletic qualities in which the athlete performs one set of each exercise within the circuit, then moves on to the next exercise. The example below has the athlete performing three times through a workout.

## Circuit Training Templates

The great thing about circuit training is that it can be applied to just about any type of workout being done. When designing a workout, close attention should be paid to the level of difficulty of each exercise, the prescribed rest periods, the total training volume and the level of training intensity.

1. **Push-Pull-Core-Leg (used for strength)**
a. Set up the circuit so the exercises apply to each training category.
   Examples: pushup − pull-up − medball chop − body weight squat; DB press − DB row − medball twists − body weight lunges; DB overhead press − upright row − MB sit-up − jump squats

2. **Push-Run-Pull-Run-Core-Run-Leg-Run (strength endurance)**
a. The same as above, except add a 25-yard run between each exercise

3. **Core-Agility-Active Recovery (speed emphasis)**
a. Perform a core exercise (medball sit-ups, medball twists, medball throws, etc)
b. Perform an agility drill lasting 5-15 seconds

c. Finally perform an active recovery exercise (light jogging, juggling with a soccer ball, shooting free throws, etc.)

*Training Key: DB= dumbbell MB= medicine ball*

## "How Do I Use Circuit Training?"

There are many different types of circuits from which to choose. You can perform circuit training for time or for repetitions. For example, if you want to improve fitness, perform circuit training for time. If you want to focus on strength, perform circuit training for repetitions. There also are partner circuits or even team circuits. These are good for training with a teammate, or your entire team. For example, if you have 18 players on your team, create a nine-circuit station workout. Have two players per station performing the same exercise. The players must look at the next station to see what exercise is being done while performing the correct exercise at their present station. This example is also time efficient for the end of your training practice.

## Injury-Proof Your Circuit Training Workout

Safety and injury prevention is always the first concern when performing circuit training. Here are a few guidelines to ensure a quality workout.

1. Be aware that athletes tend to get excited easily; therefore they are prone to do too much too soon resulting in burnout.

2 Always implement a thorough warm-up and cool down.

3 Make sure all players are familiar with equipment being used.

4. Be aware of the sports surface in relation to the exercises that will be implemented.

## Circuit Training Has No Boundaries

By following certain key training principles, the circuit training method can be applied to just about anything.

- **Specificity** Workouts should reflect the demands of soccer and the player's position. If the position requires short bursts with many changes of direction, the circuit will not include exercises with a long duration of time.

- **Overload** As the body quickly adapts to training, be sure to progressively increase training load over time. This is accomplished by increasing either volume or intensity but never both simultaneously.

- **Recovery** The body is only as good as its ability to recover from work. Plan recovery periods long enough so that your players will not get too tired too quickly during the workout. Many players burn out too soon during circuit training due to lack of recovery time.

- **Variation** Add variety to your training. The body will become quickly accustomed to a routine so be sure to change up exercises every so often.

- **Progression** Make sure the circuit workout fits into your overall training plan. The goal is to gradually increase each workout from simple to complex and easy to difficult. Unwanted fatigue from a workout will cause a breakdown in skill.

## Where To Go From Here...

This is only the starting point to help you on your way to designing cutting-edge circuits. You now have the structure of circuit training. The next step is to attempt using circuit training to see what works for you.

In addition to these training principles, manipulating the following training variables will allow you to get the results you want.

- Time/duration of work
- Number of repetitions
- Frequency (number of trips)
- Number of players
- Number of exercise stations
- Recovery duration
- Exercise Order
- Training Load

Here are some practical suggestions for program application. Be aware that manipulating any one of these variables can have a dramatic outcome on the results of your program.

- The number of players influence the amount of recovery time based on the number of stations used. In a team environment, the fewer number of stations, the greater the recovery time. This scenario would be appropriate during in-season strength training or speed training

- In most cases, the greater the number of exercise stations, the fewer number of trips will be completed. Completing two trips of 18 stations is much different than completing three trips of 8 stations

- Exercise order is critical in program design. Circuits should be influenced based on the time of year (preseason, in-season, post-season, off-season), player positions and the needs of the individual players. Leg-based circuits and total body circuits are appropriate during the off-season and preseason, while modified total-body circuits and upper-body based circuits are more appropriate for in-season training

Combining the training principles and program design variables discussed in this article with the following six-step circuit design system will get you on your way to designing cutting edge circuit training workouts for your players.

1. **Determine your training objective.**
   What is the goal of the session? (Speed-Strength-Endurance) How does it fit into the overall yearly program?

2. **Know your training environment.**
   Will you be inside a gym or outside on the field? How much space is available?

3. **Select the appropriate exercises.**
   What equipment, if any, is needed?

4. **Determine the exercise station setup.**
   What is the exercise order? How much space is required between each station?

5. **Create the circuit.**

6. **Train hard and have fun.**

Ilustration generation copyright © 2003 Circuit Training Generator www.athletebydesign.com.

*Jeremy Boone is a nationally recognized Soccer Conditioning Consultant. He is the former speed and conditioning coach for the Atlanta Beat (WUSA). Jeremy works with athletes, teams, and youth clubs who struggle with getting fit, fast, and strong. If you would like to learn more about how Jeremy can help improve your performance, please call email him at Jeremy@carolinaadi.com.*

# Designing Strength Training to Be Soccer Fit

## Vern Gambetta

Designing strength-training programs for individual players or a team may sometimes be a bit confusing but it doesn't have to be impossible.

However, there is more to program design than just following solid training principles. A successful strength program also is based on the structure and sequence of the actual training components that make up the program. The following are a few design rules to keep in mind.

## Strength Training Design Rules

### Number of Exercises

It is best to carefully choose and limit the number of exercises. Keep a focus on the workout. Determine the essential "need to do" exercises from the "nice to do" exercises. In other words, bicep curls and tricep extensions may not be necessary in the workout. Too many exercises will dilute the training effect.

### Sets/Reps

For bodyweight exercises a range of 10 to 20 reps is necessary to force adaptation. For weight training the traditional paradigm of sets and reps is still very valid. Higher reps are good for hypertrophy development, while lower reps with multiple sets are good for neural development.

### Mode of Resistance

Depending on the objective and the phase of the program, the following resistance modes can all be used:
Bodyweight
Stretch cord
Medicine Ball
Power Ball
Dumbbells
Barbell

Each mode has its advantage or disadvantage, depending on the specific objectives of the training program.

### Progression

Progress from bodyweight exercises to external resistance exercises both within the workout and throughout the training year. In addition perform balance/stability work and core work first within each workout. Start with simple exercises that the athlete can perform, then progress to more complex movements. Do not allow the athlete to proceed further into the program until the exercises have been mastered. Failure to progress appropriately may result in a higher risk of injury.

### Frequency

There are several options to choose from that work well when planning a training week, all of which work quite well, depending on the objective. The choices are:

Total Body Routine – Alternate Days. For example Mon/Wed/Fri or Tue/Thu/Sat
Split Routine – Training on consecutive days. For example Mon/Thu Legs & Total Body and Tues/Fri Upper Body

### Duration

Generally it is best to keep the entire strength training session in the time range of 60 to 90 minutes, as this will ensure optimum results.

### Time of the Training Year

Obviously the greatest emphasis on strength training should be in the off-season and pre-season, but it is important to develop a manageable program that can be continued throughout the season. This will be a time where strength training intensity dominates over volume.

## Exercise Selection Criteria

### Multi-joint

Use as many joints as possible to produce force; conversely, use as many joints as possible to reduce force.

Close the chain to utilize gravity and ground reaction forces. Wherever possible, exercises should be performed standing.

### Tri-plane motion

Movement occurs in all three planes, sagittal, frontal and transverse. The key to performance is movement in the transverse plane; therefore, it is important to include rotational movement wherever possible.

### Amplitude

Work over the greatest range of motion that is possible to control.

### Speed

Incorporate speed of movement that is safe and the athlete can control.

### Proprioceptive Demand

Challenge the joint and muscle receptors to provide feedback regarding joint and limb position and reposition accordingly. The proprioceptors assist the system to generate movement in a form that it is appropriate to the demands placed upon the system. This will ensure that the strength will transfer to performance.

Applying these strength program design rules, the exercise selection criteria and the previously covered training principles will set your strength program up for success on the field. In our next column we will take a look at how the role of recovery can make or break a team's performance and what strategies can be used to ensure a team is ready to play.

In our last two installments we explored the concept of soccer specific speed and then provided a weekly training template for speed development.

But focusing on speed training alone will ensure less than optimal athletic performance.

Strength training for soccer has long been a gray area for a number of coaches. With so many different training philosophies and misleading information available, it is sometimes confusing as to what is the optimal way to make gains in strength.

Some coaches believe only strength training for the legs is necessary, while others focus on the total body. Yet others focus on having their players lift heavy weights with machines, while other coaches insist on using light dumbbells and high repetitions. Still others refuse to believe that any strength training is necessary at all!

To clear up some of that confusion, let's take a look at a few strength-training principles based on sports science and practical research that you can immediately apply to your program.

## Principle #1

### Develop Soccer Specific Strength

The strength program should be based on the demands of soccer, the varying positions, and the qualities of each individual athlete. The goal is to develop strength that the athlete can use on the field, not to prepare for a weightlifting competition. Be aware that "just because you can lift it, does not mean you can use it on the field!" For example, how strong does a forward have to be in order to score a goal from 20-25 yards?

## Principle #2

### Body Weight Before External Resistance

Bodyweight work essentially is preparation for heavier lifting that will follow. This type of work will help strengthen tendons and ligaments as well as muscles in preparation for external loading in whatever form. Examples of bodyweight work include performing pushups, pull-ups, body weight squats and bodyweight step-ups.

## Principle #3

Train Movements, Not Muscles
The central nervous system (CNS) is the command station that controls and directs all movement. The CNS calls for preprogrammed patterns of movement that can be modified in countless ways to react appropriately to gravity, ground reaction forces, and momentum. Isolation of specific muscles does not appropriately emphasize dynamic, multi-dimensional strength development. For example, have players perform a bodyweight lunge instead of a leg curl exercise, which isolates leg muscles.

## Principle #4

Train Core Strength Before Extremity Strength
A strong stable core consisting of the lumbo pelvic hip complex – the hip, abdomen and low back – is the cornerstone of a strength-training program. The core works as a transmission to transfer force from the lower to the upper extremity and vice versa. For example, striking a soccer ball is greatly affected by an athlete's level of core strength. Therefore, a strong stable core is the key to efficient movement. This needs more than "ab work" done lying on the ground; it involves dynamic whole-body rotational movements.

## Principle #5

Develop Strength Before Strength Endurance

In order to build strength endurance, first it is necessary to build strength. Otherwise, what are you enduring? Only when a strength base has been established can you work to add an endurance component. Moving from longer rest periods to shorter rest periods between exercises over a period of four to six weeks will help establish a proper strength progression.

All of these principles can be applied within the context of a normal soccer team's training environment with a minimal amount of equipment. The most important ingredient is a commitment to devote a dedicated amount of time to strength training each week. How the principles are applied gives detail to specific programs for specific positions and individuals.

Key Points to Consider
- What is the program's goal?
- What do you want each player to look like at the end of the program?
- What are the qualities unique to each player?
- Have they gone through puberty?
- Are they early or late developers?
- Who needs to gain muscle mass?
- Who needs to lose extra body weight?
- Do your players lack experience in strength training?

Asking yourself these questions and applying these principles will be sure to get you on your way to designing a solid strength-training program. Our next installment will look at factors to consider when designing a program and provide a weekly strength-training template for youth soccer players along with some suggested exercises.

## References:

Gambetta, Vern. *Multi-Dimensional Strength Training* Video

*The SoccerFit™ team helps individual coaches, teams, and youth clubs improve their training and conditioning programs. For any comments, questions, or further information please contact Jeremy@carolinaadi.com or vgambetta@aol.com.*

# Strength and Conditioning for Youth Soccer Players

## Lynn Pantuosco Hensch, D.P.E.

In the premier club I work with, we have started our own small-scale strength and conditioning program which focuses on performance enhancement, as well as, injury prevention. Our program focuses on providing strength and conditioning experience and education to players in a developmentally appropriate manner.

I will briefly describe our strength and conditioning program. More importantly, information necessary to incorporate strength and conditioning activities into your soccer program will be provided. Also, a brief review of current research and practices in the field of youth strength training will be highlighted in order to substantiate what we do with our own soccer programs.

## Youth Strength Training

Experts define strength training as, "a specialized method of physical conditioning that involves the progressive use of a wide range of resistive loads to enhance or maintain one's ability to exert or resist force" (Faigenbaum, 2001). Research over the past 10-15 years strongly supports youth strength training, suggesting that it can be safe and effective if conducted properly. Major professional organizations such as the *American College of Sport Medicine* and American *Academy of Pediatrics*, among others, encourage participation in appropriately designed and supervised youth strength training programs. Numerous health and fitness benefits of strength training have been identified including increased muscle strength, improved body composition, and resistance to injury to name a few. Strength training can also influence psychological well being, self esteem, and attitude toward physical activity and sports. Studies have shown that children can have

muscular strength gains of approximately 30-50% following short term strength and conditioning programs (Faigenbaum, Westcott, et al., 1996; Faigenbaum, Zaichkowsky, Westcott, Micheli & Fehlandt, 1993; Ramsey et al., 1990). Furthermore, the evidence on the use of strength training to prevent sports injury is equally convincing. According to scholars with the *American College of Sports Medicine,* as many as 50% of youth sports injuries are preventable. By strengthening the supporting structures, improving muscle performance, and increasing balance around joints, sports injuries may be avoided.

Despite the many supported benefits of youth strength training, there are still myths that surround the growing trend. Some beliefs suggest that strength training is unsafe, can damage growth plates, or cause other long term harm. Researchers have not reported any data to suggest growth plate damage due to strength training. Nor is there any published evidence of a decrease in stature in children who perform strength training in a controlled environment (Faigenbaum, 2001; Faigenbaum, Kraemer, et al., 1996; Lavallee, 2002). And interestingly, evidence suggests that strength training produces fewer injuries than many other sports such as football, basketball, baseball - and soccer (Lavallee, 2002). The misconceptions regarding youth strength training are now outdated. Well planned and supervised programs can be a safe and effective supplement to any soccer training program. Ideally, strength training should be incorporated into a dynamic soccer program, rather than just added to it. Guidelines for implementing strength training activities into youth soccer programs (and more advanced programs) will be outlined.

## Strength and Conditioning Guidelines

Most research on youth strength training and sport specific fitness emphasizes the importance of safety and proper technique. Program design should be grounded in safe practices and sound technical instruction. Several basic fitness principles should be followed in regard to program implementation (Faigenbaum & Micheli, 1998).

**Principles of Fitness.** Progression, overload and specificity are important fitness principles to follow. *Progression* suggests the building from simple to complex over time. Any safe program should start slow and progress to more sophisticated exercises and increased training volume. This holds true for strength training, as it does for soccer training. The principle of *overload* implies that an individual must train at a higher intensity than normal to elicit continued results. Essentially, an individual must go "over" their normal training level to see improvements. And lastly, the principle of *specificity* is vital for optimal training benefits. Soccer players must specifically replicate the demands of soccer in their strength and conditioning training. Often the use of specificity with a particular sport is referred to as functional training.

In addition to following these basic fitness principles, a few other general guidelines should be implemented. In order to effectively develop muscular fitness the proper environment must be created. Strength training should be cooperative, not competitive as with normal soccer training sessions. The use of simple instructions, cue words, and demonstrations are important in order to clarify proper techniques and procedures. All strength and conditioning sessions should be supervised by a qualified, responsible adult. As a coach, if you feel as though you are not familiar enough with strength and conditioning practices, read on to learn more about how to get assistance with your team or program. For those who are comfortable integrating strength and conditioning into their sessions, be sure to use a dynamic warm-up (aerobic movement and static stretching), as well as, a similar cool down. Also, coaches may want to encourage players to track their progress in a workout log or notebook. Simple charts can be found online and modified for practical use. Specific components of strength and conditioning training will be discussed.

**Strength and Conditioning Training.** Well rounded programs should include muscular strength, cardiovascular fitness (speed and agility), flexibility and dynamic sport-related movements. An effective program should utilize the FITT formula (Frequency, Intensity, Time and Type). For those familiar with typical strength training guidelines, remember to modify the expectations for children to meet their body size, experience and knowledge level.

| Strength Training Guidelines | |
| --- | --- |
| Frequency | 2-3 nonconsecutive days a week |
| Intensity | Moderate to high repetitions with low to moderate resistance (increase gradually, 5-10%) |
| Time | 1-3 sets of 8-15 repetitions of 8-12 exercises (start with 1 set of 10-15 reps) |
| Type | Body resistance exercises, free weights, other inexpensive equipment such as: steps, medicine balls, ladders, resistance bands, hoops, hurdles, jump ropes, etc. |

**Muscular Fitness.** By following the FITT formula, coaches can create well-rounded strength training programs for their players. With the 8-12 exercises, consider performing at least one exercise for each major muscle group. Focus on lower body strength, upper body strength, and core strength. Various modes of exercise can be utilized. Players can use their own body resistance in exercises such as push ups, sit ups, lunges, and Pilates. Free weights are ideal, in that they are inexpensive and highly functional, but many teams do not have access to them. If your team is able to invest in some equipment (more to come about how our club made it work), items such as steps, ladders, hoops, medicine balls, resistance bands and resistance balls are very useful. Many of these items come with lists and diagrams of suggested exercises.

**Cardiovascular Fitness.** While the focus of strength and conditioning programs isn't usually on cardiovascular fitness, it is obviously important for soccer players. It is necessary to have a solid aerobic base before moving onto speed and agility training. When running, avoid running one pace for an extended period of time. Instead, run in intervals, at different speeds and distances. Intervals are more indicative of the demands of a soccer game. Speed and agility can be developed using a number of exercises to allow change in speed, direction, and distance. Using ladders, hoops, small hurdles and jump ropes, a variety of exercises can provide improved speed and agility. Sprints which include a focus on acceleration and deceleration can be especially helpful with injury prevention. To increase the challenge level, try sprinting while holding a medicine ball (or just a soccer ball) out in front of the body or overhead. Cardiovascular exercise can be performed 3-5 times a week, while speed and agility training should be done less frequently due to the intensity.

**Flexibility.** Unfortunately, flexibility is often overlooked or emphasized at the inappropriate time. Most of us have seen soccer teams circle up and stretch prior to games and practices after little more than a jog around the field. While this is a well-intentioned practice, there is very little scientific evidence to suggest that static stretching prior to competition improves flexibility or prevents injury. The greatest gains in flexibility are made after the body is fully warmed up, which often occurs during or at the end of practices and games. Incorporating flexibility is very important for reducing injuries and optimizing performance, however it makes more sense to emphasize static stretching throughout a workout or as a part of a full cool down. Exercises for flexibility can be done anywhere from 3-7 days a week. Stretches should be held for 20 seconds and performed 1-3 times.

**Sport Related Movements.** For the creative coach, there are numerous ways to incorporate soccer movements into strength and conditioning activities. Any chance you can safely use a soccer ball to create another challenge should be taken. For instance, have players jump up on a step, then jump off and land, then volley a soccer ball, jump back up and repeat. This can be done with trapping or heading, as well. Implementing sport related movements can also help to improve the balance and coordination of players. Sport specific movements will make direct connections from training to competition, which players will enjoy.

## Implementing a Strength and Conditioning Program

With the scientific background and practical guidelines described here, coaches should have enough information to consider implementing a strength and conditioning component into their soccer programs. While the information presented here is not exhaustive, there should be enough to spark an interest. Hopefully, one or more of the coaches in a given organization have some experience or expertise in the field of exercise science. If not, encourage your organization to develop a relationship with a local college or university program. Graduate students are ideal people to work with teams and players. They are usually very enthusiastic about what they are learning academically and anxious for more practical experience. And, most graduate students appreciate an opportunity to make some extra money! With our club, we have initiated a relationship with a local college with a specialized graduate program in strength and conditioning. We were able to coordinate this with a graduate student who was an ODP and collegiate soccer player - really a perfect fit!

Prior to initiating the relationship with the local college, we started off with a small scale, in house program. Several coaches volunteered to work with players from any of our teams (U13 and up) during an eight week period during the spring season and then a six week summer session. We charged the players a reasonable fee and put all of the income toward purchasing equipment for our club. We were able to buy steps, ladders, hoops, medicine balls, resistance bands and jump ropes. We had players pay for their own resistance balls because they are large and difficult to store. Since the resistance balls are inexpensive and very functional, we wanted to include them in our program. In our first year we were able to involve a number of players from our club and most of my own team. Although our program is still small, the opportunity to expand is large. We're already brainstorming about what to offer next to better our club, improve soccer performance and reduce the likelihood of injuries. With the right people and a positive direction, similar programs are possible in any number of soccer settings. Plenty of informational resources are available with a few phone calls and some online homework. Best wishes for stronger and healthier soccer teams!

## References

Faigenbaum, A. (2001). Strength training and children's health, *Journal of Physical Education Recreation and Dance, 72*(3), 24-30.

Faigenbaum, A., Kraemer, W., Cahill, B., Chandler, J., Dziados, J., Elfrink, L., Forman, E., Gaudiose, M., Micheli, L., Nitka, M., & Roberts, S. (1996). Youth resistance training: Position statement paper and literature review. *Strength and Conditioning Journal, 18*(6), 62-75.

Faigenbaum, A., & Micheli, L. (1998). *Youth strength training,* Current comment from the American College of Sports Medicine.

Faigenbaum, A., Westcott, W., Micheli, L., Outerbridge, A., Long, C., LaRosa Loud, R., & Zaichkowsky, L. (1996). The effects of strength training and detraining on children. *Journal of Strength and Conditioning Research, 10,* 109-114.

Faigenbaum, A., Zaichkowsky, L., Westcott, W., Micheli, L., & Fehlandt, A. (1993). The effects of twice-per-week strength training program on children. *Pediatric Exercise Science, 5,* 339-346.

Lavallee, M. (2002). Strength training in children and adolescents, Current comment from the American College of Sports Medicine.

Ramsey, J., Blimkie, C., Smith, K., Garner, S., Macdougall, J., & Sale, D. (1990). Strength-training effects in the prepubescent boys. *Medicine and Science in Sports and Exercise, 22,* 605-614.

# Improving Speed in Training

## Michael R. Thyron

As in most sports, movement speed or tempo or pace, as it is called in modern soccer, has become increasingly faster over the past few years. In part, this is because modern players can run faster, execute technical skills quicker and make tactical decisions better.

Speed, or lack of it, is directly responsible for many games being won or lost. It is not uncommon to hear coaches complain about their players not being fast enough.

"If only my defender was just a step faster" or "We do not have anybody fast enough to mark their forward" are typical comments from coaches. What, then, is soccer speed, and how does a coach or trainer improve it? The following defines and describes the various components of soccer speed as recognized in Germany.

Soccer speed can be defined as the ability to react to a stimulus in the least amount of time through cyclical or acyclical movements with limited resistance. Explained another way, soccer speed is a complex mixture of psychophysical components. These components include perception, anticipation, decision-making, reactions, movement at maximum speed without a ball, actions with a ball and reading the game. All of these components are interrelated and have a significant influence on the speed of the soccer player.

During a soccer game, each player is bombarded with countless pieces of visual and auditory stimuli. While this information is coming in, each player has to process it and ultimately make a decision from a variety of choices depending on a particular situation. The ability to do so is called perceptual speed.

**Perceptual speed** is enhanced through playing experience. For example, an experienced player can make a quick decision on what to do with an incoming ball before it is received. All that is needed is a quick glance. By comparison, an inexperienced player has to concentrate on the flight of the ball, and because of this, is unable to see other options. It is often too late to do something constructive with the ball once it is received.

Like perceptual speed, **anticipation speed** is also strongly influenced by playing experience. Anticipation is the athlete's ability to predict the probability and the end result of a situation. Because they can predict what will happen, they can execute a desired action. The more playing experience an individual has, the better able he/she is to pick up clues and predict what is going to happen. For example, the experienced player shows his/her ability to anticipate a situation by being in the right place at the right time with no wasted effort. By contrast, inexperienced players either get to a situation too quickly or too late. Because of this, they must react to make up for their lack of or abundance of anticipation. Finally, a good soccer player is always "on the ball" during a soccer game, even when without the ball. Only through constant reading of the game can a player's ability to anticipate be improved. So many goal attempts in soccer fail to score because players with the opportunity to shoot and score wait too long and are unable to quickly decide what to do, wasting a scoring chance. This typical situation reveals that perceptions alone are not enough.

After analyzing a situation, players must decide what to do. This ability is called **decision making speed.** Decision making is related to the complexity of the situation. The more complex, the longer processing takes, thus slowing the decision. Kicking the ball with the dominant leg is an example of a simple process that has a short decision making time. Dealing with balls on the non-dominant foot, on the other hand, is more complex and slows the decision making process.

Like anticipation speed and perceptual speed, decision making speed improves with experience. For example, if a center forward is given the opportunity to deal with crosses from a variety of angles, over time his/her ability to make quicker decisions will improve. Decision making is also influenced by one's disposition. Some people enjoy making decisions, whereas others hesitate and squander any opportunities to do so. Experienced players need less information to make quick decisions, whereas inexperienced players require more information, thus resulting in a slower decision making process.

**Reaction speed** is another important component of soccer speed. Reaction speed is the ability to react to a previously performed action or stimulus. An example is trying to save the ball after it has just been shot on goal. Every position from the goalkeeper to the forward relies on the ability to save or score potential goals at some point.

Reaction speed training therefore is an important component in the development of the individual soccer player. Reaction speed is influenced by many factors such as type of reaction, sex, age, constitution, motivation, emotions, intensity of the stimulus, fitness, time of day, fatigue, amount of sleep and muscles involved.

Reaction training should be done after a thorough warm-up and while the players are still fresh, such as at the beginning of the training session. Reaction training should focus on quality and not quantity in order to see heightened performance take place. Finally, reaction speed is better in individuals who have a good basic

level of aerobic fitness. As individuals become fatigued, reaction speed slows.

Along with reaction speed, **movement speed** is perhaps the single most important quality that a soccer player can possess. Movement speed can be divided into two types, cyclical and acyclical. Cyclical movements differ from acyclical movements because they are continuous and require space. Examples are running for loose balls, eluding markers and explosive starts. In contrast, acyclical movements are single action movements, such as sudden stops, body fakes, tackles, jumps, turns and changes of direction.

Cyclical movement speed can be divided into three types. The first is starting speed. This is the most important type for the soccer player. The ability to get to the ball first, on defense or offense, is the surest way to achieve success. Most movements in soccer require the ability to accelerate. Studies have shown that soccer players run between 40 and 100 sprints in a game. The majority of them are up to a distance of 25 meters. The most common distance is the first five meters. Game analysis has shown that this distance was sprinted twice as much as any other distance.

A second type of cyclical movement speed is sprint endurance, which is the ability to execute quick starts throughout the game with little or no sign of fatigue. Sprint endurance is directly related to recovery and is influenced by several factors such as muscle fiber type, enzymatic activity in the muscle and aerobic conditioning level.

The last type of cyclical movement speed is speed endurance, which is the ability to run at maximum speed for extended periods without any noticeable signs of fatigue. An example is the 200-meter dash to the 400-meter dash in track and field. This is the least important of the cyclical movements for soccer and should be cautiously utilized during training.

In contrast to movement speed, **action speed** involves the ball. Action speed emphasizes the coordination and technical components of soccer-specific speed. During the run of play, the next action of the ball is how the individual perceives the situation. Anticipation, decision making and reactions also come into play when carrying out action speed. In addition, the faster the ball moves, the less accurate the ability to manipulate it. This has definite consequences for training and should be worked on in the form of complex technical/tactical games and exercises which improve this ability.

The final component of soccer speed is **game action speed**, which is the most complex form and relies on all the other components for its execution. It is the ability to make fast, effective decisions during the game in relation to technical, tactical and conditioning possibilities. The ability to process information during a game quickly is individual and can vary within the same player depending on the level of play. Game action speed is concerned with doing the right thing at the right time. Finally, game action speed is influenced by motivational factors and emotions.

In conclusion, seven distinct types of soccer speed exist. Once they are understood by a coach or trainer, plans to improve them can occur more efficiently. Hopefully, the grumbling coaches who fear that speed is only a gift from God will realize that improvement is possible. An athlete's speed performance can and should be improved by using both physical and psychological measures. Training to improve technique, tactics, motivational factors and experience contributes to speed success and should be employed to give an edge that the athlete may not naturally possess.

*Editor's note: This article originally appeared in the newsletter Performance Conditioning for Soccer (Vol. 3, No. 8). Coach Thyron is the boys coach at Prairie High School, Brush Prairie, Wash.*

# Off-Season Conditioning for Soccer

## Bob Bradley
## US Men's National Team

*US Men's National Team coach offers a word of advice to soccer players about the importance of off season conditioning.*

If you want to impress your coach when team practices start up again in the fall, make good use of the summer. The long break between the spring and fall seasons is the time to train smarter and more consistently than the players you will be competing against for a spot on the team, the starting 11, or the opposition.

Your primary objective during this time should be to increase your soccer-specific conditioning level and to keep your skills sharp. Following are some guidelines for off-season training for soccer.

## Aerobic Exercise

Aerobic fitness is the foundation of soccer-specific fitness. Without a strong cardiovascular system, you won't have enough energy to play hard through an entire practice or game. The best way to build aerobic fitness is through sustained, moderate intensity movement. Two workouts per week lasting 30 minutes each is a minimum for increasing aerobic fitness. You can run, bicycle, swim, or do any of a number of other activities that you enjoy. If you run, make sure you have good running shoes. And if you have access to mulched trails, by all means use them, as this will reduce wear and tear on your lower extremities.

## Intervals

Soccer involves shorter, high-intensity movements than sustained, moderate-intensity movements. For this reason, off-season soccer conditioning should include some interval running. The basic format for an interval running workout is an easy jogging warm-up followed by several high-speed running efforts separated by short rests, and finally a jogging cool-down. In general, the high-intensity intervals (not sprints) should last 15 to 30 seconds. The rest periods should be 2-3 times run time when first starting out; as you gain fitness, reduce the rest periods until they are equal to the run times.

These workouts increase a player's ability to recover between periods of hard running and play during games, so you're not spent after the first half. One to two interval workouts per week would be adequate. You can combine aerobic exercise and intervals by extending your warm-up and/or cool-down or just alternate days (i.e. aerobic training on Mondays and Wednesdays, intervals on Tuesdays and Thursdays).

## Speed & Agility Work

Raw sprint speed is also an important ability in soccer. But soccer-specific speed is a little different from the kind of speed you need for track, because soccer requires quick changes of speed and direction (about every 5-6 seconds in a game), plus dribbling or kicking on the run. To develop your soccer speed, first of all do a few short sprints of up to 40 yards, some straight, others with sudden changes in direction. Try all kinds of different start positions, from standing to kneeling to facing backwards.

Running straight ahead trains you to run straight. So, do some sprints while dribbling the ball changing directions and speed frequently. Lastly, do some agility drills, like creating a "slalom" course with cones or other markers and sprinting through it. If you neglect agility work, you will be quite sore after the initial sessions when you arrive to camp.

## Strength Training

Soccer players need strength for the many physical challenges the game demands. I recommend that soccer players emphasize "functional" exercises that strengthen movement patterns rather than individual muscles. The lunge is functional; the biceps curl is not. Be sure to work on the whole body and not just the legs. Also, keep in mind that you need to strength train at least twice a week to see results.

## Stretching

Stretching improves your flexibility and agility and helps prevent injuries. An active warm-up with some stretching is a good way to begin practice. A cool-down involving more sustained stretching is very important at the end of the training session. The really serious flexibility training is done after the workout. Soccer players need to give special attention to their hamstrings, quadriceps, groin muscles, and calves.

## Ball Work

Do you remember those Nike TV commercials that show a player juggling a ball during his morning routine at home (showering, eating breakfast, etc.), beginning the moment he wakes up? Admittedly, this is a little extreme, but there is something to be said for spending a lot of time playing around with a soccer ball. No matter what position you play, it is important that you have a high level of "feel" for the ball, and feel comes from nothing else but accumulating experience with a ball on your foot (all parts of it), not to mention your thighs, chest and head (and hands, if you're a goalkeeper).

Now, there are plenty of people who can juggle, but can't play a lick of soccer. But it is very rare to see a good player who can't juggle. Looking for some tricks? Visit Nike's soccer web site. There are over 50 clips of juggling tricks sent in from around the world, even from Ronaldinho. Go to nikefootball.com, click on the little arrow next to the 5 small screens at the bottom until the screen 'showdown' appears, then click it for dozens of clips of players showing their best stuff (the first clip is amazing). You never know until you try. Young basketball players are often much better about messing around with the ball on their own than young soccer players. Follow their example!

Juggling is one good way to develop ball feel. But even better is kicking the ball against a wall and playing rebounds in different ways. The best thing about this type of practice is that most players enjoy it. A 4-wall handball court is also a fun venue for this type of practice. Make up games: modify handball rules, all walls, no hands and a ball. To speed it up and make it harder, use a #3 ball.

## Scrimmaging

There is no substitute for playing the game. If you were to do only one kind of training for soccer, it would have to be scrimmaging. Game opportunities may be limited during the summer, but even a game of two-on-two with a few friends in your neighborhood is better than nothing. The only fitness drawback to pickup games is the relatively low intensity of play compared to your competitive team. But because there is little pressure to perform, you can try out new moves and tactics.

## A Note about Nutrition

Most youth players fail to take full advantage of all that is known about fueling muscles before, during and after exercise. Players should use only a quality sports drink to supply all of their body's hydration, energy, and nutrition needs while working out and playing. Water does not replace the vital electrolytes lost in sweat nor does it provide energy. Other drinks such as sodas and fruit juices do not provide energy in its fastest-acting or most digestible form.

A good sport drink with its electrolytes will hydrate players faster than water alone and provides plenty of carbohydrates to fuel the muscles and delay fatigue. Remember, most goals happen late in the game. But not all sports drinks are the same. A new generation of sports drinks based on the latest exercise nutrition research also contains some protein that has been proven to deliver energy to the muscles even faster than a conventional sports drink, resulting in better endurance. The ideal ratio of carbs to protein is 4:1.

In a University of Texas study, a 4:1 carbohydrate-protein sports drink (Accelerade) was found to increase endurance by 24% more than a conventional sports drink and by 57% more than plain water. Sports drinks with protein also accelerate recovery between workouts. In a Springfield College study, two groups of athletes drank either a carbohydrate-protein sports drink or a regular sports drink during a 90-minute rest between a hard bike ride and a run to exhaustion. The athletes in the carbohydrate -protein group lasted, on average, 21 % longer in the second workout.

## Summary

As in any other sport, the recipe for success in soccer is equal parts talent and preparation. There's not much you can do about talent, but there is a lot you can do to prepare. By training smarter and more consistently than other players (and fueling your training properly) during the off-season, you can move ahead of them while they're not looking.

*Bob Bradley was head coach at Ohio University, Princeton University, the Metro Stars, Chivas and is now the head men's national team coach for the United States*

# The Problem of Over-Competition

## Dr. Don Kirkendall

There is an old quote often attributed to Mark Twain that goes something like this: "Everyone talks about the weather, but no one does anything about it" (Actually it's supposed to have originated with one Charles Dudley Warner). The soccer equivalent might be: "Our kids are playing too much" but no one seems to be reducing the number of games the kids are playing.

Most of the problems are isolated to the traveling teams; the elite teams, not the recreational leagues. The opportunities for competition are staggering. Soccer magazines and websites carry an ever increasing number of competitions for any age group in all areas of the country. By the time you add up all the league matches, cups, school matches and tournaments, a player might be playing in 80-100 games a year.

A team manager was heard saying something like, "We have to do it to be competitive. Hey, that's what the pros are doing." Are they? Is that a good comparison? A 17-year-old in the US should not to be compared to a Brazilian professional. While a team like Arsenal might have 80 matches a year, they do this with a squad of 35-40 first line players. Sao Paulo FC can have well over 80 matches a year, but they carry over 40 players on their squad. This is quite different with "AnyTown FC U18" playing 80 games a year with 18 players if they are lucky. The pros rotate players. You can't buy a ticket for any random Real Madrid league match and guarantee seeing Beckham, Figo, Zidane, Roberto Carlos, AND Ronaldo play that day.

The pros are different. It's a business and the owners are not making any money if the turnstiles aren't turning. The Champions League is to feature the best against the best, right? Don't forget the TV contract and ticket sales that, on a per match basis, far exceed the take from the domestic leagues. But youth clubs? OK, teams sponsor tournaments as a fund raiser. It may be their biggest fund raiser of the year. So, tournaments are not all bad. But how many tournaments does one have to go to?

A national staff coach was asked a question regarding player development. What was most important? Training or competing? The coach responded by saying that training was about development, where players learned and practiced new skills and tactics. Matches were about applying that development. The coach continued that so many clubs will train 2-3 times a week and that in the upcoming tournament may play two games on Saturday and two on Sunday. Will each player play to their ability or will they pace themselves to conserve energy for all the games? Players will play more conservatively to avoid mistakes that might knock them out of contention. Generally, the tournaments selected are outside of the league season when players might not be in league fitness meaning the players will pace themselves even more. At least the injury reports from tournaments haven't shown more injuries than in season. Tom Turner in Ohio observed that, "The only time the players get any rest is when they are injured.." An aside about tournaments, like the NY Marathon, once a tournament gets scheduled, lightening is about the only thing that will alter the match schedule. In the mid 1990's, the USA Cup in Blaine, MN was played in oppressive heat and humidity. Only after the medical staff threatened a walkout did the organizers shorten the games leading to reduced heat illnesses.

An interesting thing happened in the 1992 European Championships. Denmark was the last team eliminated in the qualification rounds. Then Yugoslavia was excluded at the last minute and Denmark's team was assembled 10 days before the opening match. Half the players had been off training for 3-5 weeks, but not inactive...they did their normal off-season workouts. The other half was still playing in the domestic Danish league. The entire team was together for only 6 days. And Denmark won. A lack of staleness and mental fatigue was considered to be a primary factor in Denmark's run to the title.

Sepp Blatter, the president of FIFA, has thrown his considerable influence into the concept of over-competition. He has suggested that club matches be limited to about 60 per year. Mr. Blatter was concerned over what he thought was poor form by some teams and players at the 2002 FIFA World Cup®.

He wasn't alone. UEFA commissioned a study of the 2001-2002 domestic season as it led up to the World Cup and then the performances of the European players in the World Cup. Ekstrand J, M Walden, M Hagglund studied a congested football calendar and the well-being of players as correlated between match exposures of the players before the World Cup 2002 and their injuries and performance during that World Cup.

The authors had two basic observations. First, while there is considerable variation in the number of matches per season, top level players will play in a congested calendar at the end of the season that precedes the World Cup (in some leagues, players had 2 weeks or less between their league and the World Cup push). Second, match congestion can lead to physical and mental fatigue leading to underperformance.

The interesting figure is the training : match ratio. Many clubs that train 2/week and play 2 matches on a weekend for a 1:1 ratio, or train twice for 1 game a weekend for a 2:1 ratio. Scholastic teams sometimes do better. Colleges have their own limits because the NCAA puts restrictions on matches, season length, and coaching contacts. Development comes from practice. Before the 2001 season, The UEFA researchers selected 14 of the top European clubs (of the Arsenal, Man Utd, Real Madrid, Juventus quality) and got full participation from 11 clubs. Attendance records at training and matches were recorded for 1 year (July 2001-July 2002). A common definition of injury was followed and all rehabilitation was recorded. There were 266 players in the project and 65 played in the World Cup. Each national team continued keeping the injury records during preparation and competition. Three former national team coaches from Europe reviewed World Cup game tapes and rated the 65 player's performance as over, normal, or underperformance for each World Cup match. Here are some of the findings:

- Soccer exposure was 70,000 hrs (58,000 training and 12,000 competing)
  - That's 5 hrs of training for every hour competing
- Matches ranged from 46-70
  - Obviously, teams that played more, trained less
- The 266 players averaged 175 training sessions and 36 matches (a 4.8:1 training : match ratio)
  - Players in the World Cup played an added 10 matches
  - The training : match ratio now dropped to 3.9:1
- The overall rate of injury for the World Cup players was less than for the non-World Cup players (3.2 v 5.5 per 1000 hrs of exposure). However, the match injury rate was not different between groups.
- The last 10 weeks of the season was of interest. National team players played more often (.97 matches/week in the first 36 weeks vs 1.12/week in the last 10 weeks). The non-World Cup players played fewer games.

- The 65 players played an average of 11 matches in the last 10 weeks of the season
- 29% of the World Cup players were injured during the World Cup
- 32% 'underperformed' during the World Cup

- these players averaged 12.4 matches in the final 10 weeks of the season.
- Those players that performed 'above expectations' played an average of 9 matches in the final 10 weeks of the season.
- The players who performed 'above expectations' played 25% fewer matches leading up to the World Cup than those who played 'below expectations.'
- Of the 65 World Cup players, 61% played more than 1 game per week in the last 10 weeks of the season and 2/3 of this group either underperformed or suffered an injury.

# ACL Injury Prevention:
# Why it should be on Every Coaches "To Do" List

## Lynn Pantuosco Hensch

What do professional soccer player Brandy Chastain, basketball player Rebecca Lobo, and beach volleyball player Liz Masakayan all have in common? If you answered, an ACL injury you were correct. In addition to these high profile names, most soccer coaches can list off the names of a number of their own players who have also injured an ACL (Anterior Cruciate Ligament). While it is the injuries of professional athletes that we hear most about in the media - the overall numbers are staggering.

Did you know that 1 in 10 female collegiate athletes will injure their ACL this year? Or that 1 in 100 female high school athletes will injure an ACL, as well? These ratios result in 2,200 female collegiate athletes with ACL injuries and thousands more at the high school level. The NCAA ACL injury rates are highest for women in basketball and soccer. And although females are 4-6 times more likely to injure an ACL than males, the number of male injuries continues to increase, as well.

As coaches, there is no doubt that we already have too much to do, in too little time. Yet in light of the increasing ACL injury rates, I challenge coaches to add one more important task to their "to do" lists, which is ACL injury prevention. The purpose of this article is to give an overview of what an ACL is, how knee injuries occur, and why females are more susceptible to these injuries than males. And more importantly, the article will provide preventative strategies for use with your players and teams.

## What is an ACL Injury?

The ACL is one of the four ligaments within the knee. The ACL crosses from underneath the femur (thigh bone) to the top of the tibia (shin bone). It serves as the primary restraint to forward motion of the tibia and contributes to the overall stability of the knee. Unfortunately, ACL injuries have become all too common in soccer, especially for women.

An ACL injury occurs from contact or non-contact. Most injuries are non-contact (over 75%). When asked about the professional athletes previously mentioned, if you knew that all three women experienced non-contact ACL injuries you really aced the quiz. The non-contact injuries are typically a result of inappropriate cutting, jumping/landing, pivoting, or even just running (acceleration/deceleration), which causes excessive rotational force to the knee.

Common symptoms of an ACL tear include: sudden giving way of the knee; hearing a "pop" at the time of injury; sudden swelling of the knee; and pain in the knee when walking (Cluett, 2005). And while recognizing the symptoms of ACL injuries is useful, the more valuable skill is in preventing these injuries from happening in the first place. Before establishing a prevention program it is necessary to understand why ACL injuries occur and why females are at a greater risk.

## Risk Factors Contributing to ACL Injuries

Researchers have established a number of risk factors that set females a part from males in terms of ACL injuries. The risk factors are body types, hormonal differences, body positioning, and muscle imbalances (Ahmad, et al, 2006; Hayward, 2001; Hewett et al, 2006; Moeller, et al, 1997). Each risk factor will be described in brief:

- **Body Types.** Women generally have a smaller intercondylar notch in the knee (place where ACL passes through the joint). Therefore, because of smaller, narrower knees, less stress is needed to tear ligaments in a female knee compared to that of a larger male knee. In general, females have wider hips then men and tend to rotate them more which places females at great risk for injuries.

- **Hormonal Differences.** Hormonal changes during the menstrual cycle lead to muscle tissue becoming more elastic than at other times for women. Studies have shown that estrogen levels may affect ligament laxity for some women.

- **Upright Body Position.** Females tend to bend their knees less during typical soccer and athletic movements compared with males. Females are more apt to land flat footed and with straight legs compared with males, who are more likely to have soft landings. Overall, women play soccer and other sports with a more erect posture than males which increases the risk for injury.

- **Muscle Imbalances.** Males and females have stronger quadriceps than hamstrings. But with females the muscle imbalance tends to be greater (>quadriceps and < hamstring strength). Female athletes have been shown to utilize hamstring muscles less than male athletes, resulting in improper movements and greater occurrence of injuries.

## Research on Gender Differences

A wide variety of research has been conducted to explore the gender differences which put females at greater risk for knee injuries compared with males. Interestingly, a study done with the UNC Chapel Hill men's and women's soccer teams, resulted in similar gender differences. The female soccer players flexed and recruited the muscles around the knee differently from the males. According to researcher Michael DiStefano, "the females had more erect posture, rotated their hips more, and had more quadriceps flexion than the males when performing the maneuvers" (DiStefano, 2004). The conclusion was that these ACL related gender differences were not influenced by the skill level of the soccer players. If the talented Carolina women are at risk, so are our female soccer players!

## Factors Athletes Can Control

Athletes cannot control genetics and anatomical structure (body type, hormones, etc.), but other risk factors may be altered. Both muscle imbalances and upright body position can be changed through proper training. Newer research suggests that preventative training can significantly reduce the number of non-contact ACL injuries (Myer, et. al, 2004; 2006; Wilkerson, et al, 2004).

## ACL Injury Prevention Programs

Available research supports ACL injury prevention programs, but the exact protocols are still up for debate. While experts suggest a variety of exercise prescriptions, there are some common themes and guidelines that tend to hold true across various protocols. Experts agree that learning proper techniques and patterns to avoid unnecessary stress on knees is paramount to any successful injury prevention program. Other important concepts include learning to jump, land, pivot, and run properly. Several primary components should be the basis for an injury prevention program, including core strength, leg strength and balance.

- **Core strength.** Develop a strong trunk of the body to improve stability. Various exercises using physio balls, Pilates, or abdominal exercises can build core strength. The stronger the core, the better the all around support of the body will be, especially in competitive soccer.

- **Leg strength.** Create balance in quadriceps/ hamstring strength. In order to build leg strength and create muscular balance, exercises which involve the hamstrings are key. Jumping programs such as plyometrics (explosive jumping movements) involving, boxes, hoops, and agility ladders can be helpful. Resistance bands are also a practical, inexpensive tool to incorporate. For those with access to more sophisticated equipment, weight training which focuses on hamstring strength and safe, lateral movements can be very valuable. Exercises such as lunges (which can be done without equipment) can be worked into any soccer program. Lunges with both legs, in forward, backward, side and diagonal directions are an inclusive set of exercises to add to any practice.

- **Balance.** Training for balance, agility and coordination will increase dynamic balance. Exercises which require shifting balance, direction, and speed are helpful. These types of movements can be done with or without a soccer ball. Simple equipment such as hoops, ladders and boxes can be utilized.

## ACL Exercise Guidelines

Well rounded programs should include muscular strength, balance, and dynamic sport-related movements. Injury prevention programs should promote motor control and body awareness with players. Exercises such as plyometrics are valuable, but should be used with caution. An effective program implements a variety of exercises, including:

- Exercises that promote a "ready position" with bent knees and light feet
- Exercises that require one leg at a time
- Exercises that require changing direction
- Exercises that require acceleration and deceleration
- Exercises that involve shifting balance
- Exercises that encourage soft landings

## Outlook on ACL Injury Prevention

The bottom line with ACL injury prevention is that something can be done to reduce the alarming injury rates. Researchers suggest that injury prevention programs and exercises are advantageous. Current research is in progress which should specify which types of programs, protocols, and exercise prescriptions are most effective for injury prevention. For example, U.S. Soccer team physician, Dr. Bert Mandelbaum leads the group which created the Prevent Injury/ Enhance Performance (PEP) program for knee injury prevention in southern California. The PEP program requires a 15 minute routine, consisting of a warm-up, stretching, strengthening, plyometrics, and sports specific agilities, which is performed 2-3 times per week. A comparative study showed a dramatic reduction in injury rates for female soccer players who utilized the PEP training during 2000 (88%) and 2001 (74%) (www.aafla.org/3ce/acl_frmst.htm). Longitudal outcomes will be helpful for future program design. Other studies suggest significant changes may occur in as little as 6-8 weeks of training, which is reassuring for the busy soccer coach (Hewett, 2000). In essence, learning proper movement techniques is vital. And like any other soccer technique taught, players will need plenty of repetition before mastery. Coaches can fight the odds of ACL injury by being proactive in terms of education and prevention.

# REFERENCES

Ahmad, C., Clark, A., Hellmann, N., Schoeb, J., Gardner, T. & Levine, W. (2006). Effect of gender and maturity on quadriceps-to-hamstring strength ratio and anterior cruciate ligament laxity. *The American Journal of Sports Medicine, 34*(3), 370-375.

Cluett, J. (2005). ACL Injury. Orthopedics, http://orthopedics.about.com/cs/aclrepain/a/acl.htm

DiStefano, M. (2004). *Comparison of trunk, hip and knee kinematics during a side-step cutting maneuver between male and female Division I collegiate soccer players.* Kinesiology Publications.

Hayward, R. (2001). ACL injuries: Why more prevalent in women? *Journal of the American Academy of Physicians Assistants, 14*, 38-40, 43-45.

Hewett, T. (2000). Neuromuscular and hormonal factors associated with knee injuries in female athletes: Strategies for intervention. *Sports Medicine, 29*, 313-327.

Hewett, T., Myer, G. & Ford, K. (2006). Anterior cruciate ligament injuries in female athletes: Part 1, mechanisms and risk factors. *American Journal of Sports Medicine, 34*(2). 299-311.

Hewett, T., Stroupe, A., & Noyes, F. (1996). Plyometric training in female athlete: Decreased impact forces and increased hamstring torques, *American Journal of Sports Medicine, 24*, 765-773.

Moeller, J. & Lamb, M. (1997). ACL Injuries in female athletes: Why are women more susceptible? The Physician and Sports Medicine, 25(4), http://www.physsportsmed.com/issues/1997/04apr/moeller.htm

Myer, G., Ford, K. & Brent, Jensen, L. (2006). The effects of plyometric vs. dynamic stabilization and balance training on power, balance, and landing forces in female athletes. *The Journal of Strength and Conditioning Research, 20*(2), 345-353.

Myer, G., Ford, K. & Hewett, T. (2004). Rationale and clinical techniques for anterior cruciate ligament injury prevention among female athletes. *Journal of Athletic Training, 39*(4), 352-364.

Sullivan, D. (2001). On mended knee: In the past decade 1.4 million female athletes have suffered ACL injuries – twice as many in the previous 10 years. Are you next? Not if we can help it. *Sports Illustrated for Women, 3*(1), 62-67.

Wakeham, T. (2004). Knee injuries: The major problem of female athletes and how to prevent them. *Coach and Athletic Director, 73*(7), 64-68.

Wilkerson, G., Colston, M., Short, N., Neal, K., Hoewischer, P. & Pixley, J. (2004). Neuromuscular changes in female collegiate athletes resulting from a plyometric jump-training program. *Journal of Athletic Training, 39*(1), 17-23.

# Proper Feeding

**Dr. Lynn Pantuosco Hensch**
**Westfield State College**

Youth, club, and high school soccer is more demanding than ever. Practices and games are longer, more frequent and more intense than in years past. In light of the increasing demands on young soccer players, coaches, parents, and players alike are doing all they can to keep up with the competition.

| Game Day Nutrition | |
|---|---|
| Before | √ Hydrate with water |
| 2 – 4 hours | √ Small carbohydrate rich meal<br>√ Avoid fiber, caffeine, fats<br>√ Continue hydration |
| 1 – 2 hours | √ Snack and fluids |
| Minutes Before | √ 1 – 2 cups water |
| During | √ Water every 15 – 20 minutes |
| After | √ Carbohydrate rich meal<br>√ Replenish lost fluids |

Believe it or not, the nutrition of your players can make a significant difference on the soccer field. Strong nutritional habits can help fight fatigue longer and improve recovery rates for soccer players. It is likely that players are not achieving peak performance, in part because of poor nutrition.

Although images of young players drinking Gatorade or eating PowerBars at halftime or after practice are quite common, what do players really know about sport nutrition? While players and coaches may have some knowledge about sport nutrition, many are unfamiliar with the science of successful sport nutrition. Soccer players should

be educated about the relationship between nutrition and performance. Nutrition, coupled with proper training, just might make that vital difference in the final minutes of play.

## Not the Same as Adults

Given the mainstream adult world full of fad diets, supplements and other nutritional products, it is important to remember that what may work for adults doesn't necessarily apply to children. It also is critical for professionals and parents alike to recognize that despite the sophisticated nature of some youth soccer programs, children are not miniature professionals. Young soccer players have specific needs and concerns, especially when it comes to nutrition.

For example, children lose more electrolytes in their sweat, dissipate heat differently, are impacted more severely by dehydration (higher core temperature) and have a higher energy cost for activity than adults (3, 4, 5). Also, the nutritional needs of children and adolescents are some of the highest of any sporting subgroup because of both the demands of sport and those of growth and development.

Interestingly, limited information is available on the nutritional needs of children in sport. Many of the research methods commonly used with adults are not justified for use with children. From the existing data on adults, scientists theorize that energy and nutrient needs increase with exercise training in young athletes. Young athletes have to meet the needs of their training in addition to those of regular daily living. The relevant, available nutrition information for youth soccer players will be highlighted here. Practical suggestions for coaches will be provided. Sport nutrition knowledge can be another successful strategy in your coaching playbook.

## Energy in, Energy out

As any nutrition expert would attest, it's all about calories in and calories out. Caloric balance is important, especially for soccer players. Young soccer players expend more energy while moving than their older counterparts due to their inadequate coordination and relaxation of muscle contractions.

Did you know that an average-sized boy or girl burns more than 500 calories during 90 minutes of competitive soccer? The USDA recommends 2,000 calories a day for girls who are active for at least 60 minutes a day and 2,200 calories for equally active boys (13). Some estimates suggest that young athletes require 500-1,000 calories more than the basic nutritional guidelines suggested for inactive children (8). The calorie requirements are clearly more significant for soccer players than the typical sedentary child. However, it is how and when those calories are obtained that is more important for enhanced performance.

## Nutrients

**Carbohydrates** As a coach from an Italian-American family, I am the first to promote a team pasta dinner; however, the notion of "carb loading" prior to competition for youth soccer players is not as necessary as is typically thought. It is more important to focus on quality carbohydrate selection every day, not just on game day. As in older athletes, carbohydrates are considered a valuable source for energy during sporting events. Carbohydrates can enhance performance by fueling the muscles.

Studies have shown that consuming carbohydrates before and during exercise can improve endurance and maintain blood glucose concentration and sparing of muscle glycogen in adults (3). For young athletes, it is suggested that approximately

Nutritious Snacks On The Go...

√ Whole grain bagel
√ Whole grain cereal
√ Nuts (low salt)
√ Seeds
√ Low fat yogurt
√ Low fat cheese
√ Fruits (berries, melons)
√ Vegetables (& low fat dip)
√ Peanut butter with whole grain crackers
√ Real fruit juices

50 to 60 percent of total energy intake come from carbohydrate sources (1, 7, 12). Selecting "good carbs" such as whole grain breads and cereals, rice, pasta, vegetables and legumes can make the real difference. Avoiding simple carbohydrates such as soda and pre-packaged snacks, which are full of empty calories, and refined sugar, is equally important for athletic performance (11).

**Protein** Maintaining the appropriate balance between energy and protein intake is critical for growth and development of all children. Studies have shown that protein needs for active children and adolescents may be as high as two times the recommended daily allowance (10). Protein is an essential nutrient for cell growth, maintenance and repair, especially prior to and during adolescence. Protein also is used as an auxiliary fuel source during exercise.

Young athletes are recommended to consume 15 to 20 percent of energy intake from protein (typically 1g/kg body weight/day) (10, 11). However, be cautious, as too much protein can result in too few carbohydrates and too much fat, which ultimately hinders athletic performance (6). In order to obtain the suggested amount of protein, soccer players should utilize high quality sources such as lean meats, poultry, fish, low-fat dairy products, nuts and seeds (11). Protein supplementation is rarely necessary for young athletes.

**Fat** Surprisingly, children and adolescents use more fat and less carbohydrates than adults during prolonged exercise. Fats are considered a major source of energy during competitive soccer. The role of fat is to form the structural part of cell membranes and be a precursor to several hormones. Young athletes are advised to consume less than 30 percent of their total calories from fat. Specifically, soccer players should focus on consuming unsaturated fats while avoiding the more harmful saturated and trans fats. Unsaturated fat is found in vegetable oils and other plant-based products. Examples include peanut butter, nuts, seeds and reduced fat cheeses (11).

**Vitamins and minerals:** As with adults, children likely will consume enough vitamins and minerals in a normal, well-balanced diet. Parents and coaches should encourage players to consume a wide variety of wholesome foods. A balanced diet will provide sufficient quantities of important vitamins such as calcium, iron, folic acid and zinc (6). If a deficiency is observed, children are recommended to adjust their diets rather than consume supplemental vitamins or minerals (7). In general, a multi-vitamin is helpful, but not necessary.

In particular, iron and calcium are of concern for young athletes. Iron carries oxygen to the muscles. Iron deficiency may cause symptoms such as chronic fatigue, lethargy, elevated resting pulse, mood change, decreased appetite, headaches, muscle cramps and nausea – all of which hinder performance. While iron supplementation is unnecessary, it is helpful to be aware of the symptoms should they arise so iron levels may be restored. As many know, another important

mineral for young athletes is calcium. As players enter adolescence, calcium becomes increasingly important. Calcium reduces the risks of low bone density, irregular menstruation and stress fractures during soccer.

## Are Supplements Necessary?

Nutritional supplementation is not recommended for young athletes (4, 9). The human body does not know if nutrients are coming from expensive supplements or as part of a balanced diet. Encourage players and parents to save their money and put it toward wholesome, nutrient-dense foods. Due to the lack of long-term scientific research findings, supplements should be used by children only after consulting a dietician, physician or other professional. Some nutritional supplements can be effective in cases of deficiencies, special needs or other circumstances.

## Before, During, After Competition

Once players have an understanding of their energy demands, caloric needs and nutrient requirements, it is time to put theory into practice. There are some simple competition-related nutritional guidelines that can help soccer players maximize their training and boost their performance.

**Before competition:** Players should consume a carbohydrate rich meal two to four hours before competition. Closer to game time (within two hours), a snack and fluids are helpful. Most young athletes need at least one to two cups of water prior to competition. Pre-competition snacks may include bananas, plums, peaches, melons, bagels, cereal, yogurt or fruit juices. Individual needs will vary. Be sure to limit fiber, avoid fats, restrict caffeine and continue hydration (1, 12).

**During Competition:** Hydration is more important than nutrient replacement during competition. In conditions in which competition is continuous for less than 90 minutes, carbohydrate replacement

Fats: < 30%
√ Unsaturated vs. saturated & trans fats
√ Vegetable & plant based sources

Carbohydrates: 50 – 60%
√ Whole grains
√ Complex, not simple

Proteins: 15 – 20%
√ Natural sources
√ Lean/low fat sources

typically is unnecessary. A sport drink like Gatorade can be helpful but is not required. A half-cup of water is recommended every 15 to 20 minutes of competition. It may be beneficial to get in a pattern of substituting players regularly to encourage fluid replacement, if nothing else. Even key players need to rehydrate during each half. In hot or humid weather, consider treating players to watermelon or orange slices at halftime (1, 2, 12).

**After competition:** After the big win, a trip out for ice cream to celebrate may be fun, but it isn't enough. In order to replace muscle glycogen stores and promote recovery, a post-competition meal is valuable. A balanced meal rich in carbohydrates should be coupled with fluid replacement. Water is sufficient, but sport drinks also are effective.

**Hydration:** Maintaining fluid balance is important both for overall health and athletic performance. Fluid replacement and hydration are extremely important for soccer players. As little as a two percent loss in body weight affects performance. For young players, fluid consumption is especially important because they don't sweat as much as adults and are less capable of naturally cooling their bodies. Children also absorb heat more easily than adults. Also, acclimating to exercise in the heat is more gradual for children than adults.

Collectively, these factors increase the likelihood of dehydration in children. Parents, coaches and players should be aware of the symptoms of dehydration, such as dry lips and tongue, sunken eyes, bright colored or dark urine, infrequent urination, apathy and lack of energy (1, 2, 8, 12). Children should be encouraged to drink cool fluids before, during and after practices and games, especially if symptoms of dehydration exist. Fluids should be consumed regularly throughout the event (every 15 to 20 minutes). Players should not rely on thirst to guide fluid consumption, since the thirst mechanism is so weak. Once children are thirsty, they already are somewhat dehydrated.

While water is sufficient for hydration and rehydration purposes, children may be likely to consume greater quantities of flavored fluids (4, 8). Fluids like Gatorade are more palatable and may encourage more rapid fluid replacement by children. A beverage with glucose and small amounts of sodium chloride is useful (4, 5). Beverages that are high in sugar, such as sodas and juices, should be avoided by young athletes. Monitoring children's weight before and after games can be an effective means for maintaining fluid balance, particularly in hot, humid environments. Soccer players also should arrive at practices and games hydrated and bring water bottles when applicable. A water bottle should be a mandatory part of the soccer gear.

## Take-Home Message

As can be seen, the science of sports nutrition can be applied to the needs of soccer players. In summary, soccer players should be encouraged to have nutrient-dense, balanced meals, including the proper concentrations of nutrients, vitamins, minerals and fluids. After developing an understanding of the nutritional needs of young soccer players, an effective game plan must be established. Designing a practical approach to sports nutrition can be a rewarding challenge.

On a related note, eating on the go often is a must for busy soccer families. Families may be apt to stop at a drive-through window on the way home if they didn't take the time to plan ahead. Experts suggest that planning ahead can make a great deal of difference in immediate recovery and future performance. Nutritious snack foods also should be considered an essential part of the soccer gear. Packing a brown bag or cooler of supplies certainly is recommended over the fast food alternatives. Items to take along to the soccer field include fruit, cut-up vegetables, low-fat string cheese, low-fat yogurt or smoothies and unsalted nuts.

### References

1. A guide to eating for sports (2005). Retrieved from www.kidshealth.org.
2. Athlete tip sheet: hydration game plan for safety and performance (2005). Retrieved from www.gssiweb.org.
3. Bar-Or, O. (1994). Nutritional requirements of young soccer players. *Journal of Sport Sciences, 12*, S39-S42.
4. Bar-Or, O. (2000). Nutrition for child and adolescent athletes. *Gatorade Sports Science Institute, 13* (2).
5. Bar-Or, O. (2001). Nutritional considerations for the child athlete. *Canadian Journal of Applied Phisiology*, S186-S19.
6. Clark, N. (1995). Growing pains: common questions about nutrition and sports training during kids' growing years. *American Fitness, 13* (1), 10-11.
7. Hellemans, I. (1994). Nutritional need and concerns of young athletes. *Journal of Physical Education New Zealand, 27* (4), 8-10.
8. Nelson, S. (1999). Sports nutrition for children. *Athletic Therapy Today, 4* (6), 48-49.
9. Reimers, K. (1996). On youth and nutritional supplements. *Strength and Conditioning, 18* (6), 26-27.
10. Thompson, J. (1998). Energy balance in young athletes. *International Journal of Sport Nutrition, 8,* 160-174.
11. Williams, M. H. (2002). *Nutrition for health, fitness, and sport* (6th ed). Boston, MA: McGraw-Hill.
12. Winning nutrition for athletes (2005). Retrieved from www. pueblo.gsa.gov.
13. USDA nutritional guidelines (2005). Retrieved from www.usda.gov.

© Janpietruszka / Dreamstime.com

# Here's Proof Sports Drinks Work

## Don Kirkendall

A local radio station has a contest in which the caller has 10 seconds to name five things on the DJ's list. Things like "Conference USA teams" or "Characters from the TV show 'M*A*S*H'." Here are mine for you: 10 seconds – name five sports drinks. Pretty easy. Next question: How do those five drinks differ? Mostly in taste. There are some minor differences in the amount and type of carbohydrate and maybe the concentrations of electrolytes. Other than that, they are all about the same.

Sports drinks were introduced nearly 40 years ago after research done by Dr. Robert Cade at the University of Florida. He thought that the addition of some electrolytes and carbohydrate to water would facilitate fluid and energy replacement during exercise. Cade's thinking was proven correct and sports drinks were born. Multiple research projects have since shown that a sports drink is more effective than water for replacing fluids, reducing stress on the cardiovascular system, managing heat stress, and improving athletic performance.

Trivia question: Name the first sports drink. Wrong, it was called GookinAid; its contents were the same as the sweat of a runner named Matt Gookin.

Cade's original work focused on hydration, but interest then shifted to a drink as a source of carbohydrates and energy. The energy for games, like soccer, comes from carbohydrate stored in muscle called glycogen. The problem is that the amount stored is limited. Thus, to exercise longer or harder you have to either put more glycogen in the muscle at the start (glycogen supercompensation, a special precompetition diet/exercise regimen) or consume a carbohydrate supplement during exercise to augment muscle glycogen. Having just the right amount and type of carbohydrate was the next direction of research, with hundreds of studies showing that carbohydrates taken by mouth during exercise can improve performance. A look at the ingredients on most drinks today will show similar amounts and sources of carbohydrates.

But could a drink be improved upon? Most everyone knows that carbohydrates are helped across the muscle cell membranes by insulin, a necessary process for the cell to get that energy. When blood sugar rises, insulin is secreted to help bring blood sugar down to more normal levels.

Some curious researchers, knowing that protein also can elevate insulin, wondered if protein in a drink might get more carbohydrates into the muscles (you can't just add more carbs, as that slows emptying by the stomach). The folks at the University of Texas had shown that carbohydrate intake right after exercise maximized the rate of making new glycogen to be ready for the next bout of exercise.

So, if we know that exercise breaks down protein and protein can speed up carbohydrate movement into cells by increasing insulin and immediate post-exercise carbohydrates refills the glycogen tanks in the muscles the fastest, then maybe a sports drink should have some protein to help with all of these factors. Here are some recent publications which clearly show the benefit of protein in a sports drink.

*Zawadzki KM , BB Yaspelkis, JL Ivy. Carbohydrate protein complex increases the rate of muscle glycogen storage after exercise. J Appl Physiol 1992; 72:1854-9*

This group at the University of Texas compared the use of carbohydrate, protein and carbohydrate-protein supplements to see if they could speed up the replenishment of muscle glycogen after prolonged exhaustive exercise. Nine men cycled for two hours on three occasions to deplete their muscle glycogen. Immediately after and two hours after each bout they ingested a carbohydrate, protein or carbohydrate-protein supplement. Blood and muscle tissue was sampled throughout recovery.

The replenishment rate of muscle glycogen storage during the carbohydrate-protein treatment was 38 percent greater than carbohydrate and more than three times faster than the protein treatment.

*Niles ES, T Lachowetz, J Garfi, W Sullivan, JC Smith, BP Leyh, SA Headley. Carbohydrate-protein drink improves time to exhaustion after recovery from endurance exercise. J Exercise Physiol online, 2001 4:45-52.*

Ten men were studied to investigate the effects of two different supplements on endurance, one a carbohydrate and the other a carbohydrate-protein drink of equal calorie amount. After a muscle glycogen lowering exercise, two drinks were administered with a 60-minute interval between dosages. Then they rode to exhaustion. The athletes went 20 percent longer when using the carbohydrate-protein drink than the carbohydrate-only drink, which correlated with elevated insulin in the carbohydrate-protein condition.

The researchers concluded that a carbohydrate-protein drink consumed after glycogen depleting exercise may lead to a faster rate of muscle glycogen re-synthesis than a carbohydrate only beverage. This would hasten the recovery process and improve exercise endurance during a second bout of exercise performed on the same day.

*Ivy JL, HW Goforth Jr, BM Damon, TR McCauley, EC Parsons, TB Price. Early post-exercise muscle glycogen recovery is enhanced with a carbohydrate-protein supplement. J Appl Physiol 93: 1337-1344, 2002*

This group compared a carbohydrate-protein supplement and a carbohydrate supplement of equal calorie content. After 2.5 hours of intense cycling to deplete their thigh muscles of glycogen, the subjects received each drink. After four hours of recovery, muscle glycogen was the highest for the carbohydrate-protein treatment when compared with the carbohydrate treatment.

*SL Miller, KD Tipton, DL Chinkes, SE Wolf, RR Wolfe. Independent and combined effects of amino acids and glucose after resistance exercise. Med Sci Sports Exerc. 2003, 35:449-55.*

This study assessed the separate and combined effects on muscle protein metabolism of amino acids and/or carbohydrate consumed at one and two hours after weight lifting. Volunteers performed leg exercise and then ingested one of three drinks (protein, carbohydrate, or carbohydrate-protein) at one and two hours after exercise. The greatest uptake of protein three hours after exercise was with carbohydrate-protein and least with carbohydrate.

In fact the carbohydrate-protein drink was 38 percent more effective than the protein drink in resynthesizing muscle proteins (weight lifters, take note). This means the muscle is gathering the pieces to make new protein. This study concludes that more protein is taken up by the muscle when the protein is mixed with carbohydrate, more evidence that a drink containing a mixture of carbs and protein is more effective than either alone.

*Williams MB, PB Raven, DL Fogt, JL Ivy. Effects of recovery beverages on glycogen restoration and endurance exercise performance. J Strength Cond Res 2003; 17:12-9.*

This study compared a high carbohydrate-protein beverage containing electrolytes and a traditional carbohydrate-electrolyte sports beverage. After a glycogen-depleting exercise, each subject exercised to exhaustion at 85 percent of maximum. Ingestion of the carbohydrate-protein beverage resulted in a 92 percent greater insulin response, a 128 percent greater storage of muscle glycogen compared with the CHO and a 55 percent increase in endurance performance in the second exercise bout. These findings indicate that the rate of recovery after exercise is coupled with muscle glycogen replenishment and suggests that recovery supplements containing protein and carbohydrate should be used to maximize muscle glycogen as well as fluid replacement.

*JL Ivy, Res P, Ding Z, Widzer MO. Effect of a carbohydrate-protein supplement on edurance performance during exercise of varying intensity. Int J Sports Nutr and Exerc Metab (in press).*

This study compared a carbohydrate and a carbohydrate-protein supplement on endurance performance. Trained cyclists exercised at variable exercise intensities for three hours, and then they cycled 85 percent VO2 maximum until exhausted. 200 ml of each of the three supplements (water, CHO, carbohydrate-protein, Accelerade) was provided every 20 minutes. The carbohydrate-protein increased time to exhaustion by 36 percent over the carbohydrate supplement and 55 percent over water.

## Comments

Just as our approach to training for soccer has undergone dramatic changes leading to greatly improved level of play, sports drinks continue to evolve to further improve the nutrition and performance of the soccer player by supplying more fuel so the player can run at higher intensities for greater distances, especially late in the second half, which is prime time for goal scoring and injuries. The well-fueled team scores more, yields fewer goals and may be injured less, outcomes all coaches would prefer. These concepts can be used in tournament settings when recovery time between games is limited.

Players who follow these suggestions will be far more ready for the next game than their opponents who hit the fast food drive-thru. Remember, after genetics and training, the factor that can have the biggest influence on performance is nutrition.

Another point is that during that critical immediate post-exercise or match period, a drink with carbs and protein improves the efficiency of storing glycogen. That means that fewer carbs (i.e. calories) are needed to store the same amount of glycogen. This is an important consideration for female athletes, many of whom do not eat enough food in an attempt to control weight.

The overall observation is that a sports drink with some protein helps get carbohydrates into the muscle faster and the muscle damage that happens after exercise gets the building blocks of repair quicker when the amino acids (protein) and carbohydrates are combined. The basic recipe is four units of carbs to one unit of protein. If the nutrition information on the label says 24 grams of carbs, then the drink should have six grams of protein, a 4:1 ratio. You have to read those labels.

The conclusion should be obvious: a drink combining carbohydrate-protein helps on two fronts – improving endurance during exercise and helping speed the recovery process. And it is even better than a pure protein drink at repairing damaged muscle protein.

*Editor's note: Don Kirkendall is in the Department of Orthopaedics at the University of North Carolina at Chapel Hill.*

# The Road to Recovery

## Jeremy Boone

The demands on young soccer players today are ever increasing, as soccer has now become a year-round sport. Not only do players play high school soccer and club soccer in the fall, winter and spring, but now players participate in summer leagues as well. Coaches now feel time constraints more than ever before training their players. However, recovery methods unfortunately do not receive the same attention. Applying principles of recovery and regeneration will be sure to give your team a winning edge.

## Plan for Recovery

In order to better understand the concept of recovery, coaches should be aware of the following factors that affect the recovery process. Based on feedback from your players, these factors will help you in planning your future training sessions.

## Eight Factors Affecting Recovery

- Stress
- Environment
- Social factors
- Sleeping patterns
- Psychological factors
- Nutrition
- Fatigue
- Training and conditioning

In planning a training session, you must identify how each of these factors affects individual players and the team as a whole. Begin by determining what days your team will practice and when tournaments will occur. Next, plan your recovery sessions. Be sure to distribute active and passive rest accordingly. Finally, plan your actual training sessions. Progressive planning will ensure

your players are continually improving. When performance levels begin to decline, ask yourself if you are allowing your players time to recover. Review your plan, make the appropriate changes, and you will soon be on your way to successful soccer play.

## Recovery in a Training Session

Inter-recovery occurs within a training session. The interplay of the variables below determines whether or not your session will have a training focus or a recovery focus.

- Session volume
- Distance
- Duration
- Density
- Number of sets
- Number of repetitions
- Frequency
- Session intensity
- Number of players
- Size of field
- Touch restriction
- Number of available balls

For example, in midseason when two games might occur in one week, rather than playing 11 v. 11 full field, an alternative would be to play with a zonal focus. Divide the field into thirds: defensive, midfield and attacking. When the ball is in the attacking third, the defensive players must stay in their zone. This will dramatically reduce the total volume of player distance covered within the session, keeping physical stress at a minimum level. Another alternative would be to keep the number of play restrictions low by playing unlimited touch. This will keep the training intensity low, both physically and psychologically.

## Performing Team Relays

An additional factor to consider during your training session is the work-to-rest ratio while performing team relays. The greater the number of players per group, the greater the recovery time. Likewise, the smaller the number of players per group, the greater the work rate. For example, your players just finished playing 4 v. 4 during a 10-minute period. While player fatigue has now set in, a team relay with large numbers of players per group will allow adequate recovery. This will keep the flow of practice moving and the quality of performance high.

Let's now take a look at some basic principles of recovery and regeneration that you may immediately begin to integrate into your overall coaching plan.

## Principle #1: Players Are Only as Good as Their Bodies' Ability to Recover

As coaches we must recognize the importance of recovery for our players. Traditional thought in terms of physical preparation for soccer success is determined by what kind and how much training is being performed. This belief does not take into account one's ability to recover, thus potentially preventing an increase in one's fitness level or speed. Recovery is the actual time when the body makes gains in strength and fitness. Be sure and plan recovery just as you would actual training.

## Principle #2: Variation and Specificity Apply to Both Training Methods and Recovery Methods

Incorporate a variety of recovery methods into your coaching plan. The human body adapts very quickly to all forms of stimulation. Once this adaptation occurs, the same intensity, load and volume of the stimulus has a decreasing effect. A variation in the stimulus is required to continue to make improvements. In practical terms, this means always performing the same cool-down jog after a game, getting a massage after every intense practice or having a contrast bath multiple times per week will not be as beneficial for your players.

Recovery also should be specific to the activity and the needs of the individual. For example, post-game recovery will be different for goalkeepers than for field players.

## Principle # 3: Cool-down is Key!

Performing a cool-down session post-practice or post-game is critical for a player's recovery and preparation for future play. Without a proper cool-down, it takes up to four to six hours for the body to remove lactic acid and toxic wastes from the blood. Something as simple as a light recovery jog at 50 percent intensity for 10-20 minutes can help remove 80 to 90 percent of lactic acid within the body one hour after play. Be sure not to exert too much effort during the cool-down. The glycogen stores in the muscles already are depleted and an intense cool-down will only deplete them further.

## Principle #4: Active Recovery is the Best Type of Rest

Two forms of recovery are passive (no activity performed) and active (any activity not specific to soccer that does not induce a training effect). Soccer players are accustomed to training and playing on a continual basis. Implementing passive recovery measures (e.g. being a coach potato) is actually a shock to the nervous system. Therefore, it is ideal to have players perform active recovery activities such as roller-blading, ultimate frisbee or, best of all, a pool session on days off. A simple rule to remember by Gary Winckler, track coach at the University of Illinois, is "this is a time when muscles work and nerves rest."

## Principle #5: The Concept of the 24-Hour Athlete

It is not always what is done with the players during the two hours or so that is spent on practice. Just as important, if not more so, is what the player does during the other 22 hours in their day. What are their nutritional habits? Are they getting enough sleep? What are their social habits? These are but a few of the questions to be aware of. Being an athlete is a lifestyle, not a part-time job. It is our responsibility as coaches to educate players on skills such as time management, nutrition, etc.

## Principle #6: Training is Cumulative

When planning your training session, be aware that training occurs day-to-day, week-to-week, month-to-month and year-to-year. Use this simple sequence to help create a systematic and progressive practice plan for your team in terms of applying training load, volume and intensity.

The concept of recovery may seem rather complex. However, by implementing the principles and concepts found in this article, you may now have a better understanding of recovery and its role in successful soccer performance. Below are a few practical recovery templates for all levels of soccer. And remember, a team is only as good as its ability to recover!

The SoccerFit™ team helps individual coaches, teams, and youth clubs who struggle with getting fit, fast, and first to the ball. For any comments, questions, or further information please contact Jeremy Boone at Jeremy@carolinaadi.com or Vern Gambetta at vgambetta@aol.com.

## Recovery Implementation Tips

**Recovery: Recreational Level**
- Require players to bring a water bottle
- Implement multiple water breaks during a training session; "entire practice is a water break"
- End sessions with a flexibility focus
- Educate parents
- Implement simple sports nutrition concepts for post workout recovery

**Recovery: Club Level**
- Includes recreational recovery model
- Dynamic warm-up and cool-down
- Implement nutritional strategies such as a post-workout beverage (4:1 carbohydrate to protein)
- EMPHASIZE the importance of good sleeping habits
- Begin to implement individualized flexibility routines
- Begin to teach self-massage

**Recovery: College/Professional Level**
- Recovery now becomes a complex model
- Include both recreational and club models
- Implement external means of recovery (massage, sauna, whirlpool, micro current)
- Nutritional supplementation

# Chapter 5:
# Coaching and
# Team Management

# The Craft of Coaching

## Many qualities and attributes are needed in moving players to new levels

### By Jeff Tipping
### NSCAA Director of Coaching

Bill Beswick, renowned sports psychologist formerly of Manchester United and now with Middlesborough F.C., has a saying which should inspire all coaches: "A good coach is able to take a player where they have never been before and will not get to on their own."

This in many ways gives meaning to what it is to coach and encapsulates the primary purpose of the coaching profession. This article explores coaching as a craft, a professional endeavor which requires pride of performance, acquisition of highly valued skills, and has an objective which is both enormously satisfying and develops an insatiable appetite for more.

At an NSCAA Academy a few years ago, a disgruntled graduate from a highly successful Division I college program said, "I didn't learn one thing in four years of college; I haven't improved since I left high school." It was astonishing to discover how disenchanted this player had been with his college experience. He had played in several Final Fours, one of which his team won. It is clear that serious players want more from a coach than winning trophies. They want to prepare for the next level. They want to get better.

Many would argue that the ultimate acid test of a player is "What impact did you have on the game?" Surely the ultimate acid test of a coach is "What impact did you have on your players?"

It would be disingenuous to assert that a player's sole means of improvement is through good coaching. Coaches take too much credit for producing good players and too much criticism for producing poor ones. Playing with and against better players is, ultimately, what improves a player. Players also improve from modeling, – watching and imitating good players. Improvements are accelerated for players immersed in a soccer culture where good play is appreciated and the game is revered.

Player improvement also does occur, undeniably, from participating in focused, dynamic and well-structured practice sessions. The objective of the NSCAA Academy is to explore the coach's role in the development of players and to explore coaching and teaching as a craft, a highly prized skill.

## Managing and Coaching

It is important to highlight the difference between managing and coaching if only to distinguish the difference between winning trophies and improving players. Many successful programs emerge because the coach is a good recruiter, scheduler, fundraiser, negotiator and manager of people. The management of a team or club is a vital task in winning and building a winning culture. The managerial aspects of coaching are critical and are receiving greater attention in our Academies. It is possible, however, for programs to have exceptional winning records where players do not improve.

It is not entirely surprising to hear of players from winning programs who are dissatisfied with the quality of coaching they receive on the training ground. They have been recruited for their ability

## Observation – Match Analysis:

To discover what the players need to practice, the coach must observe them play in a game. The game tells us what the players need. The observations the coach makes during a game will give the practice session a focus. Consequently, the soccer coaching model on game day is quite different from football, basketball or lacrosse which encourages a high degree of interaction between players and coaches. Possibly baseball or ice hockey are better models for soccer wherein the coach quietly observes the game, writes notes and occasionally exhorts players to perform.

### Match observation and analysis

This is a very difficult skill. Some useful tips to develop this skill include:

- Watching a lot of soccer games
- Sitting quietly with a pad and pen to put down observations. Some coaches have an assistant do the writing while they observe
- Developing the ability to look away from the ball. This is difficult as the ball is a magnet for attention. Here are three classic scenarios where looking away from the ball might be important
  - If midfielders get caught in possession, you may accuse them of indecision. Had you looked away from the ball at the forwards, however, you would have seen that they had not checked, made runs, etc.
  - Your forwards have the ball outside opponent's penalty box. Are your backs pushed up to the half line to compact the team defensively?
  - Your team plays a 4-4-2. When the right flank has the ball, does left flank come inside to become a third center forward, or does he/she stay wide? This has implications for getting into penalty area if a cross is delivered or leaving space for overlapping left back
- Compartmentalizing observation into categories:
  - Individual
    - Evaluation of your players' technical, tactical, physical and psychological performance.
  - Small group
    - Observation of backs, midfielders, forwards, etc.
    - Observation of vertical thirds, left flank, central, right flank
    - Observation of players within 12 yards of the ball
    - Observation of first and second attackers
    - Observation of first and second defenders
  - Team
    - Does team exhibit ability to apply principles of game?
      - Attack
      - Penetration
      - Support
      - Mobility
      - Width
      - Creativity
      - Defense
      - Pressure
      - Cover
      - Balance
      - Compactness
      - Predictability

The scope of match analysis is way beyond the limits of this article, but covered more fully in the NSCAA Advanced National and Premier Diplomas. Match analysis provides the delineation of the themes that must be developed in practice.

but they stagnate as players due to a lack of interest or lack of skill of the coach to help them. How much better would it have been for the player previously mentioned to have won trophies and improved as a player? How much more rewarding would have been the player's experience if the coach had taken player development as seriously as managing the program? The very best coaches we have, obviously, do both.

## Coach as 'Craftsman'

The craft of coaching players comes down to four basic tasks. The end results are carefully designed and focused practice sessions in an environment which closely resembles the competitive pressure of a game, and in which players improve. The four basic tasks are:

- Observation
- Organization
- Instruction
- Motivation

## Organization – Developing Practice Sessions:

Soccer players learn to play better soccer by practicing soccer-like exercises. Contrived drills, excessive standing in lines, scrimmages with no focus, running laps have very little benefit to players. We explore many different methods of coaching in the Academy but the purpose of all the methods is to help the coach organize training sessions which improve players by having them play soccer.

### Facilitating learning

"The Game is the teacher" is a phrase which we constantly hear. This maxim, in practical terms, means that the soccer coach organizes conditioned soccer games to improve players. The kind of conditions the coach puts on the games will help teach the players. This process is called facilitating learning. Part of the skill of an advanced coach is to design exercises that specifically address problem areas. The conditions the coach puts on games are examined in detail in the NSCAA Academy, but basically fall into the following categories:

- Numbers of players (e.g. 4 v. 2, 8 v. 8, 6 v. 6 + 1, etc.)
- Size and shape of field (narrow and long for vertical passes, short and wide for shooting or crossing)
- Goals or methods of scoring (shooting into a full goal, dribbling across a line, 6 passes equals a goal, etc.)
- Numbers of touches (1 touch to encourage passing and support play, 2 touches to encourage receiving)
- Zonal games (field marked off by cones with restrictions as to who can go into certain zones)

The methods a coach uses to improve the players depend on such factors as age, ability, and ultimate purpose of a practice. The methods of a coach of 7-year-olds uses are completely different than those of a college coach. A coach preparing to play an opponent may be more concerned about the future game than the one which is past.

### Basic guidelines of teaching:

- **Focus:** Improvements will more likely occur when concentration is on two or three concepts.
- **Progression:** Sequencing of exercises follows logical progression. The coach may work with the back four versus two center forwards before putting them into an 11 v. 11 game. Having a 9-year-old practice dribbling in 1 v. 1 may precede playing in a 5 v. 5 game.
- **Duration:** Practices should be about the same length as a game. Very little quality learning happens in the final half hour of a two-and-a-half hour practice.
- **Practice Plan:** All coaches are encouraged to write down a practice plan regardless of age group of the players. Practice plans should delineate practice sequencing and duration of exercises.

Practice components: Practices consist of four main components:

- **Warm-up** – 20 percent of time. Should be related to theme and focus of practice (e.g. passing in pairs, circle routines)
- **Teaching exercises** – 50 percent of time. Two or three exercises that focus on observations the coach makes from games. Coach may split team up (e.g. goalkeepers and defenders in one end, midfielders and forwards in other)
- **Final game** – 20 percent of time. 11 v. 11 or even-numbered game. Coach emphasizes points from the practice
- **Warm-down** – 10 percent of time. Players jog, stretch together; led by captain, assistant coach.

Some coaches will do fitness between final game and warm-down. The coach may meet with players prior to session to explain what they will be doing in practice. Some coaches will show video clippings of the previous games to highlight their observations. This is also helpful in changing the players frame of mind and preparing them, psychologically, for practice.

# Instruction – "The Teachable Moment":

Possibly the biggest difference between skilled coaches and novice coaches is in the quality and quantity of their instruction. There are certain "teachable moments" which occur in a practice session when the skilled coach speaks and addresses a player or group of players. The number of instructional stoppages and the timing will be very much a matter of choice for the coach. It will also depend on the age group; 14-year-olds will need more instruction than pros.

The "teachable moments" happen at fairly predictable times:

- When something is done incorrectly
- When something is done correctly
- Between exercises, during water breaks
- When the players are clearly fatigued and will welcome a rest and instructional moment
- Ball out of play

Instructional points can be made to an individual, group or a team. They can be made while play continues or play can be stopped. Most importantly, *they must focus on the actual teaching theme or goal.*

Different instructional examples to improve players:

**Tony DiCicco, U.S. Women's National Team 1998**
Conducting a practice session for the Women's National Team, Tony's stoppages almost universally came at the moment a player did something right. He brought the players' attention to what it looked like when done correctly, praised them and moved on. He never made any corrections to address mistakes the players made.

**Bob Gansler, Kansas City Wizards 2002**
He conducted a practice session, which contained three dynamic exercises each lasting 20 minutes. He never stopped any of the sessions once. He made all of his coaching points during water breaks and between changeovers in exercises. A true proponent of "the game is the best teacher."

**Helmut Schoen,**
**German National Team Manager**
1974 Paul Breitner relates how Schoen walked over to the 2 v. 2 exercise where he and Beckenbauer played. Schoen never said a word, but Breitner related how Schoen's presence burned a hole in the back of his neck. He redoubled his efforts in the exercise. Sometimes silence can be the coach's greatest ally.

Clearly there are no absolutes as to how the coach gets improvement out of players. Coaches must understand what is best for their environment and fits their personality. Avoid:

- Too many stoppages which prevent any flow from developing
- No instruction at all. The coach merely supervises exercises which have no meaningful focus and in which the players receive no guidance

## Motivation –
## Light a Spark in a Player:

One of the great rewards of coaching is helping to energize a player and stimulate a player so that he or she wants to improve. Players will improve only if they want to improve but the coach can offer extrinsic motivation which lights a spark in a player. The coach does this in a number of ways.

### Methods of motivation

- **Quality practices:** Practices which are organized focused and facilitate clear improvement.
- **Specific instruction:** Coaching points which specifically relate to the focus of the session.
- **Mixture of positive and negative re-inforcement:** Coaches must be demanding at times. The best coaches understand how to mix praise with honest observation in such a way as to challenge the player to improve.
- **Appearance and participation:** The coach should have a modicum of physical fitness and dress like a coach. Players like it when a coach occasionally joins in a practice. (Hint: make yourself the +1 who cannot be tackled).
- **Realistic expectations:** The prudent coach sets realistic goals and targets for the players. They keep the game within the context of how good the team is compared to who they are playing. The coach is wise to forewarn players, parents and supporters that, in soccer, nothing is ever guaranteed.
- **Humanity:** Personal honesty and integrity are respected by players. Players will clearly respond to a coach who displays an interest in them aside from their soccer ability.

Enjoy your coaching.

© Craig Bohnert

# Defining the Word "Coaching"

## Bill Beswick

*Following is a summary of a lecture given by Bill Beswick to the NSCAA Academy coaching staff in connection with the NSCAA Convention in Baltimore. Beswick also made two clinic presentations at the convention. Beswick is a mentor/adviser to soccer coaches in England, including Howard Wilkinson, Steve McLaren and Steve Round.*

**B**eing the head coach of a team is a lonely job; it takes courage to be a coach. In fact, the majority of the final decisions relating to a team fall on the coach's shoulders. But when there is a dip in the team's performance, the coach may need someone to give ideas as to the why the team is in decline.

Nevertheless coaching itself is, for many, a search for self-fulfillment and that process is what keeps the profession, while sometimes frustrating, also exciting. Coaching's highs provide wonderful moments that keep coaches' interest and involvement while they search for perfect practices and perfect games.

Beswick said he tries to work with coaches in terms of how they develop their philosophies as well as how they relate to their players. Coaches must begin with the end in mind; they must know what they want in the long run. They must keep the "big picture" in front of them; "don't lose it in the details."

There are several core issues with which coaches are concerned:

- Did we get the preparation right? Were the players in the right frame of mind?
- The process. Do we pick the right players? The right substitutes?
- Are the players fit enough?
- Are we playing them in the right positions?
- Do we have the right shape as a team? Are our tactics right so that we can play well in that shape and get results?
- Do the half times help or hurt us? If the coach makes good suggestions and is right, then players start to believe and change themselves.

Beswick's definition of coaching: "Coaching is taking players somewhere new." He asked his audience what came to mind as that definition was broken down.

The word "coaching" evoked the following responses: "enthusiastic," "committed," "want to improve," "positive role model," "good listener," "presence," "problem solver," "solution-oriented," "loyal," "sense of humor," "ethical," "creative," "knowledge-giving," "respected," "good character," "inspirational," "people skills," "vision," "mentor, "imposing," "influencing," "honest," "inspiring," "preparing" and "teaching."

Beswick noted that all of the responses were positive. He said coaches need to be passionate – but controlled. He added "caring" to the list, noting that modern coaching is about "selling, not yelling." "Effective coaching" was another addition with the reminder that the ultimate objective of coaches is to achieve perfection. "Motivating" was added with the eventual goal of the coach to make players self-motivating. Good coaches are also "other-oriented" and build a sense of trust within the team. The exemplary coach also is disciplined, including self-disciplined. The coach also uses a sense of humor to defuse matters. "Worry prolongs, humor eases" is something for coaches to keep in mind.

Good coaches are usually good story-tellers. They come up with an appropriate tale related to the coaching issue at hand.

The words "is taking" brought these responses:

"teaching and leading," "growth," "planning-progression," "probing," "exciting," "enjoyable," "encouraging," "direction," "organized," "experience," "goals and goal-setting," "persistence," "analytical," "philosophy," "methodology," "psychology," "timing," "leading," "supporting," "vision," "challenging," "empowering," "unbalancing," "shaping," "sculpting," "executing," "evaluating," "risking," "doubting," "observing," "forgiving," "ethical," "motivating," "mentoring," "perfecting," "inspiring" and "adjusting."

A coach must have a clear sense of purpose. The coach must create the plan and establish goals to achieve the desired end result. As part of the coaching process the coach must share "the why" of everything. The importance of practice needs to be constantly stressed to the players. "Don't expect anything new at game time" was a reminder to coaches.

Other Beswick thoughts:
- The players need to do the simple things well
- Be organized, be compassionate and the results will occur
- Mistakes are part of the process; it is not the falling down that is important, it is the getting up following mistakes that is important

The word "players" evoked the following responses:

"commitment," "desire," "dealing with criticism," "ability," "belief," "passion," "self discipline," "coachability," "sense of fun," "sense of enjoyment," "acceptance of pain," "humility," "supporting," "challenging," "empowering," "risking," "teammate" and "potential."

Beswick, who noted that "multi-cultural" is also important in modern coaching where a variety of personalities from different backgrounds make up team rosters, added "Lifestyle commitment."

He also noted that humility is something that players of quality possess and players must understand and accept their roles within the team in order for it to be successful.

Finally, the phrase "to somewhere new" evoked the following: "where we are headed" and "perfection." Beswick believes that "relevant excellence" is what coaches should strive for as they seek to bring their players and teams to a higher level of play. Coaches need to have the right vision for their teams. "Sell the dream and they'll give you the effort" Beswick said. Coaches must be careful not to defeat the potential of both the team and the individuals on the squad. Finally, coaches should let the team's goals unfold as naturally as possible.

The process of developing a learning environment was addressed. One mark of a successful coach is that he or she is able to creatively repeat lessons and not leave the players bored. "Repetition without repeating" is part of the art of coaching.

McLaren, when viewing videotape with the Manchester United team never mentions mistakes to players in the final or attacking third of the field. He doesn't want to discourage players from taking chances in that area of the field that places huge demands on individual creativity. Mistakes exhibited in the middle third of the field may bring questions from him, but not necessarily critical questions. Mistakes made in the defending third of the field will bring criticism as they can be fatal to the team's chances for success. In using motivational videotape it is important to show everyone. Give everyone some attention.

Coaches need to learn to handle defeat – and victory. Dean Smith believed the coach should take care of the losses and give the wins to the players.

All coaches share a consistent desire to win games but the evolution of the modern coach includes the following differences from yesterday's mentors:

- The traditional coach focuses on the task and communicates to the group, whereas the modern coach achieves the task with a more "play-centered" approach and a far higher level of both team and individual communication
- The modern coach is interested in maximizing the potential in the player, he or she is player-centered. The traditional coach is task-centered and more interested in development of the collective unit
- Formerly coaches might have been labeled as being "results-oriented" vs. the "excellence-dominated" coach of today
- Today careful planning of a more long-term nature (Beswick termed it "the journey to excellence") is the rule against what has been termed "instinctive coaching." "Small details win big games"
- Coaches today believe they can influence soccer results more (64 percent of goals scored are via set pieces; three substitutes can affect results) vs. the player-dominated "let the boys sort it out" philosophy of the traditional coach
- Yesterday's coaches were isolated and unto themselves; today's coaches have assistants to share the workload or mentors to lend perspective to their coaching
- Coaching has evolved from "me" to "we"
- Authoritarian approach of the more traditional coach has given way to a more democratic methodology
- Today's coach is intent on listening carefully, then speaking. Selling rather than yelling
- The coach is no longer seen as a trainer, but rather as a teacher
- The traditional coach was often simply an ex-player; today's coach is qualified as a coach

- The traditional coach was seen as a hard worker; today's coach is seen as a smart worker — it isn't the hours you put in that matter, it is the quality of the time; work not longer, but smarter.

*Editor's note: Bill Beswick is a former coach of the English National Basketball Team and also has worked with the English FA's U-18 , U-21and full national soccer teams as a sports psychologist.*

© Craig Bohnert

# Fitting Practices to Ages

## US Soccer Federation

The U.S. Soccer Federation has made these recommendations for formats for the best practices for youth development:

- To promote the implementation of small-sided games as the vehicle for match play for players under the age of 12 throughout the United States.
- To promote and encourage an appropriate development environment for players that is based on both age and ability

## Recommendations by Age Group:

U-6:
- Game form – 4 v. 4 (3 v. 3 is an option)
- No goalkeepers
- Game duration – 4 x 8 minutes
- Substitution – free
- Goalkeeper status – none required
- Field size – 4 v. 4 (40 x 25 yards) or for 3 v. 3 (30 x 20 yards)
- Ball size – 3

U-8:
- Game form – 5 v. 5 (4 v. 4 is an option)
- Game duration – 2 x 20 minutes
- Substitution – free
- Goalkeeper status- used last defender as goalkeeper in 5 v 5
- Field size – 5 v. 5 (45 x 30 yards) 4 v. 4 (40 x 25 yards)
- Ball size – 3

U-10:
- Game form – 7 v. 7 (6 v. 6 is an option)
- Game duration – 2 x 25 minutes
- Substitution – free
- Goalkeeper status – players rotate as goalkeeper in game
- Field size – 60 x 40 yards
- Ball size – 4

U-12:
- Game form – 9 v. 9 (8 v. 8 is an option)
- Game duration – 2 x 30
- Substitution – free
- Goalkeeper status – goalkeepers share time in order of priority
- Field size – 100 x 50 yards
- Ball size – 4

U-14:
- Game form – 11 v. 11
- Game duration – 2 x 35
- Substitution – no re-entry in half
- Goalkeeper status – goalkeepers chosen based on ability
- Field size – 110 x 60 yards (minimum)
- Ball size – 5

U-16/U-18:
- Game form – 11 v. 11
- Game duration – 2 x 40 or 2 x 45
- Substitution – no re-entry
- Goalkeeper status – goalkeepers chosen based on ability
- Field size – 110 x 70 yards/20 x 70 yards (minimum)
- Ball size – 5

## Development of Goalkeepers

The implementation of goalkeepers in youth soccer is an issue that creates considerable discussion among coaches. Requiring a player to be only a goalkeeper at too early an age may have a negative effect and eliminate him/her from future soccer participation. Children grow at different rates and times. It is impossible to predict who will be the best goalkeeper at age 20 when they are age 10. Early selection as a goalkeeper may not be in the player's best long-term interest. Development of a goalkeeper must be carefully monitored and conducted. The progressive teaching of technical skills is important given concerns for safety at this position.

## Recommendations:

- U-6 – No goalkeeper required for 3 v. 3 or 4 v. 4 games
- U-8 – No goalkeeper for 4 v. 4. Use the last defender for 5 v. 5 game
- U-10 – Rotate players on the team as goalkeeper
- U-12 – Goalkeeper is identified within the team; goalkeepers share time in a priority order determined by the coach
- U-14+ – Goalkeeper chosen on ability and contribution to the team

## Maximum competition:

Multiple games being played on one day or one weekend can have a negative effect on the quality of the experience and development of the individual player. Similarly, playing schedules that include so many tournaments and games that there is never an "off season" for players can retard the development of players.

## Recommendations:

- For tournament managers and schedulers:
  - Players allowed to play a maximum of one full-length game plus overtime period per day per weekend (maximum two games per weekend)
  - Where multiple games are a necessity:
    - Schedule full-length games with a day of rest between games
    - Play shortened halves for games played on back-to-back days
    - For players U-I4 a maximum of 100 minutes of competition per day
    - For players U-15 and older a maximum of 120 minutes per day

- Kick-off times for games should allow players reasonable opportunity to prepare properly for competition. This encompasses rest and recovery, nutrition and adequate time to warm-up
  - Coaches prioritizing events:
  - Objectives are identified and a seasonal plan is developed that balances practice, competition, rest and recovery
  - The best interests of the player must be considered when scheduling competition. The quality and the choice of the events must be carefully considered when developing a seasonal plan

# From Looking Good to Winning

## Jeff Tipping

*The KNVB and NSCAA teamed up to offer a course for coaches at the KNVB Sports Center at Zeist. The following is a summary of the course that dealt with coaching methods and the training session.*

The perspective from Holland is important because the Dutch have always been able to make soccer and the teaching of soccer simple. Although there are some similarities between the U.S. Soccer, NSCAA and KNVB perspectives, the Dutch Vision does have some specific and interesting nuances. The Dutch have long been known for playing wonderful soccer. The emphasis in Holland for many years was "looking good while playing the game." Winning was a secondary concern.

Even after losing the World Cup final in Munich in 1974, the Dutch were satisfied because they played "much better than the Germans." Many in the international soccer community viewed "The Orange" as the quintessential underachievers. That all changed in 1988. The Dutch won the European Championship in Germany and they beat arch-rival Germany in the semi-final. The Dutch discovered that winning was fun. As a result of that win, the KNVB changed the focus of soccer teaching and coaching in Holland. In a 1991 meeting of all KVNB staff at Zeist, the entire curriculum was redefined. The distinction between playing pretty soccer and playing to win became an integral part of the KNVB curriculum. The role of the coach and objectives of coaching at each age level were made very clear to all soccer coaches in Holland.

## Coaching Objectives by Age

The first step was to determine what should be taught to young players in each age group.

Winning became important, but playing the game "the Dutch way" remained a goal. The Dutch wanted to ensure that there was a natural progression to teaching soccer in the whole country. Winning would be emphasized, but not until after the foundation was set. Age group goals were determined:

### 5 to 6 Year Olds
- Ball touch/learn to master the ball
- Skill games in which direction, speed and precision are emphasized

### 7 to 11 Year Olds
- Begin to teach the basic game – start to develop maturity on the ball
- Technical skills and game insight have to be developed by playing in simplified soccer situations – small-sided and small-group games
- Instructions by the coach should be confined to technical matters

### 12 to 16 Year Olds
- Game maturity develops in 11 v. 11 situations
- Team functions are taught for each third of the field through small-sided and full-field games
- Position functions have to be developed through small-sided and full-field games
- Instructions by the coach for both technical and tactical matters

### 17 to 18 Year Olds
- Full competition with emphasis on winning – soccer maturity begins to develop
- Game coaching with tactical emphasis
- Stress on efficiency of play and mental aspects of the game

With these overall objectives in mind, it is important to understand that at age 11 the emphasis changes from technical training to the development of tactical considerations. In youth soccer up to the age of 11 the main objective is to learn the technical skills. The starting points for the coach are defined as:

- Technique is not an objective by itself but leads to soccer maturity
- There must always be a relation with soccer as a whole and the aforementioned objectives
- Soccer insight and technical skills should be developed through game-related situations. Small-sided games are best for this

For juniors (from 11 to 18 years) that means:

- Development of the tactical aspects of the game
  - This begins with vision, awareness and communication
  - Working together as a team in small groups and the whole team
- Playing soccer with a given and specific task or goal as a team
  - Players must be aware that the most important thing is winning the game
- Reading the game:
  - Recognizing and judging the situation with good decision-making

To try to make the distinction between "pretty soccer" and winning, the KNVB asks all coaches to remember the following golden rule:

*Technical activities should not be considered as the be-all and end-all for soccer and for training sessions. The game, playing maturity, playing matches and pleasure in playing should be most important. Technical activities such as heading, turning, feinting, ball control, passing, etc, are too often exercised individually and in a way that is out of context with the game. They are taught as individual "tricks of the trade" and very seldom*

*incorporated into playing the game. All technique must be taught within the context of the game at all times.*

## Mechanism of Coaching

The best teacher of the game is the *game itself.* It is the most natural, efficient and loved way to lead the players to the goal of "game maturity." Therefore, in the total learning process the role of the coach is:

- Simplifying the game to basic forms. That is best done with small-sided games
- Constructing basic game forms to compensate the negative influence of modern society. The coach must plan for the session to be successful
- To realize the difference between football "real" and football "strange" training activities. Are all drills realistic? Do they have a goal?
- To use training exercises as a means to reach the coaching goals for the different development levels (age groups)

In order for the coach to do this or to do the job well, it will help:

- If the coach has a lot of soccer experience
- If the coach knows as much as possible about the game at all levels
- If, with the know-how, the coach has the qualities to bring the training exercises to life, i.e. to demonstrate them
- If the coach can read the game and transfer this game intelligence to his or her pupils

The Dutch understand that the game is the best teacher and that the players play the game. However, the coach can influence the players. How can the coach influence the players? It is not a simple process. Here is a step-by-step presentation:

- Structure soccer in the three main moments that occur in a soccer game
  - Possession by your team
  - Possession by the opponents
  - Changing possession

- Observe and listen to improve insight into the game
  - Learn to read the game

- Concentration
  - Is there close attention by the players?
  - Is there an atmosphere to perform and to learn?

- Technique
  - The players must learn to master the ball in relation to the game
  - The players must have an insight into the game
  - Do the players know the team intention?
  - Do the players recognize the situation?
  - How is the organization, the formation and field occupation?
  - Is the space used optimally?
  - Are the players positioned well in relation to each other?

- Communication
  - Do the players understand each other?
  - Are the players working together?
  - Are all the players alert?

In a major difference between the Dutch objectives or goals and the contemporary goals of teaching in the USA, the Dutch know that insight into the game, technique and communication can be distinguished from each other, but they can't be separated. They influence one another and are dependent on each other. The best players have competency in all three areas.

## Preliminary Stage

The first developmental period is defined as the preliminary stage that takes place from 5 years old to 11 years old. The preliminary stage leads to what the Dutch call basic game maturity. This must be accomplished before the players can move into the second phase, where winning becomes important.

The main goal is defined as an attempt to lead the player toward development of the basic individual qualities necessary to cope with the game and game situations. If done well, the player moves toward simplified game maturity and is ready for stage two. The KNVB realizes that the best, most natural and most efficient means to this end is playing daily on the street, on the beaches or in the park with other players where space and time are reduced naturally. The players work hard to survive in these situations. The Dutch try to replicate this play environment in training.

The KNVB works together with professional clubs, amateur clubs, regional and local federations to ensure a common curriculum. The United States has not been able to do this. It is essential in this age group to find a balance between playing games (usually small-sided) and training activities that can be fragmented. The Dutch are adamant that the best teacher is the game.

## The Second Stage

The second developmental period is from ages 12 to 18. The coach must begin to combine match related maturity and competitive maturity.

The main goal at this level is team building. The Dutch connotation of team building is not quite the same as our understanding of team building. The coach must build on the simplified maturity attained in the preliminary stage and begin the 11 v. 11 process. Team building the Dutch way is a complex process and entails a number of factors:

## Team Organization

To perfect the team, organization is probably the main task of a coach. To have 11 players on the same page is difficult. Team organization includes defining the three functional lines, understanding the evolution of the game, the selected style of play, the quality of players, the team tactics, the course of the game and the quality of the opposing players.

## Team Mobility

Players must understand the three moments of the game and understand their roles in positions to master mobility.

## Team Efficiency

Team efficiency suggests that players must continue to perfect the activities with a ball. This technical ability combined with an understanding of player roles, team style and team tactics will lead to team efficiency.

## Winning the Duals

The team that wins the highest number of individual duals within the context of the team will win. This takes perfect technique and an understanding of the team style and tactics. Winning is important.

In order to accomplish this, the KNVB maintains that each training session must have four different characteristics or requirements.

## Soccer-related Objectives

- To score goals
- To build up
- Possession
- Defending
- Etc.

## Many Repetitions

This takes planning and making sure the coach has all the right equipment.
- Many turns
- Many passes
- Many shots

## Understanding the Group

- Age
- Skill level

## Correct Coaching

- Influence the players
- Intervene
- Give instruction
- Demonstrate
- Ask players questions
- Become engaged

The Dutch want the game to be the teacher, but they know that the role of the coach as a person of influence or as a facilitator is important. They understand that a progression is important, that creating a foundation is important, but there is a time when winning becomes important.

# Teaching the Game
## Each coaching method has its advantages and disadvantages

### Jeff Tipping

*"Practice doesn't make perfect, practice makes permanent"*

Coaches have many means of addressing the teaching of the game of soccer in practice settings. I would like to offer the following methods as means of coping with the teaching of the game with the strengths and weaknesses of each approach listed as part of the discussion.

## 1. Condition Play

Dependent upon the desired outcome, coaches can seek to impose conditions on practice play. The following restrictions attempt to arrive at the following outcomes:

| Restriction | Emphasis |
|---|---|
| 1-Touch | Quality of support and passing |
| 2-Touch | Quality of first touch and passing |
| 3-Touch | Quality of shielding and dribbling |

Diagram 1: Condition play: The teams are playing 6 v. 6 soccer on a reduced size field (44x60) with the condition that all players must take two touches of the ball.

Advantages
- Coach controls aspect of play
- Habits ingrained in players to prepare the ball when on attack
- Normally played in game-like situation.

Disadvantages
- Conditions of game become more important than good soccer (i.e., there are times to take more touches)
- Takes away players' judgment
- How to punish player when condition is broken? Generally practice has to stop and flow of game is disrupted

## 2. Drills

Diagram 2: The players are practicing a basic wall-pass drill which ends with a shot at goal.

60 yards

44 yards

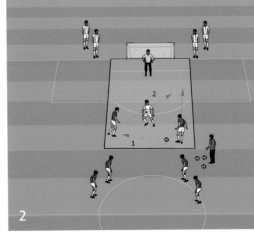

This is an example of practice of certain techniques and skills by constant repetition and movement. This normally involves players forming a line and it is generally not position specific (i.e., everybody performs same technique). It is normally done without opposition.

Advantages
- Coach closely supervises large group or even two-three groups
- Isolation of special technique or movement.
- Good for team spirit/morale
- Repetition takes place

Disadvantages
- Not position specific, i.e., there are not a lot of opportunities for backs to execute wall passes in central areas of the field or shoot from central positions per Diagram 2
- Lining up produces inactivity, cold weather could produce muscle strains, etc., if too much inactivity
- Lack of opposition makes practice unrealistic

## 3. Repetitive Pressure Training

Diagram 3: Pressure shooting by a center forward. Usually the player receives a continuous supply of services with little time between serves. One player's shooting techniques are put under

pressure by four feeders who give him continuous service in rotational order.

Advantages
- Good for technical, functional training
- Initially enjoyable
- Good for fitness
- Good for imprinting habits

Disadvantages
- No opposition generally
- Servers are normally static
- Limited tactical choices
- Fatigue leads to sloppy technique
- Working player dependant on quality of services

## 4. Shadow Play

Done in groups or over the whole field, normally against imaginary opposition.
- Used to imprint a style of play (direct or indirect).
- Method used the day before a game to rehearse patterns of play with guaranteed success (the confidence factor) and eliminating the danger of injury.
- Good for choreographing functional movements (i.e., fullback plays ball to winger and overlaps, winger dribbles inside and reverses to fullback who then crosses the ball to the center forward. CF heads to goal).
  - Establishes a passing rhythm.

Advantages
- Good warm-up
- Good refresher in pattern play
- Players achieve success easily
- A good 'hurry up' technique when time is limited

Disadvantages
- Sometimes little transfer to competitive match
- Players get complacent and bored if used excessively
- Can create bad habits

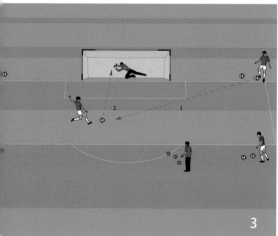

3

## 5. Functional Play

Diagram 4: Play is 2 v. 2 down a narrow central channel. The coach can instruct either the functional play of center forwards or the functional play of center backs.

## 6. Phase Play

Diagram 5: The prior functional practice has been enlarged to one-third of the field where the attacking team plays vs. the defensive unit. The service starts with one of the central players receiving the ball.

Coaching is done with small groups of players in a specific area of field, i.e., two center forwards vs. two center backs at top of penalty box.

Advantages
- Players get individual attention from coach
- Challenging and enjoyable as it is related to the technical and tactical demands of positions
- Can easily be incorporated into bigger game.
- Coach works on very specific, functional weaknesses or strengths of players

Disadvantages
- Excludes large numbers of players
- Exercises are isolated from live game situation
- Physically burdensome if done to excess

A direct progression from functional play frequently used to highlight previously practiced small group functional play in a large game setting. Normally practiced over at least half of the field. Phase play would normally utilize a 'trigger-man' who begins each repetition or movement. This practice can be used to instruct either attacking or defending play.

Advantages
- Realistic
- Easily supervised
- Repetitive
- Involves large groups of players

Disadvantages
- Numerous stoppages to re-start exercise
- Defenders sometimes frustrated if they have no goal or reward
- Players 'cheat' knowing that 'trigger-man' re-starts with same service

## 7. Coaching Grids

Diagram 6: Grids are used to give meaningful practice to the squad, e.g. shooting and goalkeeping drills in area 40x30 (area A); 4 v. 2 possession play in 20x20 area (area B), and 1 v. 1 dribbling, counter-attack practice in area 10x20 (area C).

Squares or rectangles (normally 10x10 yards) marked on a training field. Utilize to work on various aspect of play-giving coach easy flexibility to expand or combine squares. Used for effective teaching of techniques or basic tactical play.

Advantages
- Easily organized and coach can easily view a lot of activity at one time
- Good for specific training (i.e.. 1 v. 1 in a 10x20-yard area)
- Can be easily expanded

Disadvantages
- Players have difficulty transferring how the practice fits into a full game
- Normally non-functional (i.e., wall passes by backs, etc.)

## 8. Coaching in 11 v. 11 Game

Coaches frequently finish a practice with an 11 v. 11 game. Can be used for testing to see if previous training has been effective or to highlight a particular team concept (i.e. defending as a team).

In an 11 v. 11 game the coach sets up an attacking situation from the defensive third of the field.

Advantages
- Very realistic
- Players like it
- Facilities teamwork and tactical understanding

Disadvantages
- Very dependent on coach's ability to break down complex situations in a complex setting
- Exposes poor technique, (i.e., there are no tactics without technique or under pressure of opponents, technique fails)
- Too much emphasis on the competitive aspect of the game diminishes learning
- Too complex for many coaches and players to analyze
- Communication can be difficult for players not near scene of stoppage

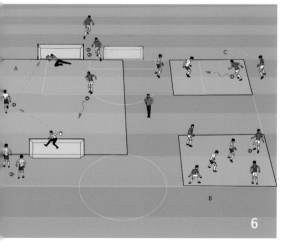

# Good Coach or Good Leader?
## Qualities are needed that will motivate players to do their best

### Nancy Feldman and Chris Cakebread

*Leaders are made, not born. They are made by hard effort, which is the price all of us must pay to achieve any goal that is worthwhile.*

*−Vince Lombardi*

It's March 20, 8 o'clock in the evening and a light rain is falling on a cold Nickerson Field at Boston University. A typical college student would be hunkered down with a textbook − in the library or in an overheated dorm room − prepping for an upcoming midterm. But, that is not happening for 18 members of the Boston University women's soccer team. They are just completing a series of soggy wind sprints at the end of a two-hour practice. It is five months until the 2003 season begins and already the coaching staff is preparing the team.

The 2002 season was a disappointment. Coming off two consecutive America East championships and two NCAA tournament appearances, the team finished with a 7-10-2 record. The Terriers find themselves in an unusual position. Rather than beginning preparation for the new season from a position of achievement, as they have over the past few years, the task is to begin to reestablish the psyche and character of a team that fully expected to compete to win its third consecutive conference crown and make its third appearance in the NCAA women's soccer tournament.

From end-of-season assessments with her staff, head coach Nancy Feldman identified what was important for the following season: to refocus on leadership principles that would re-create a successful team. If, as Coach Lombardi said, leaders are made, not born, then how are they made?

"I thought of the situations that we had to play through this year," says Feldman, "and I also thought of what I have learned as a coach and as a player that could apply. I think that these points are important to keep me grounded as a coach. I also thought that they might be helpful to other coaches especially those who are in the process of developing their ideas and philosophies."

Drawing on years of experience, first as a Division I player at the University of Massachusetts and then in a coaching career that spanned 15 years at the college level − as well as involvement with several national team programs − Feldman prepared the following list of leadership principles to reinforce for the coming season.

## Be You

Coaches and team leaders need to be able to adapt the strengths of their personalities to their role on the field and in the locker room. There is no one coaching or leadership style that fits all. Coaches by nature are controlling, but they have a responsibility to provide both learning, and − dare we say − a fun environment for their players. Passion is endemic to any sport. Players often draw their will to succeed from their coach. It is the role of the coach to capture and retain that passion and encourage and develop it throughout the season.

Therefore, sincerity is the key. Although we can all look to role models to emulate, a leader's own personality and style are the only ones that will work. Be yourself. If you are knowledgeable about the game and prepared for the season, your passion and commitment will translate to the team.

## Have (and Express) a Philosophy and Vision

Often, a coach will begin a season without a clearly defined set of objectives and goals for the team. It is not enough to just have a daily practice plan and a stance that communicates "we'll just see how things go" as the season develops. A coach should have a season-long plan, realistic but aggressive. It is vital that the coach encourage a two-way dialogue with the team so that the team shares, and has ownership of, the objectives and goals for the coming season.

This stage can provide an opportunity to identify leaders within the team. While some may receive the formal title of captain, it takes more players than the captains to help promote a team vision. Senior members of the group must feel an integral responsibility for the success of the team and must be able to communicate that, particularly to the new members.

A coach should use and develop the leaders within the group and delegate responsibilities to a number of team members, enhancing the leadership pyramid, thus strengthening the power of the plan and the vision. Senior members of the group must feel an integral responsibility for the success of the team and must be able to communicate that, particularly to the new members.

A coach should use and develop the leaders within the group and delegate responsibilities to a number of team members, enhancing the leadership pyramid, thus strengthening the power of the plan and vision.

## Establish a Culture

The Montreal Canadians are one of the most tradition-rich teams in all of sport. Established in the National Hockey League in 1918, the Canadians management has a collection of photos of former players in the Hockey Hall of Fame. Under the photos are these words in French and English: "To you from failing hands we throw the torch, be yours to hold it high!"

Every organization and every team, professional or amateur, needs to instill standards and values in their team culture. Most often a culture is reflected in the behavior and actions of the leaders. But that example must be based upon the standards set by the coach. Consistency in action and behavior is critical to this being a successful component of a team. You cannot set standards for the team and then bend the rules for individuals. Your core team leaders must buy into the standards and make clear to their peers what is valued. Coaches must nurture and support this core group, because those players will be the role models for behaviors and actions of the team.

Provide evidence that the culture established is expected to be in place not just on the field, but in every aspect of the team member's actions.

## Build a Foundation

A culture, a philosophy, is not established overnight. A coach must lay a foundation that incorporates both enthusiasm and passion for team success, as well as standards of action and behavior. How best to do that? Develop a set of formal traditions and expectations that the team members can count on. In addition, a strong foundation can best be established by making every individual player accountable for how they go about their business, both off and on the field. Find creative ways to do this as a way of involving the team and coaches so that all members of the team organization take pride in their affiliation.

## Keep Things on Track

No season proceeds exactly as planned. Inevitably, even in the most successful seasons, difficulties arise, injuries happen, and not everything can be controlled. Always be prepared to implement alternative action plans. To gain the proper perspective, be sensitive to your players and others involved with the team. Listen. Don't always be the one to carry the message. Be open to your staff, as well as to team members, and hear their feedback and concerns. Be prepared to motivate your team, particularly when things are moving off track. Surprise them. Seasons are long, and training – as well as emotion – often gets stale. Have some fun.

## Inspire

What is it that has drawn you to the sport in the first place? What is the passion and fire that keeps you motivated? Can you identify those traits and apply them within your personality? It's important that each coach be able to inspire and motivate players to do their best. No one can be expected to emulate the personality style of another coach. What each coach has to work with is his or her own personality and charisma. Be comfortable in the role that you adopt, but continue to improve on your teaching and motivational techniques. Inspiration comes from showing that you believe in and are confident about your players. Make players feel a part of the process, not just dutiful soldiers.

## Reexamine

As the season begins, every coach has a set of expectations. Coaches are not seers. Nothing ever goes precisely as planned throughout a season. What happens when a team just cannot put the ball in the net? How does a coach hold together a team that is not reaching expectations? When or how does a coach begin to question whether the principles implemented so positively in September begin to fall apart in November? A coach has to monitor each member of the team, not to mention the peripheral influences that intrude on a fragile team's psyche. It is no longer enough to confine a relationship with players to soccer, ignoring everything else. Players can be influenced by anything from cataclysmic world events to pressures from school, family and friends. Keep checking the pulse of the group and how your athletes are being affected by the many external variables.

## Reflect, Renovate and Reapply

In our harried society we often move from one stage of life to another, with little time – or desire – to look back. A season ends and a coach moves on to other responsibilities and then to pick up the thread of the next season. Reflection is not a skill taught in school. But it is a trait that should be applied by a coach during the season. Coaches should also elicit opinions from players, assistants and those close to the organization to gain a broader perspective on the actions of the team and the season. "How can we improve?" should be the focus, and not "What did we do wrong?"

Find ways to reenergize your team during and after the season. It's easy for a coach to push the same buttons in practice and during a game, week in and week out. Gradually, players begin to tune out the message. It's like seeing the same commercial on television many times. Eventually it's just white noise. Nothing penetrates the players and turning up the volume only makes it worse. Find fresh ways to restate goals, objectives and philosophies. Keep your team off balance by introducing new ideas, new situations. Be open to new developments in sport and life, not just in soccer. A coach who can draw on disparate sources can often cobble together a system or philosophy that stands out for its unique flavor and can make a significant and lasting impression on the players.

## Wrapping it up

Often individuals who gravitate to coaching are former players who by mission – or by accident – end up coaching a team. It would be unusual for an athlete not to have been influenced by experiences with former coaches. Experience is a great teacher, if it is the right kind of experience. An understanding of the game is clearly a necessity when one chooses to go into coaching. Wins, at every level, tend to validate the skills of a coach. However, it takes more than just the W's for a team to be successful.

As any experienced soccer participant knows, a coach can't just roll out the ball and develop a team by running a few drills and setting up an offensive and defensive system of play. Intrusions from a plethora of situations influence the dynamic of any team situation. When a situation, a game, or a season begins to unravel, it's the coach who becomes the focal point and it is the coach who is ultimately responsible for maintaining team cohesion. Having the ability to lead in both good times and bad is a crucial skill. Preparation is critical; adaptability is instrumental.

Good leadership comes down to working hard to look beyond the playing field and locker room. Coaches should ask themselves before, during and after the season: "How can I be a better leader?" "What can I do today to influence my team to be better as a unit," and "How can I influence each individual to perform to their best ability?" It's a big responsibility, and not one that comes easily. Stephen Covey concludes an early edition of his book, The Seven Habits of Highly Effective People with the following words: "By centering our lives on correct principles and creating a balanced focus between doing and increasing our ability to do, we become empowered in the task of creating effective, useful and peaceful lives."

Okay, so soccer coaching may not lead to a peaceful life, but applying sound leadership principles can help each coach to be more effective, and ultimately create a more successful team environment.

© Craig Bohnert

# Soccer's Building Blocks

## Christian Lavers

The resources available for training elite youth soccer players have increased exponentially during the past 10 years. Athletes in the top clubs throughout the country now are regularly provided with, among other things, both strength and power training as well as speed and agility training, benefits previously reserved solely for college and professional soccer athletes. In many regards, the training and coaching methodologies used with these youth soccer players are far more advanced than those used with athletes in other American sports.

The large increase in training tools and disciplines and the resulting necessity for top players to become not only better soccer players but also faster and stronger athletes has added an element of complexity to planning soccer training. The challenge for trainers and clubs is to provide their athletes with the proper amount of training in each discipline at the proper time without overtraining the athlete.

Adding to this challenge is the fact that, if not provided with this training by their clubs, many athletes will find it on their own. When athletes begin training with several different independent programs, the lack of coordination between the training plans often results in overtraining.

Similarly, conflicting training methodologies often can diminish the returns the athletes receive from their hard work. Because of these problems, providing athletes with one integrated and coordinated training plan becomes even more important.

What is needed is a structural framework for developing a year-long training program for elite soccer athletes. This model program will

incorporate the proper amount of training in all the disciplines essential for soccer and athletic development. Adherence to this program or one like it will develop soccer players who not only are improved technically and tactically, but also are stronger, faster athletes.

Because of the vast difference in training priorities and needs for both the very young athlete and the mature college or professional soccer player, the scope of this article is confined to 16- to 19-year-old athletes. Presuming that, for elite players, basic technical and tactical concepts are mastered before age 16, it is near age 16 when strength, speed and other training disciplines first can be incorporated most efficiently into a soccer-training program.

The U.S. Soccer Federation and most other soccer governing bodies in countries throughout the world, including the German and Dutch, have identified four basic components to the game of soccer: technical, tactical, physical and psychological. A model-training plan for elite athletes must address each of these components. Analyzing training structure through a component-based viewpoint also helps to provide a framework for developing efficient and successful training plans:

## Technical Component

Elite U-17 to U-19 players already should have mastered soccer's basic technical skills. For these players, training technique involves learning and perfecting advanced skills (bending a ball, volley finishes, etc.) while increasing the speed and consistency of execution in all technical actions. This technical training should provide high amounts of repetition at increasing speeds. As such, high quality technical training often will include a fitness element.

Finally, technical training for elite players should involve increasing "resistance" within the training activity. Though younger players may need to train primarily with no pressure or resistance (with passive defenders, for example), elite players must spend much of their time training technique under defensive pressure within a game-realistic environment.

## Tactical Component

For elite U-17 to U-19 players, tactical training still can involve reminders of the basic decision-making principles of the game – individual tactics. However, most tactical training at this age should focus on learning broader and more complex tactical cues. The majority of tactical training time should be spent in one of two areas:

- **Group/team tactics:** Group or team tactics involve learning tactical cues within lines on the field and in various systems of play. Group or team tactical training also helps individual athletes understand their roles and functions in various situations on the field.

- **Functional training:** Since by this age most players have "settled in" to a specific position or line on the field, functional training also should be a regular feature of training – involving training players in both the specific techniques and tactics of their primary positions.

## Physical Component

The physical component of the game involves athleticism – strength, quickness, agility, balance, power, etc. Because the methods for training these qualities are quite different, the physical component can be broken down into three training modules:

- **Strength and power development:** Strength and power training for soccer players should heavily emphasize the athletes' "core"

– the abdominals and lower back. Most importantly, the training must be soccer-specific; that is, the training exercises should strengthen muscle movements that actually are performed in the game.

- **Lateral speed and agility (LSA):** LSA training involves increasing foot speed, improving control of the body's center of gravity and increasing the efficiency and speed of changes of direction. Both LSA and SAS (see below) training modules emphasize quality of movement mechanics, not fitness or quantity of movement; therefore, these modules are most effectively done first in training.

- **Straight-ahead speed and acceleration (SAS):** SAS training involves improving acceleration mechanics so the body is efficiently and effectively using all body movement and positioning to increase speed. The goals of SAS training are to eliminate counterproductive movement habits and to increase muscle explosiveness.

## Psychological Component

Many coaches speak of the need for a proper mentality and the importance of psychological strength, but fail to spend time doing psychological training. At its most basic level, psychological training involves teaching the athlete how to train consistently and effectively, then how to compete effectively. More advanced psychological training involves activities designed to help the athlete perform in game situations. Psychological training can be broadly separated into two basic focuses:

- **Motivation-focused training:** Motivation-focused psychological training is designed to help the athlete learn to train and compete sharply and with high intensity on a consistent basis. Examples include goal-setting sessions, developing habits of a "competitor," etc.

- **Performance-focused training:** Performance-focused psychological training is designed to help the athlete perform successfully in pressure situations. Examples include: visualization techniques, stress-reduction techniques, etc.

Each of the four training components obviously includes a broad range of training activities. Within this spectrum of activities, basic coaching principles dictate that, whatever the training goal, developmentally appropriate training activities always be selected. Also, the activities used in any session must depend on the specific individual developmental needs of the athlete or team involved.

It is useful to think of the components not as independent divisions, but as overlapping areas along a soccer training continuum. For example, tactical training always has some degree of technical benefit and psychological training can be built into conditioned games. Well thought-out and efficient training activities can and should involve multiple components.

## Season Segmentation

During the course of a calendar year, each training component will receive greater or lesser emphasis, according to established training priorities. These priorities should be carefully identified based on the time of the year, specifically the time and focus of the particular season.

For soccer players, the calendar year can be roughly divided into four different seasons, each of varying length and each requiring very different training priorities (Table 1).

The training planning process begins each year with a three- to six-week pre-season and moves directly into the longest season of the year, the competitive season. At the conclusion of the competitive season, a period of rest and regeneration, or a recovery season, is essential. Following this recuperative break comes off-season training, which should be a time of significant individual technical and athletic improvement. Properly conducted, off-season training lays the groundwork for much of the results of the competitive season. At the end of off-season training, the players should be provided with a short recovery break before the yearly cycle begins again with pre-season training.

## Developing Training Priorities

The different realities and demands of each season will dictate training priorities and goals during that season. For example, in the competitive season, the pressure for results in competition requires that team tactical training be a high priority. Similarly, the need to help athletes deal with the stresses of game performance requires psychological development to be a high priority. Each season of the year will require similar adjustments to training priorities. Table 2 illustrates the appropriate priority level for each training component in each season.

*Table 1: Four seasons of the soccer year*

| Season | % of Year | Months |
|---|---|---|
| Pre-season | 15 | 1.5 |
| Competitive Season | 45 | 5 |
| Recovery and Regeneration | 15 | 2.5 |
| Off Season Training | 25 | 3 |

*Table 2: Seasonal training priorities*

| Season | Technical Training | Tactical Training | Physical Strength/ Power | Physical Training: LSA | Physical Training: SAS | Psychological Training |
|---|---|---|---|---|---|---|
| Pre-season | High | High | Low | Medium | Medium | Medium |
| Competitive Season | Low /Medium | High | Low | Medium | Medium | High |
| Off Season | High | Low | High | Medium | Medium | Low |

The priority level of each training area should determine the amount of weekly training time devoted to that area within the season. Although the exact weekly training frequency may vary both within and across seasons, establishing training priorities helps to provide a guidepost to the content of each training week:

- HIGH – Should be addressed in every training during the week.
- MEDIUM – Should be addressed in approximately one-half of the trainings.
- LOW – Should be addressed in one training per week.

Only after the priority level of each training area in each season is determined can a successful yearly training plan be developed. Logically, this plan will begin with the pre-season.

## The Pre-season

Ideally, pre-season training should begin four weeks before the first official competition. This will provide sufficient time to address all team needs and to physically and mentally prepare the players for the rigors of the competitive season. (At a bare minimum, pre-season training should begin two weeks before competition.) Pre-season training has several goals:

1. Sharpen technical execution
2. Develop a team system and style of play
3. Refine fitness levels
4. Establish set piece organization

Though players may not be expected to enter pre-season in top physical form, pre-season is not a time to get fit. Elite athletes must understand that fitness is a 12-month priority and must take responsibility for maintaining high levels of fitness throughout the year. If an athlete enters pre-season expecting to get fit, chances of injury increase significantly and performance in all pre-season training will suffer. The costs of getting fit during the pre-season then will carry over to produce unsatisfactory results early in the competitive season.

During the course of a four-week pre-season, two or three friendly competitions are ideal. Spreading these competitions over the course of the pre-season will allow for adequate training time to address tactical problems that are identified during the competitions. These competitions also provide opportunities to train set plays in a realistic environment.

Pre-season training should place a heavy emphasis on refining technique, particularly the speed of technical execution. During the off-season, technical "sharpness" tends to fade without competition. Since demanding technical training also has a fitness component to it, it is also a very efficient way to provide more enjoyable fitness training.

Table 3: Model pre-season training program

| Session | Morning | Afternoon |
|---|---|---|
| Monday | Recovery or Psychological Training – 45 Minutes | Off |
| Tuesday | Technical Training 60 Minutes | LSA, Tactical Training 75 Minutes |
| Wednesday | Off | SAS, Tactical Training 90 Minutes |
| Thursday | Technical Training 60 Minutes | LSA, Tactical Training 75 Minutes |
| Friday | Off | Off |
| Saturday | Light Technical Training, Psychological Training 45 Minutes | Off |
| Sunday | Off | Friendly Competition |

Considering these goals, a model pre-season training week places heavy emphasis on refining technical execution and mastering team tactics (Table 3).

During a four-week pre-season, two-a-day training should be planned only during the middle two weeks. The lower intensity of the weeks without two-a-days will allow the athletes to "ramp up" at the beginning of the pre-season, which will help reduce injuries, and to "taper down" into the competitive season.

Similarly, two-a-day training should be planned so that the training on these days is short and of high intensity. The high-energy demand placed on the athletes during these days requires that total training time be carefully managed. If this training is too long, fatigue will cause both the concentration and performance level of the athletes to drop precipitously.

Always remember that the over-arching goal of the pre-season is to begin the competitive season with players who are healthy, fit and fully tactically prepared for success. Both over-training and under-training will compromise these goals.

Recovery training should be very light and low-impact and primarily scheduled to help the athletes reduce stiffness and soreness from previous training and competitions. As such, pool workouts, light jogs or stationary biking are excellent activities. Yoga is another activity with excellent recuperative benefits.

## The Competitive Season

The primary focus of the competitive season is on game results. As such, during the competitive season, tactical and psychological training as shown in Table 4 will provide the greatest immediate rewards.

Because technical improvement requires high amounts of repetition and thus has a longer time horizon, general technical training is a lower priority during the competitive season.

However, specific technical functional training may be a regular feature of training in order to improve an athlete's performances in executing the techniques they use most often in competition. For example, technical functional finishing activities for forwards may greatly

*Table 4: Model of competitive season training program*

| Monday | Off |
|---|---|
| Tuesday | SAS, Tactical Training 75 minutes |
| Wednesday | LSA, Tactical Training 90 minutes |
| Thursday | SAS, Tactical Training 90 minutes |
| Friday | Off |
| Saturday | Technical Training, Psychological Training 30 minutes |
| Sunday | Competition |

improve goal-scoring success during the course of the season if done consistently.

The intensity level of training must be monitored carefully during the competitive season. Because players must have opportunities to recover after competition, training the day or two after competitions should be lighter than on other days.

Most importantly, scheduling during the competitive season must remain flexible. For example, the day after particularly physically demanding competitions, it may be advisable to add a short recovery and psychological workout. Also, one strength and power training per week may be added to maintain strength gains that were made during the off-season. Finally, psychological training may play an increased role during weeks of highly emotional or important competitions.

Training the day before competitions can be very effective if planned correctly. This training should be of high intensity in order to simulate the coming competition, but must also be very short to prevent tiring the players for the next day. Psychological training on this day should consist primarily of visualizing individual performance during the competition. This primes the athlete for performance while also lowering stress.

## The Recovery and Regeneration Season

The recovery and regeneration season is both the most overlooked season of the year and the most abused. This season has only one focus: to allow the athlete to mentally, physically and emotionally recover from the stresses of a competitive season. In order to accomplish this, the recovery season must provide the athlete with an extended break from the sport.

The recovery and regeneration period is overlooked because many trainers, players and particularly parents, do not appreciate the importance of a break. Whether driven by concerns of falling behind other players and teams, boredom or whatever else, the recuperative benefits of this period often are ignored. More than anything else, this period of rest is important in preventing burnout and over-training of young soccer players. After a recovery season, players will return healthy and reinvigorated to their training. In this instance, less really can mean more.

The length of the recovery season is negotiable. It can range from 25 to 40 percent of the length of the pre-season and competitive season combined. Generally, the longer the competitive season, the longer the recovery season should be.

Table 5: Model off season training program

| Monday | LSA, Technical Training 75 minutes |
|--------|-----------------------------------|
| Tuesday | Strength and Power, Technical Training 90 minutes |
| Wednesday | Off |
| Thursday | LSA, Strength and Power, Technical Training 90 minutes |
| Friday | Off |
| Saturday | SAS, Strength and Power Training 60 minutes |
| Sunday | Off |

No team activities should be planned during this season. Every athlete should be encouraged to avoid any soccer training for several weeks during this period, even if the athlete believes this to be unnecessary. If after a few weeks an athlete desires to begin individual soccer training again and he/she is completely healthy, encourage the athlete to do so.

## The Off Season

The off season is the time of the year farthest removed from the competitive season and is sandwiched between the recovery season and the pre-season. Off season training should not begin until the athletes have had time to recover physically, mentally and emotionally from the competitive season.

Because it is far removed from the competitive season and the stresses of winning and losing that competition provides, individual training needs take priority during this period: technical development, power and strength development, LSA and SAS all can be very effectively trained during this period (Table 5).

Off season training should be specifically tailored to the needs of individual players. Technical training programs can be different for each player or each functional line. Strength and power development needs also may be different among players on the team. However, while different

individual training programs may be developed, conducting these trainings together as a team will help build camaraderie and sustain motivation.

## Conclusion

Elite soccer players require training programs that address all of their needs technically, tactically, athletically and psychologically. A program that focuses too much on one area while neglecting another will hinder the athletes' overall development. On the other hand, a program that forces the athlete to over-train or that emphasizes the wrong training areas at the wrong times will risk injury and diminish team success. Therefore, finding the correct mix of training components and developing a single integrated training plan are mandatory for long-term individual and team success.

A well-developed yearly training program accelerates overall player development, reduces the chances of injury and increases player motivation. When players know that all their developmental needs are being addressed, they also grow in confidence – both in themselves and in their teammates.

The selection of safe and developmentally appropriate activities and the final scheduling of weekly training remain the domain of the team trainer, who must combine his/her technical expertise with knowledge of specific team needs.

The best trainers also realize when additional coaching expertise is required. Often, strength or speed specialists should be brought in to develop appropriate programs and to provide expert feedback. However, even when these experts are employed, it is the team trainer who must insure that each training module addresses individual needs and is scheduled appropriately within the training program. It is in these choices where the best trainers distinguish themselves.

*Editor's note: Christian Lavers, who is on the Region II Girls ODP Staff, holds a USSF "A" License.*

# Realistic Practices Pay Off

## Kids love to compete and they gain more in a game-like setting

### Dr. Louis Pantusco
### NSCAA National Academy Associate Staff Member

As a coach of a U-10 team, boys or girls, you have certain expectations of the kids as they take the field on a Saturday morning. You want them to play hard, be aggressive, pass to each other and hopefully play to the best of their ability. Winning is a bonus.

But are you giving them the tools necessary to achieve these goals? It takes more than your desire, combined with the shouts from the other side of the field, to convert these youngsters into game-time warriors. It takes effective, realistic practice sessions.

In many of the practices at the U-10 level, coaches focus on simplicity and fun; there may be some emphasis on technique (i.e., passing, control, shooting and dribbling), but primarily coaches just try to make it fun. Take the simple drill in which two players are asked to run up the field together, 10 yards apart, passing the ball back and forth with one touch. How often does this happen in a game? Should developing players be running at top speed when learning how to pass? It's hard enough to teach the proper technique when they are standing still. Another popular practice is the hour-long scrimmage in which the score ends up 14-5.

What is the best approach to teach young players various aspects of the game during a practice session? I'm sure there is a multitude of topics or concepts that can be useful for the U-10 player, but here are three objectives that need to be incorporated into every training session: competition, repetition and position.

## The Warm-up

In the warm-up phase of a practice, U-10 coaches should focus on the technical aspects of the game. In this part of practice, repetition can be stressed. It is not necessary to introduce a new dribbling move or another technical aspect of the game every practice. Rather, an appropriate amount of time in the practice should be used to review and offer some further refinement (progression) of information covered in the last session. Hopefully the players will have worked on the material presented at the previous practice on their own so that their level of proficiency has improved.

It is here that soccer coaches can take a lesson from those teaching dance or karate, where mastery of the required technique is achieved through repetition. Once reviewed, the technical exercise should be upgraded in terms of its demands on the players. Unless challenged, soccer players will not improve.

Competition should be mixed in with repetition almost immediately. In my 15 years of coaching camps, clinics and clubs, I have found one constant: kids love to compete. Boys and girls are inspired when a contest is introduced. It does not matter if they are doing ball taps, pullbacks, push passing or shooting, competition can be introduced in all technical training.

For example, when teaching the pull back move, the coach could put a ball between two players and say "go." At that time the players try to pull the ball away from each other. The player who pulls the ball back only gets a point if he/she still has possession of the ball inside the grid after five seconds. The coach has an opportunity to instruct the players to bring the ball back behind their plant foot, turn their body away from the defender and get ready for contact. This simple drill gives the coach an opportunity to work on shielding and dribbling, but more importantly it introduces a game-like element of competition.

In another example, when players are dribbling around in a grid, using the inside/outside of either foot, the coach can create a competitive environment. One approach is to choose players to legally charge the dribbling player's shoulder as they dribble through the grid. For that youngster who isn't as technically advanced, one defender to fend off is plenty. For the better or really skillful dribbler, two players may want to assume the challenging role.

This pressure teaches the players with the ball to be more proficient dribblers. I instruct the dribbling players to step away from the ball (while still within playing distance of the ball - to be legal!) into the defender, virtually stopping the defenders progress; then after the pressure is absorbed, spin away from the defender (or get out there with the ball). Kids love the competition and they learn how to play in game-like conditions.

How many of have heard players complain about other teams pushing? What is the coach's response? The proper response would be, "Step into the pressure, absorb the push, then spin away from it." Where have they heard that before? At practice.

So once again, starting with the warm-up, U-10 teams need to play competitively in practice to get ready for the demands of the game. The warm-up should consist of repetition and competition, with emphasis on the former.

## Match-like Conditions

In stage two of the U-10 practice, the coach should set up a match-like situation. In NSCAA terminology this means introducing a goal to the exercise. In U-10 games, 2 v. 1 and 3 v. 2 situations seem to happen continuously. Introducing your team to these man-up or man-down situations is useful. The emphasis here is position, followed closely by competition. Repetition will come from the coach.

Once the ball goes out of bounds or the situation that you constructed is no longer recognizable, simply start over again. Giving the defense a point for getting the ball back to the coach is a good way to keep score and instill competition. Regardless of the situation being set up, competition is a must. If you don't want to keep score, ask an ambitious parent to assist.

In Diagram 1, we see a 2 v. 2 game established within a 20 x 25 yard grid, though this can be adjusted according to the age and skill level of your players. There are four two-player teams, dressed in blue/white, white, gray and red/white. The two teams on the exterior will either be assigned to play in goal or serve as neutral support players on the touchlines. Each team will play three games in the middle.

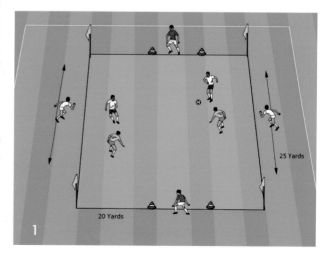

25 Yards

20 Yards

1

The interior players are put into competitive situations every time they touch the ball and with the support of the neutral players either team will have numerous 1 v. 1, 2 v. 1 and 3 v. 2 situations to recognize. The neutral players provide width to the game, though they should be limited in terms of their touches. They also might be allowed to shoot, though within two touches to keep their interest. Hopefully your goalies also will keep their focus. In arranging the two-person teams, coaches may want to work to equate competition and/or play players together (strikers together, etc.). If for some reason, parity cannot be achieved, place restrictions on the more talented team. You might limit touches or require the player's weak foot to score the goal.

This exercise provides ample opportunity to teach spacing, speed of play and movement without the ball. It also places kids in a competitive environment. If there is balance among the teams, keep score. Let the players know their record at the end of this mini-tournament within your practice.

## The Practice Match

Every practice should end with a two-goal match. Players need to learn the rules of the game, the expectations of their position and how to apply the techniques introduced throughout your practices. It is here that the coach can allow players to experience playing different positions. These games should be 8 v. 8 or less so everyone gets involved. The games should be fluid, with competition coming to the forefront while repetition takes a back seat.

When do you stop play? Ideally the coach should try to resist the temptation to continually shout instructions and let play move on. He or she should make mental notes about general themes – where to move, when to pass, when to dribble – and talk to players individually at water or rest breaks or following practice.

© Perry McIntyre

Sometimes there are correctable and teachable moments in the practice game. They should be utilized, but sparingly. If there are teachable moments, the coach needs to get his thoughts across clearly and concisely. Players should be encouraged to be aggressive, pass or share the ball with one another, though on the latter count it must be remembered that at age 10 most kids are egocentric and would rather keep the ball for themselves.

The game should be competitive, though. In addition to goals scored, teams could be rewarded for such things as successful passes, winning tackles and shots on goal. The coach also may try not to referee very "tightly." Players need to develop an ability to withstand some rough contact. By stopping play every time someone is pushed a bit, the coach does not make the game realistic or breed players who can withstand such physical pressure in games. Obviously, this type of practice management demands discretion, as no one wants liability problems to emerge from such an environment.

In my years of coaching I have been fortunate to receive many compliments from parents in regard to the work I have done with their kids. Without question the most common comment from parents is, "I am so happy to see my son/daughter be aggressive out there." Soccer is a competitive sport. It is not fair to our young players to expect them to be tough during games without training them in a competitive environment.

The competition is fun and the success obtained from developing in a competitive practice atmosphere increases the probability that the players will retain that attitude and have it carry over to their matches. Remember, practice is where the teaching is done. In games, coaches lose control over repetition; what seems to matter most is the ability to correctly apply technique in simple game situations (this plays out in your team's tactics, i.e. formation and shape) and the ability to deal with the competitive element in the game.

If your practices have had these emphases, then, in time, your players will be successful in meeting these soccer challenges.

# Making Training Game-Like

## Pat McCarry

As a coach involved in youth soccer, I have increasingly seen the value of using conditioned (restricted) games in successfully coaching technical and tactical themes.

In the past, a youth training session has often comprised a warm-up, then a series of drills or activities (often unrelated and not progressive) followed by a regular game. Even when the earlier activities have been related to a coherent theme, there often has been little transfer of those skills to the real game itself. The former activities lacked relevance in the eyes of the players and were seen as something to endure before playing a "proper" game. At this point the players would revert to old habits and show very little improvement and learning in relation to the theme as they played. The conditioned game as a bridging activity provides the vital missing link.

The progression for an effective technical practice that will use conditioned games might be:
- Warm-up on related theme
- Technical/skill development of a specific theme
- Conditioned games emphasizing the specific theme
- Game emphasizing the specific theme

There are a variety of conditions that can be placed on any game depending on the aim of the practice, including:
- Limited touches
- Use of zones to restrict or encourage movement
- Man-to-man marking
- Extra goals
- Extra balls
- Minimum number of passes before moving to a different zone (or scoring)
- Time limits
- Passive defending
- Modified playing area

Each condition is used to force the players to repeat, in a game-like setting, certain skills/ patterns of movement they currently do not use appropriately. The skill of the coach in selecting which conditions to apply, then adapting them if they are not working, is critical to the success of this type of training.

If done successfully the coach will create many perfect opportunities to coach the theme of the day (e.g. 5 v. 5 with man-to-man marking in a relatively small area to reinforce individual defending technique). It's as if he or she has rigged the game to enable the coaching points to be clearly made in context.

As well as being game-related, these activities are fun. The players are active, easily engaged and enthusiastic, which means they are better able to learn and progress. The use of these games also is a useful strategy for working with youth players or teams that may be attending practice for reasons other than a burning passion for the game.

U.K. Elites uses the conditioned game as an integral part of most sessions, whether technical or tactical. However, in certain team tactical areas our curriculum promotes exclusive use of conditioned games once the warm-up has taken place.

## Developing Tactical Skills Among Youth Players

In the United States, huge strides have been made in the quality of youth soccer. The general technical improvement is quite evident. Improved technique can be seen throughout the youth playing community. In fact, some firmly believe that the main weakness in the American youth game at all levels is still tactical. The best way to address this is within the game itself.

An effective tactical practice utilizing conditioned games may develop as follows:
* Warm-up
* Conditioned game 1: more restrictions
* Conditioned game 2: fewer restrictions
* Game

If a tactical concept is to be coached successfully in a 90-minute session, there will be little time to work on the technical aspects of the game. With this in mind, the related techniques will be delivered in the preceding session and revised in the warm-up, such as opening the body to receive the ball when switching play. To coach both the technique and the tactical understanding of this theme in one session would be to overload the youth player.

Sound planning, both short-term and long-term, and an understanding of child development are essential if the players are to receive a balanced curriculum that includes technical, tactical and (as they get older) functional elements.

Switching the play is a good example of team tactical play suited to conditioned games and is particularly relevant to coaching American children, as their traditional games are very direct. Passing backwards, sideways and diagonally with patience are not natural patterns of play in American football, basketball and ice hockey and therefore need to be conditioned within the game situation so they become considered options.

This is no easy task in the one or two sessions devoted to the theme during a particular season. Because time is limited, the coach needs to be focused on the desired result. The early part

of the session will involve rules that coerce the players to switch play so the pattern of play is established. Conditions then gradually are removed as the session unfolds. Ultimately the coach needs to give the players a tangible reason to switch the play.

It is important that the concluding game involves free play so the players can focus on the tactical (decision-making) aspect of the game. This is the part of the session that allows us, as coaches, to assess learning and see if the players are switching play at the right time and providing the team shape that enables this (width, depth and length). At this point some players will resort to old habits and attack directly in straight lines, while others will adhere rigidly to the recently-enforced habit of changing the angle of attack, even when direct penetration is the most appropriate option.

This is where effective coaching takes place; however, the interventions should be timely. To stop the game too often will prevent flow and is sometimes unnecessary, as some errors are of an individual nature and could be addressed with a quiet word at a later time.

An effective test of coaching skills could simply be to observe the results of the work. Simply put, are the players demonstrating the theme correctly and appropriately? Technical weakness inevitably will cause the games to break down, especially at a younger age. This will have implications for variables such as size of area and the number of players on each team.

In our example, the field should be short and wide to encourage the exploiting of space out wide, and the attacking team will be initially overloaded to promote success. These additional considerations will be critical to meeting your objectives.

The session plan is part of U.K. Elite's U-12 unique residential camp curriculum and its essence is modified as the players get older. At this young age, teams will have varying success in initially applying this tactic to a real game situation, but hopefully they will understand the concept.

As educators our aim is to provide them with an understanding of the game as well as the technical tools necessary to play it well. Of course, we are mainly concerned with technique and individual tactics with 5- to 8-year-olds. However, as they mature physically, mentally and psychologically, we can address team concepts.

U.K. Elite's Residential Camps and High School Team Training Weeks have experienced tremendous growth over the past three years, mainly because both the American youth

players and their coaches recognize that we are addressing more complex concepts and differentiating for the Elite player. The curriculum is customized for U-l0, U-12, U-14, U-l6 and U-18, sometimes building on themes from a younger age group, and at other times introducing new concepts. Our aim is to take the players to a new level of technical and tactical understanding.

If we are as effective as possible in our coaching methodology, then American youth players will be able to appreciate and understand the game more fully, even if their participation ends at the high school stage. This should constantly ensure a better-informed and better educated generation of soccer players and parents in the future.

# Keep Them Short and Sharp

## Ian Stokell

*A few years ago as the U.S. Men's National Team played a series of exhibition games some of the players were quoted in the media as saying that they were physically and mentally fatigued and that had accounted for somewhat mediocre performances against such teams as the Netherlands and Belgium. The views of several coaches on the motivation of players and training and practice regimens are reported in this article.*

While technique and tactics are often seen as the major components in the coaching of a soccer team, few teams could compete effectively at a high level without consideration being given to motivation and maintaining player sharpness throughout the latter part of a season.

And just as different coaches have a variety of views on the subjects, the different levels of soccer – national team, professional, college – can also influence a particular coaching approach.

At the national level, just being given the chance to play can be incentive enough. Former U.S. National Team coach Steve Sampson told Soccer Journal that "Starting time, playing time, being selected to the National Team can all be used to motivate players."

And the reverse is also true. Said Sampson, "Not selecting a player also is a major statement to a player, especially if a player has been a consistent member of the team or a part of the program, and then all of a sudden if he's not called in, there has to be a reason why. And then it's up to that player, through his play with his club team, to perform better so that he then gets the call-up for the National Team."

Then "starting" is what those players want. "Once a player is eventually called up," said Sampson, "then those players – and they are all excellent players – what they live for is 'starting.'"

And being given the chance to start often elevates that player to a new level. "It's amazing to me the mentality of a player who gets the opportunity to start versus a player who comes off the bench," Sampson said. "And so you can motivate a player by giving him the privilege of starting, and if a player who is coming off the bench performs well, consistently well over a number of games, then again you can motivate a player by starting him, as opposed to bringing him off the bench."

Bobby Clark is head coach of Notre Dame's men's soccer team and he can turn to a lifetime of involvement in soccer for his perspective on the game. He was a Scottish international who played in the 1978 World Cup and for many years was with Aberdeen in the Scottish league. He was also head coach of the New Zealand National Team. For him, just having a team in contention can be motivation enough.

"The best way to keep yourself fresh is having the team keep winning," Clark said. "That's the easiest way to keep players motivated. The big thing is to be 'in things.' Whether you're playing at college or at the professional level, if you're in things and you're winning, then your players are going to be fresh."

"Obviously we'd all like to win, at college we'd like to win the NCAA championship, but the only thing I ask for every year is to be in contention come the end of the season. Because, then, the motivation is provided just by being in contention for things."

Referring back to his days in Scotland he added, "It was hard in Europe. Say you went out of the Cup somewhere in February, then maybe you're out of the league, and you're not involved in relegation and not involved in promotion, that's when there's lethargy, there's nothing to play for. However, if you're in contention for the league and you're in contention for the Cup, I think motivation is easy."

L.A. Galaxy coach Bruce Arena agreed, saying, "If you're winning, a lot of times you have some natural momentum."

But he added that motivation and keeping players sharp at the MLS level was very different from the national and college game.

"There's individual motivation and there's team motivation," he pointed out. "We don't get into a whole lot of motivating players individually in terms of personal goals. Our motivation is as a team and our goal is to become a good team."

"We don't necessarily use wins or losses as a means of evaluating where we are. It's just an everyday process as you grow as a team, and try to become a good team, and when you've arrived you know it. Obviously, individual performances are there but we always believe it's part of the whole team process."

But ongoing success during the season can bring its own problems, such as pressure from players to do more in training. Said Clark, "If a team actually starts to do well, then the motivation takes care of itself. Half the time you've actually got to hold them back because they want longer sessions. You keep them hungry. I don't like to see the sessions drag out. I want them to be saying 'Coach, can we stay out a little bit longer?' And I say 'No, that'll do us for today.'"

Both Arena and Clark advocate shorter, sharper sessions as the season progresses, not only to

avoid injuries but also to keep players sharper. Referring to his professional days in Scotland, Clark said: "Alex Ferguson was our manager when I was with Aberdeen. When we won the league we did very little, we'd just come in because we'd usually be playing a game every Saturday and every Wednesday, and basically everything was kept for the games. The rest of it was freshening up, warming up, coming in, getting a sauna, getting a massage, doing some shooting, doing a little five-a-side, but there was very little coaching done at that point because coming to the end of a season, we were just ticking over. The team by that time was a team, and that's really what you want to be when you're coming to the end of a season."

For L.A. Galaxy, a daily training session averages about an hour and 15 minutes. To keep players fresh, said Arena, "As simple as it may seem, you give them more time off. Practices are shorter and sharper.

"A lot of people believe that you need to work harder as you get toward the end of a season," said Arena. "I think for the physical part, that's not the case. Maybe you need to work harder mentally, so you expect players to be sharper upstairs in terms of their responsibilities, on the field and off the field."

Said Clark, "You've got to really keep them fresh. If you're coming to the end of the season and you're in contention, you have to keep the players' minds occupied, but you don't want to give them too much."

"They should be a team by then. You shouldn't have to do a lot of teamwork, unless you get a lot of injuries. So there shouldn't be a lot of tactics. The guys should really know the tactics by then. So it's really just fine-tuning and keeping them fresh. Short sessions where the players are kept interested."

So what is a typical training session at that stage?

"It could be small-sided games, it could be shooting," Clark said. "It's got to be short and sharp. It could be loads of different things. It doesn't need to be five-a-side. I don't think fitness should be a problem then. I think the one thing you have to guard against coming down the line is that you don't want to get injuries, but you want to keep them occupied."

And that, perhaps, is what makes a good coach. Said Clark, "You feel it yourself. This is one of the keys for the coach. I think you follow your gut instinct. But I think the worst thing is that you try and over coach coming down the line."

Arena said L.A. Galaxy's 75-minute training sessions are focused, with "a little bit more physical work in the first half of the season than the last half. But a typical training session would be a warm-up, some type of possession game, small-sided possession game and some type of game to big goal. That's almost a daily routine with our team. And then once in a while we would throw in restarts. And once training ends as a team, players work on things individually that they need to work on."

But training sessions become more difficult for the National Team. Said Sampson, "I have to take a specific approach to my training sessions every time we get together, given that the personnel are not the same, game in and game out."

Sampson's approach will differ with the availability of players. And players can be left out of a squad if they are playing too much at the club level or a club game is too close to a National Team game, especially if they also have to travel abroad to that U.S. team match.

"So I have to prepare a team tactically for the upcoming opponent," he said. "And when we have the full squad together we can play with a level of consistency and style, but if I have a mix of full National Team players and players who

I'm experimenting with, then my approach has to be different."

Avoiding injury, again, is a primary consideration.

"As far as training techniques," said Sampson, "it's very important that we have a period before the actual core of the training session starts, and also a period at the end, where players are warming up effectively, going through a light stretching routine, to where they are properly warmed up, before we get into any kind of a tactical exercise. And then at the end of every single training session, we have a cool-down period that also involves the lowering of the heart rate, and once again, more stretching, so that we don't incur injury.

"This is especially important for players who are traveling across the ocean, or great distances, when they come into training initially at the beginning of the week."

Not trying to include too much in a session is also important.

"From a tactical standpoint," he said, "I try not to emphasize more than one, maybe two points in a training session. I try and keep it very specific and very simple."

Whether training is geared toward the individual or the team, or varying degrees of both, depends as much on the style of coaching as the level of play. While the National Team pays a lot of attention to individual requirements, because players arrive from different club schedules, professional clubs can often focus more on team aspects. Age can also be a factor.

"We have players on the National Team who are 20 years old all the way up to 36 years old," Sampson pointed out, "and you can't treat a 36-year-old the same way as a 20-year old. Also, if a player plays a game two days before you play a National Team game, you obviously have to treat him much differently than the rest of your team."

"So we have a very individualistic approach based on the needs of a player and the National Team in general. Sometimes I'll give a few players the day off while the rest of the team works. And everyone has to understand that that is the approach that has to be taken."

L.A.'s approach can be more team-oriented because the same personnel are involved all the time. As a result, training is geared more toward the team than the individual. Said Arena, "Obviously you always do individual training, but most of our individual work is often done by tapes. We look at a lot of video and we analyze what individual players do during a game and try to demonstrate to them the good and bad of what they are doing."

Arena doesn't believe in spending too much time on preparing for the opposition, and because he keeps the same personnel, he can build on training themes throughout the season.

"We don't necessarily focus on what our opponents do," Arena said. "Our concentration is on our team and constantly getting better at what we're doing. Working on concentration builds from day one all the way through the season. The themes are basically the same in terms of our team concepts and the responsibilities of individuals. As you get into the season, it's second nature."

Concentrating too much on the opposition is a mistake, he says.

"I don't think good teams anywhere dedicate most of their training to their opponents. That's my belief. You can't change what you do. Your players are the same; you respect your next opponent, you respect their strengths and weaknesses. That's the mental exercise. That's

the thing we can do after training when we meet as a team and look at video. But we are who we are and we have a style of play. We make slight adjustments in accordance to our opponents, but we don't spend a lot of time in training on our opponents. Instead, we spend it on ourselves, getting better at the things that we do."

"I think that's a classic fault of coaching — just to spend a whole lot of time on things that you don't have control over, like your opponent, in trying to predict how they're going to play and everything else, when really what you do have control over is your own team."

So with everyone giving players so much time off as the season progresses, when does the real coaching work get done? For Bobby Clark, it is in the spring for the college game, just as it was in the summer when he played in the Scottish professional game.

"I think all your coaching has to be done early on," he said. "When I was with Aberdeen, the six weeks during the summer, that's when we really bedded down, through pre-season. That's when we did all our tactical stuff, and all our work, and that's what laid the foundation for the rest of our season."

For the college game though, the spring is the best time. Said Clark, "I think for my college team, the main part of my coaching, what I call my teaching, is done in the spring. A lot of folks give teams the spring off. They maybe go just three times a week, but we go five times a week. We don't have long sessions, but we go five times a week. Sometimes a game on a Saturday to make it six times.

"I like the spring because that's the time I bed in everything. I bed in all the tactics, such as how we're going to play, that's when the real teaching is done."

For the college game then, fitness is accomplished in the summer. Said Clark, "Then the players for college must do the fitness through the summer on their own. We're quite lucky, we're on the quarter system and we don't break up until June. So I have them right through June, so they've got 10 weeks before they come back to me, and that's when they've really got to do their fitness work."

When the players return from summer break, they should have established basic fitness. Said Clark, "When they come back to me two weeks before the season starts, for college, we're not really doing any fitness work, we're just reinforcing all the lessons that we learned in the spring. That's just what I call reinforcing time, and trying to get them to get back into remembering what we were doing.

"And then once the season starts, you hope the players are in automatic. They should know what they're doing by then, they should change gears themselves. All it needs is a little bit of guidance, just know when to put on the break or put the foot on the accelerator, because it's in gear. The gears should be shifting themselves. You know when to put your foot down; you know when to take your foot off. Again, the coach has got to feel that. But I do very little work as far as hard work on fitness in the season; everything is with a ball."

For Sampson, fitness is a basic requirement when reporting to the national camp. Said Sampson, "The first thing players must understand is that if they are not 100 percent physically fit, I will not play them. And if a player comes into camp injured, I will fine him. And at times I will send him back to his club team. I have done that in the past. When you come into the National Team, you must be 100 percent physically fit."

One final word from Steve Sampson on motivation: "Degrading, screaming and yelling have never proven to me to be a tool that has ever been successful. Showing a lack of respect toward a player to me has never shown any positive results. That is to say, negative reinforcement rarely, if ever, is effective. And I think that is especially true at the National Team level."

A lot of good, dedicated coaches at all levels of play would support that view.

*Editor's note: Ian Stokell has been playing and coaching soccer for nearly 35 years. His passion for the game began at age 7 when an uncle took him to watch Arsenal beat Everton 5-3 in London. To see over the heads of the spectators he had to stand on the upturned end of an oversized rectangular biscuit tin he had brought from home.*

# Curing Common Coaching Problems

## Dan Woog

*Although every coaching problem is unique – different characters, different situations, and different circumstances – there often are similarities. In other words, the same types of problems occur season after season, year after year, from one end of the country to the other.*

*While the following problems and courses of action are by no means all-inclusive, we present them with the idea that they will provide a start toward understanding the problems and the search for solutions all youth coaches struggle with. There is universality to these situations and to their solutions as well.*

## The Player Who Wants to Play Only One Position

*"I'm a left winger."*
*"I can't play defense."*
*"I've never played halfback before."*

This is a problem best nipped in the bud. The sooner a youngster learns that a soccer player is a soccer player, period – that a soccer player plays offense and defense always, that a team needs change and that different coaches see players' abilities and roles in different ways – the better off that player will be.

There are two good ways to deal with this problem. One is through communication – explaining to the team as a whole and to the player individually how fluid "positions" must be (especially compared to specialized sports like baseball and football). This verbal communication works only if the player is old

enough to reason and mature enough to have a dialogue with his/her coach.

The second method is to ease the player into a new role during practice. Let him/her get the feel for a new spot during non-threatening, non-pressure situations. Spend time teaching new responsibilities; don't simply announce before the game, "Jordan, you're our new stopper." Follow this up with concerned questioning: "How do you like playing in the back? What's better about it, compared with striker? What's worse?" You may be surprised how many times the answer is "It's fun!"

## The Player Who Thinks the Coach's Lineup/Strategy/Substitution Policy/etc. is Wrong

This is more insidious than the previous problem. Usually the player is older, more independent. Often, in fact, it's the better player, the one with excellent skills or a solid game sense, who is apt to challenge the coach's way of coaching.

Certainly coaches can learn from their players. Someone out on the field has a different perspective than someone on the sidelines. Not always better, or worse, or right, or wrong, just different. That player's insights or suggestions often can be valuable.

But it's the coach's job to see that those suggestions are offered at the appropriate times; that is, the time designated by the coach. Time can be allocated during certain practice sessions for questions about strategy. That's when a rational team-wide discussion can be held. Possibly the halftime remark, "Anyone have any comments about the first half?" can elicit some responses. However, no coach can allow killer statements about other players or negative comments about coaching policy to disrupt team unity. Criticism by players must be restricted to private conversations with the coach. Breaches should result in loss of playing time.

There is a time for open discussion and a time for coach's authority. Any coach who does not recognize the difference, or who abrogates this responsibility, is doing the team and his/her young athletes a grave disservice.

## Parental Interference

This can get pretty hard, indeed. Dealing with peers, friends and colleagues is a lot different than dealing with children. Coaches need the Wisdom of Solomon, the patience of Job and the diplomacy of Kissinger when interacting with the numerous and varied adults who make up the so-called "cheering section."

One clever way of dealing with parental pressure is to suggest that the parent come help you coach. Often the loudest mouths are those who know the least. "You know, I really appreciate your interest. Could you help me run practices and take over next week when I'm away?" This will usually produce the response, "Oh, I couldn't, I don't know enough about the game." Use that line as a wedge to open a discussion about the need to let the coach operate without outside interference, unless the parent wishes to "put his money where his mouth is."

When the critics do know what they're talking about — for instance, your assistant or a particularly knowledgeable parent — and they're vocal enough to be undermining your authority, organize a meeting of all the adults. Calmly confront the issue head-on, ask for criticism, answer it as rationally and articulately as you can, then stress the need for a united front. The next time the critics carp, they'll be facing

pressure themselves from other parents — the middle-of-the-roaders — who will pay them less mind. To switch the maxim around, the best defense is a good offense.

## Coaching a "Superstar"

This is a problem? You bet! And it can take several forms.

One form is the player who clearly knows more than the coach, especially when everyone else knows it too. (This is almost always an adolescent problem.) The coach must be smart enough to recognize the situation and to admit it. He/She must learn from the player while not surrendering the team. Good one-to-one communication skills are a must. The coach has to impress upon the player the need for cooperation and patience, with both the team and the coach, while at the same time letting the player know that he/she is not special, that rules or expectations will not be bent or twisted on their behalf.

Another problem occurs if the superstar believes he/she is too good for the other players on the team. If a coach expects a team to always feed the ball to the star or singles that player out for constant praise and uses him/her for every good example, yet is loathe to offer criticism, this reinforces the player's feeling of being special. Good young players should be used as examples for others, but they also need to be criticized constructively, prodded and shown the necessity for working selflessly with others. Too many great athletes have stagnated as youngsters because they haven't been pushed to improve even more, pushed to develop team concepts and skills they'll need once they advance to a higher level of play.

A coach can't be afraid to sit a superstar down. If too many practices are missed, the player should sit; if a rule is broken, he/she should sit; even if the superstar is having an off day — and everyone does — the coach should resist the temptation to think that the star must be on the field at all times or the team will fall apart. As far as can be determined, no youth soccer player in the U.S. is God – and the sooner our youth soccer players learn this, the better.

## Disruptive Players

Often players disrupt practices or cause problems on the bench because they're bored. Usually they're bored because they're inactive. The cures for inactivity are simple. During practices, less talking by the coach, more movement by the players, smaller groups so each youngster touches the ball more will help. During games, don't just keep your eyes glued to the field. Ask the players on the bench questions, tell them how soon you'll be substituting them in, remind them to keep cheering for their teammates. Most children are disruptive only because they want attention.

## Information Overload

Youngsters' attention spans are short. They cannot handle as much information at one time as adults, yet there are many coaches who insist upon forcing every scrap of detail they know on their players, often at the most inappropriate times.

The pre-game talk is the wrong time to introduce a game plan. It should have been introduced in bits and pieces during practice sessions so players could have had time to assimilate the information and understand it thoroughly. New concepts should be introduced singly and completely. Similarly, while reinforcing old (previously explained) ideas before a game, concentrate on one or two key points. If you use the scattershot approach – throwing out eight or 10 different thoughts in random order as they occur to you – you'll lose your audience entirely. Older youngsters, in particular, are masters at looking straight at you as if enraptured while their minds are a zillion miles away.

This has the added advantage of refining your own coaching skills. It's easy to attack every problem in sight every single day, hoping something, sometime, will sink in. It's more difficult to pick out one or two ideas and reinforce them systematically; that requires foresight, planning and patience. It's like the introduction to a letter Abraham Lincoln is purported to have sent to a friend: "I would have written you a shorter note, but I didn't have time."

## Improper Warm-Ups Before a Match

Too many coaches are content to let their players kick aimlessly before a game. As much as possible, warm-ups should be match-related: goalkeepers should be working on their diving, jumping, catching, throwing and punting skills; field players should be working on controlling the ball, passing it on the ground and working it around as much as possible. Five against two (5 v. 2) and keep-away are two good ways to include these concepts in a warm-up.

When it comes time to practice shooting, also make it match-related. Don't always use the same angle and/or distance for the drill; include defenders as defenders, too. Be certain that your corner kickers practice these prior to game time as well, especially if you're playing away. Every corner of every field is different, and it doesn't hurt to test them all.

Many coaches sit their youngsters down for 15 or 20 minutes prior to a game and start telling them everything they need to know about soccer. Before a match, children are restless. They want to be active and do things, not sit and listen. Keep your comments to a minimum, especially with young children. Your coaching should be done in practice sessions, not just prior to kickoff.

On the other hand, don't let your players tire themselves out. A half an hour of warm-up is plenty. Any longer and they become tired and bored. If they run the risk of warming up too long, sit them down – but don't feel the need to bore them with soccer talk.

## Helter-Skelter Comments at Halftime

The need for carefully-thought-out, well-organized, judicious halftime comments is crucial. Spend the few minutes prior to halftime thinking about what you want to say. That way you won't ramble or hem and haw in the few minutes allotted to you.

Again, don't overburden your players. If things are going poorly, twelve different ideas won't change things. Concentrate on one or two. If things are going okay, you probably only need to mention one or two things they can work on in the second half. If things are going great – well, as an old Yankee once said, "If it ain't broke, don't fix it."

Of course, halftime comments should nearly always be positive. Very little is to be gained from negative criticism unless the players are old enough to handle it and it is used so seldom it makes them sit up and take notice. Whenever you offer criticism, be sure to couch it in non-threatening terms: "Taylor, you're heading the ball well, I know, but we need to keep the ball on the ground, away from their big backs."

## Failure to Communicate

There are two times communication is especially important: when a player comes out of a game and when the match has ended.

No child likes to leave the field. Much worse, though, is coming out, walking to the sidelines and being ignored by the coach. The coach should greet every child who comes out of a game personally. A pat on the head, shoulder or rump is good. Better is some verbal comment,

such as "Good work out there, I just needed to get Chris in." Or, "Wow, you really worked hard. Take a rest, and I'll get you back in the second half."

Even if a player was removed because he/she was playing poorly or couldn't handle his/her position, use the substitution situation to teach: "Pat, listen, next time you're in there and you're playing against someone that fast, this is what you do...." It goes without saying; of course, that you should never, ever, remove a player immediately after he/she commits a mistake, no matter how grievous the error. To do so can only demoralize an already desolate youngster. Whatever you want to say can wait a few minutes.

After the game is a fair time to talk a bit. You don't have to deliver an oratorical masterpiece or go over every player's performance minute by minute, but you can wrap up the game briefly. This is what we did well, this is what we did poorly, this is what we'll work on next week and practice is at the usual time. Then the coach should ask the players; any questions or problems or injuries? Thank you, goodbye. Resist the temptation (and the parents who are hanging around like vultures, waiting to drive their children to their next engagement) to let everyone leave immediately after the match.

## Too Many Substitutions, too Often

This is a mistake made most often by coaches who have never played soccer. Soccer is not football, where subs run in and out on every play bringing in secret messages from the coach. Nor is it hockey, where line shifts every 90 seconds are de rigueur.

In soccer, it takes at least 10 or 15 minutes for a player to get into the flow of the game, to understand the rhythm of that particular match, as well as to figure out the capabilities of his particular opponent, the idiosyncrasies of the field, the weather and whatever else makes every game different. It also takes that long for a player's legs to feel comfortable, nervousness to disappear and his/her second wind to arrive. To substitute without giving a chance to play at least 10 or 15 minutes (except in emergencies) is doing that player a disservice.

It's also unwise to send in subs in "waves" or "lines." Some coaches do it with notable success – the University of Connecticut's Joe Morrone comes to mind – but the feeling here is that it's bad for two reasons. One is that it disrupts the flow of the game - it takes your own players on the field longer to adjust to three or six new players than it does to adjust to one or two – plus it runs counter to the international concept of the game.

All over the world, soccer is a game of fluidity and fitness, played from start to finish with no more than two reserves. Of course, in American youth sports we want to give as many youngsters as possible a chance to participate. That's good, and every child should play in every single match; however, it's not soccer when children start thinking of themselves as "the second forward line" or "the third wave of midfielders." If they see themselves in this image, they're not thinking of themselves as "soccer players" who can play anywhere and are creative, intelligent athletes able to think and adapt under ever-changing, pressure-filling situations. This leads to another coaching problem.

## Stereotyping Youngsters by Position

It's unfair for a coach to say, "No, you can't play striker, you're a fullback" or "Why do you want to switch? You're doing fine at right midfield." Children constantly are changing, each at different rates. Some are growing into their bodies, while others are getting more awkward by the minute. Some suddenly become more aggressive, while others begin to lag in the capability to visualize the entire field at once. For

a coach to label players as capable of playing only one position harms them developmentally and harms the team tactically.

A coach must be willing to take risks with his/her players. If the midfielders are having a problem keeping together during a game, the coach must be able to look down the bench and give someone else a try or switch with someone who's playing another position on the field. Certainly in a runaway game, a coach must be willing to move players around with abandon. If you're up by several goals, it may help keep the score down; if you're down by a few, what's the harm in trying something different?

## Failure to Plan for Emergencies

Every coach should know ahead of time what to do if the unthinkable happens. Who is the third goaltender - the backup behind the backup? What formation will you use if (heaven forbid) one of your players is sent off? If you're down by one goal in a must-win situation and your sweeper is your best athlete, do you ever plan to move him/her up into the attack? How about your goalie? Would you move him/her up as the final "roving back?" At what point in the game would you do this?

These are the kinds of questions that a coach must think about before the game. If you have to spend time answering them during the match, or if you've never even thought of them before they arise, you haven't done your homework.

## Too Much Yelling from the Sideline

One of the most appealing aspects of soccer is that once the whistle blows, the players are on their own. There are no timeouts, no huddles, no strategy sessions – in other words, once the game begins, the coach has very little input into the outcome. For those of us with big egos, that's a sobering thought. For the youngsters, that's great. They're their own coaches during a game. More than most team sports, the contest is theirs to win or lose.

"Go to the ball!" "Be aggressive!" "Mark your man!" All these are bits of advice a coach can call out during a game. They're good advice, but they lose effectiveness when shouted over and over and over again. They tend not to get heard when several different people - the coach, his assistant, the parents and all the youngsters on the sidelines - are yelling them at the same time, and they are not really that revolutionary. After all, soccer players know they should win loose balls, be aggressive and mark their men. Why not try spending one or two games quietly on the sidelines? Do your teaching during practice sessions, then let the players play during the match. Limit your advice to one or two key moments each half. You may be surprised by how well your players do without hearing your dulcet tones.

## Focusing on the Score Rather than the Play

There are 1-0 games and then there are 1-0 games. By this we mean, consider the 1-0 match you've won against a team you usually beat 7-0. Then consider the 1-0 match you've lost against a team you've never held below five goals. Too many coaches look only at the final score. They tell their team "Great game!" in the first instance without realizing the opposition is getting a lot better or without warning their team that they might be getting complacent. They also tell their team "Well, you lost again" in the second instance without congratulating them for how close this game was or giving them encouragement that perhaps the next time the score finally will be different.

We hate to use clichés, but this one happens to be true. "It's not whether you win or lose, it's how you play the game." You can play well and lose,

just as you can play poorly and win. Your team knows after a match whether it won or lost. It's your job, as coach, to tell them how they played the game.

# Training Session for U-6 Players

## George Perry
## NSCAA Senior Staff

*NSCAA Senior Staff member George Perry offers his advice on organizing and running a season for the U6 level.*

U-6 players are a unique group. They are shy, outgoing, very honest, inquisitive, quiet, loud, energetic, passive, and most import to me, extremely bright. And this is just the tip of what they are like, which is why they are so enjoyable to work with.

When I meet with this age group for the first time, I like to sit on the ground with them. I introduce myself, making sure they know what to call me. I prefer Coach or Coach Perry but you use whatever is comfortable for you.

While we are sitting there, I explain my rules, how I like to run my sessions. I tell them that there are three rules they have to pay attention to:

- When I am talking, they have to listen
- When I call on them, I promise I will listen to them
- They cannot just kick a ball...

What do I mean by this, "you cannot just kick a ball"? What can you do when you play soccer? Where I lead them in the discussion is that I want them to understand that you can dribble, shoot and pass the ball. I always want them to try to do something constructive with the ball. With this age group, I am particularly interested in them learning how to be comfortable with the ball (dribbling), controlling the ball (receiving), and how to score (sometimes that is shooting and sometimes they dribble the ball into the goal). Passing is not something I emphasize at all with this age group. Their egocentric mentality has them wanting to keep the ball and not share it. That can come later.

Too often I hear from the sidelines (from both coaches and parents), "kick it", "send it", "great kick", and even "pass it"... I would prefer to hear, "great turn", "good job controlling the ball", "great dribbling", "that's the way to go to the ball", "great shot", "what a great goal" "that's the way to help your teammate", and many more! I am not sure teaching these young players to pass the ball is in their best interest. At this age we want them to learn what they can do with the ball and feel more comfortable with it. Certainly some will pass the ball and it is good to reinforce that but it should not be a high priority with this age group.

In the last couple of U-6 programs I have run, I organize the session like a clinic. One of the programs, the Boys & Girls Club in Crawfordsville, IN, I had about 80 players. We had it set up so there were 10 teams of 8, each team having a coach (volunteer parent). We would meet once a week. The other program I am working with now is the YMCA program in Monmouth, IL. Here I have about 35 players, age range from pre-kindergarten to 2nd grade. When they play the games, each day, they play with different players of similar age and/or ability. The programs ran for eight to ten weeks.

The purpose of running the "clinic" is that I am the only one who has to prepare activities for each session. The coaches (my players, parents or other volunteers) just have to show up and follow my "lead." Since we do the program for eight to ten weeks, this offers the coaches eight to ten 30 minute clinics on how to interact with the players and hopefully learn from me how to let the players be individuals, to explore the game for themselves. More often than not, they take me to a different path of what they are capable of doing. Every group has been similar and yet unique. That is another reason I never tire of working with this age group. After helping me for a season or two, I hope the coaches will be ready to take a group (not as large as I do) for themselves.

For the first 25-30 minutes, I run a "clinic" for the players, working on the various skills previously mentioned. All of the coaches, and sometimes some of the parents, would be my assistants. After the "clinic", they would go to their field and play games. In Crawfordsville, we had ten, 25 yards x 15 yards fields set up and they would play a game consisting of four, six minute quarters. In Monmouth, I have three fields, one for the pre-kindergartners, one for the kindergartners, and one for the 1st and 2nd graders. The "coaches", parents and players of mine, would oversee the games. I would move around during the games, sometimes helping out if needed but mostly watching and enjoying the players having fun with the game. I encouraged the coaches to be supportive but not to do too much coaching during the games. Let the game do the teaching now.

For the 25-30 minute clinic, I like to have every player with a ball or at least a ball for every two players. The space I use is 2 or 3 of the playing fields that I have set up for the program with 80 players and one field for the program with 35 players. I put cones on the outside of the area, one every four or five yards. After I am done talking with the players at the beginning (something I do every time we meet for consistency), I have the players pair up and go sit in between two cones. This takes a little bit of time the first session or two, but with the help of the coaches and parents, it goes very quickly. By the second or third training session, the players, with the exception of a few, can do it on their own.

To get started, I have one of the players in the pair come into the middle of the area with their ball. I will do an activity with them for 45 seconds to a minute and then they will switch

places with their partner. I have each group do the same activity. This way, you can get by with 10 activities but I like to have a few extra in mind in case one does not work with this group. Sometimes you will only get to 8 activities. I always go with the flow of the players. They tell me through their actions if I should repeat the activity again or go to a new one. Remember to give the players plenty of water breaks, especially in the heat. But even if it is cool, this gives them a break to get away from the working space and when they return, they can re-focus on what you are doing. Here is a sample of what I might do at one of these sessions:

- Every player in the middle has a ball and dribbles within the playing space. On my command, "stop", they put a foot on the ball. Once I have seen they all have their foot on the ball, I say "go" and they continue dribbling. They do this for 45 seconds and then switch with their partner

- Every player dribbling their ball but this time I will call out a body part, "knee", and they have to stop the ball with their knee. I will often say "left knee" to help them begin to learn, if they do not already know, their left from their right

- I will show them how to turn the ball by using the inside of their foot and taking the ball back in the direction they came from. I will then ask them to do that every time I say "turn." If I say "stop" they have to put their foot on the ball as they did before (teaching change of direction)

- Now I will show them how to turn the ball by placing their foot on top of the ball and pulling it back, again, taking the ball back in the direction they came from

- I will show them how to do step-ups, light touches on top of the ball, alternating feet each time. Make sure they do not step on the ball. For those having trouble, I do it with them on their ball so they can follow my feet. After they get that, I will ask them to do as many as they can in 15 seconds. The second time I have them do it for 15 seconds, I will ask them to do 2 more touches than the first time

- I have them dribble within the space and then I will say "stop." Again, they put their foot on the ball. I ask them to point to an open space near them and then I ask them to dribble as fast as they can to that space. If it gets crowded, just slow down. I repeat the "stop" but this time I ask them to continue dribbling and every time they see an open space to dribble as quickly as possible to that space. Hopefully this will get them to pick their head up while they are dribbling to find space

- This next activity needs the help of all the coaches. We will play a game of tag. The players are to dribble throughout the playing area and try to avoid being tagged by one of the coaches. If they are tagged, they have to do 5 step-ups and then continue dribbling, trying to avoid being tagged again

- Freeze tag. Again, the coaches are "it" and the players are trying to avoid being tagged. When they are tagged, they are "frozen" and have to stand still with one foot on top of their ball. Another player, who is not "frozen", can dribble to them and tag them which "un-freezes" them. They can continue dribbling and try not to get "frozen"

- Hospital Tag. I use the same playing space but add a small square (the hospital), about 5 yards square on the edge of one of the sides of the playing space. Again, an appropriate number of coaches are it. As the players dribble throughout the playing space, the coaches are trying to tag them. Every time a player is tagged, they have to put a hand on the body part that was tagged. So if

I tagged you left shoulder, you would have to put your hand on your left shoulder. You still continue dribbling. If you get tagged again, let's say you hip, you must put your other hand on your hip. If you get tagged a third time, you have to go to the hospital. Dribble to the hospital and perform a task, 10 step-ups. This "heals" you and you can re-join the dribbling with your hands free. Now the game starts over for you

- Sharks and Minnows. Have the players (minnows) on one side of the playing space, each with a soccer ball. Have the coaches (sharks) in the middle. On your start command, the minnows try to dribble to the opposite side of the space. The sharks try to take the ball from them. If a shark takes the ball away, they have to dribble the ball to the side-line. The minnows try to get their ball back. This encourages the players to not just stop when they loose the ball in the game. The coaches should let the players win their ball back. As players do loose their ball, they do not sit out. They join the sharks in the middle and go after the minnows that crossed the water. Make sure you do not have too many sharks. When you have fewer, you will see that some of the players will learn to watch what is happening and time their runs when the sharks are busy after others

After the 25-30 minutes are up, you organize the players into their games. Now it is all them and we just supervise to make sure it is a safe environment, encouraging them to have fun and let them be themselves, not what "we" want them to be.

As I tell all the coaches I have had the pleasure of working with in all the NSCAA Academies I have taught and programs I have been a part of, yes, it is important that the players have fun, but most important is, YOU HAVE FUN! It is infectious.

# Athletes First, Winning Second

**Frank L. Smoll, Ph.D.,**
**Ronald E. Smith, Ph.D.**
**Department of Psychology,**
**University of Washington**

As a form of competition, sport involves a contest between opposing individuals or teams. An athletic event is a struggle for supremacy in which every coach and athlete seeks to emerge victorious.

The common notion in sports thus equates success with winning – scoring more points, runs or goals than the opponent. However, in a youth or developmental model of sport (Smoll & Smith, 1999), the measure of success goes beyond records and standings. Success is a personal thing and is related to one's own standards and abilities.

With respect to the educational benefits of sport, youngsters can learn valuable lessons from both winning and losing. But for this to occur, winning must be placed in a healthy perspective. We have therefore developed a four-part philosophy of winning (Smith & Smoll, 2002a; Smoll & Smith, 1981).

The purpose of this article is to present an overview of the philosophy and to consider ways of conveying it to athletes. Hopefully, the article will serve as a guide for developing your views and orientation toward winning. Moreover, by successfully implementing this philosophy in your role as coach or teacher, you will be able to maximize young athletes' enjoyment of sports and their chances of deriving the positive outcomes of participation.

## Part 1: Winning Isn't Everything, Nor Is It the Only Thing.

Young athletes can't possibly learn from winning and losing if they think the only objective is to beat their opponents. On the other hand, it would be naive and unrealistic to believe that winning is not an important part of youth sports. Winning is an important goal, but it is not the most important objective.

> *Success is peace of mind, which is a direct result of self-satisfaction in knowing you did your best to become the best you are capable of becoming.*
>
> *– John Wooden, former UCLA basketball coach*

Most programs seek to develop desirable psychological and social characteristics as well as physical skills. However, as we all know, some coaches get caught up in a "winning is everything" orientation and place an overemphasis on winning. When this occurs, they may temporarily lose sight of other important objectives and values of their program. This does not mean that coaches should not try to build winning teams, but sometimes winning becomes more important for the coach than it is for the athlete.

Our research has shown that coaches for whom athletes enjoyed playing most, and who were most successful in promoting youngsters' self-esteem, actually had won-lost records that were about the same as coaches who were less liked and less effective in fostering feelings of self-worth (see Smoll & Smith, 2002).

Another finding was that athletes on winning teams believed that their parents liked the coach more and that the coach liked them more than did athletes on losing teams. This is an interesting commentary on children's perceptions of adult values. Winning made little difference to the youngsters, but they knew that it was important to the adults in their lives.

Given that sport is heavily achievement-oriented, seeking victory is encouraged. However, to create the most valuable experience for athletes, coaches should help them understand that there is more to get out of sports than just a won-lost record. This can be done by reducing the ultimate importance of winning relative to other prized participation motives (e.g., skill development and affiliation with teammates).

Most notably, in recognition of the inverse relation between enjoyment and competitive anxiety, fun should be highlighted as the paramount objective (Scanlan & Lewthwaite, 1984; Scanlan & Passer, 1978, 1979). If young people leave your program having enjoyed relating to you and to their teammates, feeling better about themselves, having improved their skills and looking forward to future sport participation, you have accomplished something far more important than a winning record or a league championship.

> *The bottom line in youth sports should not be based on pressure to win. Instead, it should be on the enjoyment of competing and the opportunity to develop positive attitudes toward other people.*
>
> *-- Lute Olson, University of Arizona basketball coach*

## Part 2: Failure Is Not the Same Thing as Losing.

Athletes should not view losing as a sign of failure or as a threat to their personal value. They should be taught that losing a game is not a reflection of their own self-worth. In other words, when individuals or teams lose a contest, it does not mean that their worth is less than it would have been had they won.

## Part 3: Success Is Not Equivalent to Winning.

Neither success nor failure need depend on the outcome of a contest or the numbers in a won-lost record. Winning and losing apply to the outcome of a contest, whereas success and failure do not. How then can we define success in sports?

## Part 4: Athletes Should Be Taught that Success Is Found in Striving for Victory.

The important idea is that success is related to commitment and effort. Athletes have complete control over the amount of effort they give, but they have only limited control of the outcome that is achieved. If you can impress on your athletes that they are never "losers" if they commit themselves to doing their best and give maximum effort, you are giving them a priceless gift that will assist them in many of life's tasks.

Comments by two well-known college coaches indicate that their philosophy of winning agrees with the orientation presented above.

Penn State football coach Joe Paterno stated, "We can't let people get hold of our kids and make them think they've got to win. The winning is great. You strive for it. You try to do it. You compete to win. But if you lose, you lose. I've never seen a football game where there wasn't enough glory for everybody – winners and losers."

Similarly, former UCLA basketball coach John Wooden once told a group of coaches: "You cannot find a player who ever played for me at UCLA that can tell you he ever heard me mention 'winning' a basketball game. Yet the last thing I told my athletes, just prior to tip-off, before we would go on the floor was, 'When the game is over, I want your head up – and I know of only one way for your head to be up – and that's for you to know that you did your best. This means to do the best you can do. That's the best; no one can do more. You made that effort.'"

With a developmentally oriented philosophy of winning, coaches are urged to focus on athletes' effort and enjoyment rather than on success as measured by statistics or scoreboards. In other words, you are encouraged to emphasize, "doing your best," "getting better" and "having fun" as opposed to a "win at all costs" orientation.

Although formulated prior to the emergence of achievement goal theory (Ames, 1992; Dweck, 1999; Nicholls, 1989), this approach clearly is consistent with a task or mastery orientation (see McArdle & Duda, 2002). Moreover, focusing on effort rather than outcome is consistent with Dweck's (1975) highly successful attributional retraining program with low-achieving children.

> *The only successful youth sports program is the one with the coach who will accept losing along with winning, last place in the league along with first place, and still be able to congratulate his team for their efforts.*
>
> *– Roger Staubach, former Dallas Cowboys quarterback*

Children who received Dweck's intervention showed improved performance (in a math problem-solving task) and were better able to cope with failure. Within the realm of sport, one might expect this approach to lessen the effects of failure, thereby reducing stress for athletes.

## Behavioral Guide for Coaches

A number of research-derived guidelines for enhancing relationship skills are presented in our book *Way to Go, Coach!* (Smith & Smoll, 2002a). They constitute the core of our scientifically validated coaching education program, which is known as Coach Effectiveness Training (see Smith & Smoll, 2002b; Smoll & Smith, 2001).

Two of the guidelines have direct relevance to developing a healthy philosophy of winning. First, reinforce effort as much as results. It's easy to recognize and praise an athlete who just made a great play, but coaches usually are less likely to reward a player who tried hard but did not make the play. Perhaps the second athlete deserves (and needs) positive feedback even more.

Let your athletes know that you appreciate and value their efforts. Make sure their efforts are not taken for granted. As we stated earlier, athletes have complete control over how much effort they make; but they have only limited control over the outcome of their efforts. By looking for and praising athletes' efforts, you can encourage them to continue or increase their output.

A second coaching guideline is pertinent to our philosophy of winning: Encourage effort, don't demand results. Most young athletes already are motivated to develop their skills and play well. By appropriate use of encouragement, a coach can help increase their natural enthusiasm. If, however, youngsters are encouraged to strive for unrealistic standards of achievement, they may feel like failures when they don't reach the goal. Therefore, it is important to base encouragement on reasonable expectations. Again, a coach encouraging effort rather than outcome can help avoid problems.

## Reducing Fear of Failure

Fear of failure can be an athlete's worst enemy. High levels of competition anxiety not only reduce performance, but also make the athletic situation threatening and unpleasant rather than enjoyable. In fact, many young athletes drop out of sports because of the stress created by their fear of failure (see Smith, Smoll, & Passer, 2002).

How does fear of failure develop? Usually, it arises because the young athlete has been punished for failing to achieve a desired outcome. Such punishment may come from coaches, parents or peers, or it may be self-administered by athletes themselves when they fail to measure up to their own performance standards.

Because the punishment and resulting decrease in self-esteem are so distasteful, athletes may come to fear and dread the possibility of failing. They dread making a mistake or losing a contest. Their fear, by disrupting performance, increases the likelihood that they will perform poorly. It is easy to understand why some athletes "choke" in pressure situations. Instead of enjoying competition and developing a positive drive for achievement, some athletes are driven by the negative motive of avoiding failure.

How can coaches help to prevent development of fear of failure in their athletes? We believe that John Wooden had the answer when he emphasized to his UCLA teams that success lies in doing one's best, of giving maximum effort regardless of the final score. If coaches only demand that athletes give their best, and if they reward their efforts rather than focusing only on outcome, athletes can learn to set similar standards for themselves. As far as winning is concerned, if athletes are well trained, give maximum effort and are free of performance-disrupting fears of failing, winning will take care of itself within the limits of their ability.

## A Final Thought

Tremendous concern has been shown for the amount of emphasis placed on winning in youth sports. Yet to be for or against competition is not the issue. Sport competition is neither universally good nor bad for kids. The important thing is how the competition is organized and conducted. The philosophy of the American Sport Education Program, "Athletes first, winning second," reflects a proper perspective on winning (Hanlon, 1994). In other words, the most important coaching product is not a won-lost record. It is the quality of the experience provided for the athletes.

## References

Ames, C. (1992). Classrooms: Goals, structures, and student motivation. *Journal of Educational Psychology, 84,* 261-271.

Dweck, C. S. (1975). The role of expectations and attributions in the alleviation of learned helplessness. *Journal of Personality and Social Psychology, 31,* 674-685.

Dweck, C. S. (1999). *Self-theories and goals: Their role in motivation, personality, and development.* Philadelphia: Taylor & Francis.

Hanlon, T. (1994). *SportParent.* Champaign, IL: Human Kinetics.

McArdle, S., & Duda, J. L. (2002). Implications of the motivational climate in youth sports. In F. L. Smoll & R. E. Smith (Eds.), *Children and youth in sport: A biopsychosocial perspective* (2nd ed., 409-434). Dubuque, IA: Kendall/Hunt.

Nicholls, J. G. (1989). *The competitive ethos and democratic education.* Cambridge, MA: Harvard University Press.

Scanlan, T. K., & Lewthwaite, R. (1984) Social psychological aspects of competition for male youth sport participants: I. Predictors of competitive stress. *Journal of Sport Psychology, 6,* 208-226.

Scanlan, T. K., & Passer, M. W. (1978). Factors related to competitive stress among male youth sports participants. *Medicine and Science in Sports, 10,* 103-108.

Scanlan, T. K., & Passer, M. W. (1979). Sources of competitive stress in young female athletes. *Journal of Sport Psychology, 1,* 151-159.

Smith, R. E., & Smoll, F. L. (2002a). *Way to go, coach! A scientifically-proven approach to coaching effectiveness* (2nd ed.). Portola Valley, CA: Warde.

Smith, R. E., & Smoll, F. L. (2002b). Youth sports as a behavior setting for psychosocial interventions. In J. L. Van Raalte & B. W. Brewer (Eds.), *Exploring sport and exercise psychology* (2nd ed., pp. 341-371). Washington, DC: American Psychological Association.

Smith, R. E., Smoll, F. L., & Passer, M. W. (2002). Sport performance anxiety in young athletes. In F. L. Smoll & R. E. Smith (Eds.), *Children and youth in sport: A biopsychosocial perspective* (2nd ed., 501-536). Dubuque, IA: Kendall/Hunt.

Smoll, F. L., & Smith, R. E. (1981). Developing a healthy philosophy of winning. In V. Seefeldt, F. L. Smoll, R. E. Smith, & D. Gould, *A winning philosophy for youth sports programs* (pp. 17-24). East Lansing, MI: Institute for the Study of Youth Sports.

Smoll, F. L., & Smith, R. E. (1999). *Sports and your child: A 50-minute guide for parents.* Portola Valley, CA: Warde

Smoll, F. L., & Smith, R. E. (2001). Conducting sport psychology training programs for coaches: Cognitive-behavioral principles and techniques. In J. M. Williams (Ed.), *Applied sport psychology: Personal growth to peak performance* (4th ed., pp. 378-400). Mountain View, CA: Mayfield.

Smoll, F. L., & Smith, R. E. (2002). Coaching behavior research and intervention in youth sports. In F. L. Smoll & R. E. Smith (Eds.), *Children and youth in sport: A biopsychosocial perspective* (2nd ed., pp. 211-231). Dubuque, IA: Kendall/Hunt.

ISBN: 9781841262789
E-Book: 9781841265728
$ 17.95 US/$ 29.95 AUS
£ 12.95 UK/€ 16.95

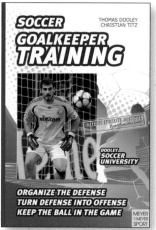

ISBN: 9781841263069
E-Book: 9781841267104
$ 16.95 US/$ 29.95 AUS
£12,95 UK/€ 16.95

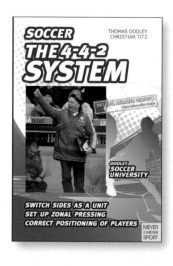

ISBN: 9781841263076
E-Book: 9781841267098
$ 16.95 US/$ 29.95 AUS
£12,95 UK/€ 16.95

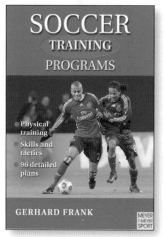

ISBN: 9781841262741
E-Book: 9781841265742
$ 17.95 US/$ 29.95 AUS
£ 12.95 UK/€ 16.95

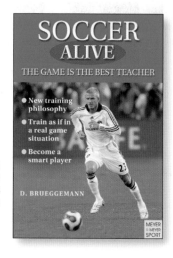

ISBN: 9781841262352
E-Book: 9781841265735
$ 19.95 US/$ 32.95 AUS
£ 12.95 UK/€ 19.95